Durable Inequality

Durable Inequality

CHARLES TILLY

UNIVERSITY OF CALIFORNIA PRESS
Berkeley   Los Angeles   London

The Irene Flecknoe Ross Lecture Series was established in the Department of Sociology at the University of California, Los Angeles, in 1987. The series is supported by a fund established by Ray Ross in memory of his wife, a distinguished public health nurse in Los Angeles. The lectures bring social science theory and research to bear on significant social, political, and moral issues, often in novel, even unorthodox ways. Prior Ross lecturers include Jerome Kagan, Edward Shils, S. N. Eisenstadt, William Julius Wilson, Alan Wolfe, Howard S. Becker, Craig Calhoun, and Charles Tilly.

University of California Press
Berkeley and Los Angeles, California

University of California Press, Ltd.
London, England

© 1998 by
The Regents of the University of California

Tilly, Charles.
  Durable inequality / Charles Tilly.
    p. cm.
  Includes bibliographical references and index.
  ISBN 0-520-21171-5 (alk. paper)
    1. Income distribution. 2. Equality. I. Title.
  HC79.I5T388 1998
  339.2—dc21   97-31570
                                                CIP

Printed in the United States of America

9 8 7 6 5 4 3 2 1

The paper used in this publication meets the minimum requirements of American National Standard for Information Sciences—Permanence of Paper for Printed Library Materials, ANSI Z39.48–1984.

To the memory of Laurence John Tilly, 1930–1995
rugged individualist and infectious collectivist

Contents

Acknowledgments

The pages that follow offer you heavily edited and greatly expanded versions of the Irene Flecknoe Ross Lectures at the University of California, Los Angeles, delivered October–November 1995. I am grateful to William Roy for organizing my participation in the lectures, Robert Emerson for presiding over them, and the UCLA audience for providing searching questions. Adam Ashforth, Karen Barkey, Matt Bothner, Herbert Gans, David Goodman, Alex Julca, Yagil Levy, Anthony Marx, Cathy Schneider, Arthur Stinchcombe, Alexei Waters, Viviana Zelizer, members of the Columbia history-sociology colloquium (fall 1996), and three anonymous critics for the University of California Press read earlier versions of the whole manuscript attentively. Members of a special workshop convened by Harrison White at Columbia's Center for the Social Sciences (fall 1996, with notable participation from Duncan Foley,

David Gibson, Ann Mische, Richard Nelson, Shepley Orr, and the irrepressible White himself) tore apart four chapters of the manuscript and
then helped paste them back together. Although none of these demanding critics got everything she or he wanted, and despite the fact
that some of them will feel I ignored splendid advice at my peril, they
caused sweeping alterations in the book and even forced some changes
in my thinking about its problems.

Thanks also to Art Stinchcombe for his permission to quote from a
semi-published paper he never bothered to republish, and for his re-
minder that I might inadvertently have lifted some ideas from a sprawl-
ing, arboreal, unpublished manuscript of his that I reviewed for him
decades ago, from one branch of which he eventually carved his extraordinary (and unaccountably neglected) *Economic Sociology.* Certainly, at-
tentive readers of Stinchcombe will notice affinities between his way of
approaching these matters and mine.

If Eric Wanner holds the book up to the light and squints, he will
see the first substantial report of the work for which the Russell Sage
Foundation gave me a bountiful visiting appointment and support for
a small research group in 1987–1988; I am grateful to Eric for tactful
abstinence from nagging in the meantime.

I have adapted a few pages from my "Stratification and Inequality,"
in *Encyclopedia of Social History,* ed. Peter N. Stearns (New York: Garland,
1994); from "The Weight of the Past on North American Immigration,"
Research Paper 189, Centre of Urban and Community Studies, University of Toronto, 1994; and from "Social Movements and (All Sorts of)
Other Political Interactions—Local, National, and International—Including Identities: Several Divagations from a Common Path, Beginning
with British Struggles over Catholic Emancipation, 1780–1829, and Ending with Contemporary Nationalism," Working Paper 207, Center for
Studies of Social Change, New School for Social Research, 1995. I have
also drawn ideas and a bit of text from *Work Under Capitalism,* by Chris
Tilly and Charles Tilly, forthcoming from Westview; although he bears
no responsibility for the final shape this book has taken, Chris gave me
acute economist's-eye challenges to my lecture texts.

Excerpts from earlier versions of the book's text appear in "Durable

Inequality," Working Paper 224, Center for Studies of Social Change, New School for Social Research, 1995; and in "Mechanisms of Inequality," Working Paper 37, Work–Organization–Economy Working Paper Series, Department of Sociology, Stockholm University, 1996. I owe thanks to Peter Hedström, Richard Swedberg, Ronald Burt, Trond Petersen, Mario Bunge, Walter Korpi, and other participants in Stockholm University's conference on Social Mechanisms (June 1996) as well as to Paul DiMaggio and Anton Schuurman (who were not in Stockholm) for criticism of the latter paper.

As a canny builder modifies the structure where the architect's plan would have produced sagging walls and open joints, copy editor Mary Renaud eliminated hundreds of burrs and blurs from my manuscript. One sign of her prowess is this: except for a single split infinitive, she found every outright error I had marked in my copy of the manuscript after submitting it, and many more I had not noticed.

Sweden's great Humanistik-Samhällsvetenskapliga Forskningsrådet financed and organized the stay in Stockholm that permitted me to devote most of my time over five months to the book. I am especially grateful to Bo Öhngren and Marianne Yagoubi of HSFR for their help, guidance, and encouragement; to Richard Swedberg for hosting my stay at Stockholm University's Department of Sociology; and to Mattias Widman for keeping the department's infrastructure glued together.

On the grounds that *(a)* if I can't summarize here what I said elsewhere, it probably isn't worth mentioning and *(b)* if I find other people's repeated self-citation irritating, they probably feel the same way about mine, I have suppressed the recurrent urge to cite reports of my research on popular contention, residential segregation, migration, population change, state formation, capitalist transformation, and related topics, from which examples in the text frequently come.

New York City
March 1997

1 Of Essences and Bonds

We could reasonably call James Gillray (1757–1815) Britain's first professional cartoonist (George 1967, 57; Hill 1976). He left us unforgettable images of public and private affairs under George III. Very few handsome people figure in Gillray's caricatures. In the savage portrayals of British life he drew, etched, and colored toward 1800, beefy, red-faced aristocrats commonly tower over other people, while paupers almost invariably appear as small, gaunt, and gnarled. If Gillray painted his compatriots with malice, however, he also observed them acutely.

Take the matter of height. Let us consider fourteen-year-old entrants to the Royal Military Academy at Sandhurst to represent the healthier portion of the aristocracy and gentry, and fourteen-year-old recruits for naval service via London's Marine Society to represent the healthier portion of the city's jobless poor. At the nineteenth century's start, poor boys of fourteen averaged only 4 feet 3 inches tall, while aristocrats and gentry of the same age averaged about 5 feet 1 inch (Floud, Wachter, and

Gregory 1990, 197; for the history of the Marine Society as an aristocratic benefaction, see Colley 1992, 91–93). An average beginning military cadet stood some 10 inches taller than a newly recruited mariner. Because poor youths then matured later than rich ones, their heights converged an inch or two by adulthood. Nevertheless we can imagine their counterparts in the army: aristocratic officers glowering down half a foot or more at their plebeian troops. Such an image vivifies the phrases "high and mighty," "haughty," and "look down on someone."

Poor people have few good times. But the years around 1800 brought Britain's low-income families especially bad times. In the short run, massive diversion of resources and labor power to French Revolutionary and Napoleonic wars depleted domestic production as it drove up consumer prices. Over the longer run, the urbanization, industrialization, and sharpened inequality promoted by capitalist expansion were then aggravating the hardships faced by Western Europe's poorer households. As poor people ceased producing their own food faster than agricultural productivity rose, hardship extended to their daily bread.

In his Nobel Prize lecture, economist and economic historian Robert Fogel points out that at nutritional levels prevailing toward the end of the eighteenth century, from 3 to 10 percent of the English and French work forces had too little food to sustain any effective work at all, while a full fifth of the population commanded too little for more than a few hours of light work per day (Fogel 1994, 371–374). At those low nutritional levels, furthermore, English and French workers were extremely vulnerable to chronic disease, hence liable to work lives disrupted by illness and early death. Fogel speculates that malnutrition itself thereby accounted for the stunning proportion of beggars—up to 20 percent of the entire population—reported in various regions of eighteenth-century Europe.

Over population categories, regions, and countries, as Fogel and other researchers have recently established, material well-being and stature vary in strong relation to each other (Floud, Wachter, and Gregory 1990; Fogel 1993, 1994; Fogel and Costa 1997; Komlos 1987, 1990, 1994). Richard Steckel sums up:

Stature adeptly measures inequality in the form of nutritional deprivation; average height in the past century is sensitive not only to the level
of income but to the distribution of income and the consumption of basic necessities by the poor. Unlike conventional measures of living standards based on output, stature is a measure of consumption that incorporates or adjusts for individual nutritional needs; it is a net measure
that captures not only the supply of inputs to health but demands on
those inputs. (Steckel 1995, 1903)

Well-being and height link through food consumption; victuals invigo-
rate. Although genes set variable limits to height distributions in human
populations, childhood nutrition strongly affects the degree to which
any individual approaches her or his genetic limit. Low birth weight,
which typically results from a mother's illness and malnutrition, predicts reliably to a child's health problems, diminished life expectancy,
and smaller adult size.

Within a given population, furthermore, short stature itself generally
predicts to higher levels of morbidity and mortality—most likely not
because of height's inherent advantages but because, on the whole, short
stature correlates with unfavorable childhood health experiences and
lesser body strength. Rising height across an entire population therefore
provides one of our clearest signs that the well-being of that population
is increasing, and marked adult height differentials by social category
within the male or female population provide a strong indicator of durable inequality.

That average heights of adults in Western countries have typically
risen 6 inches or so over the past century and a half reflects a significant
rise in living standards. That even in egalitarian Sweden recent studies
reveal lower birth weights for the newborn of less-educated women (in
this case, most likely a joint outcome of smoking and nutrition) tells us
that material inequalities persist into prosperity (*Dagens Nyheter* 1996).
That at my modest altitude I easily see over the heads of many adult
males with whom I travel on New York subways—especially those
speaking languages other than English—signals that in capitalist countries we still have profound inequalities of life experience to identify
and explain.

Since sexual dimorphism prevails among primates and since humans commonly live in mixed-sex households whose members share food, one might suppose that female/male height differences, unlike class inequalities, derive almost entirely from genetic predisposition. Not quite. Nature and nurture are disentangled with difficulty when it comes to such matters as sex differences in body size. As James Tanner puts it:

> Variation between the heights of *individuals* within a subpopulation is indeed largely dependent on differences in their genetic endowment; but the variation between the means of groups of individuals (at least within an ethnically homogeneous population) reflects the cumulative nutritional, hygienic, disease, and stress experience of each of the groups. In the language of analysis of variance, most of the within-group variation is due to heredity, and most of the between-group variation is due to childhood environment. (Tanner 1994, 1)

What counts, however, as a subpopulation, or group? Surely not any cohabiting population, regardless of social divisions within it. For "group," read "category," to recognize that class, gender, race, ethnicity, and similar socially organized systems of distinction clearly qualify. (I will follow current conventions by speaking of "sex" in reference to X and Y chromosome–linked biological differences, "gender" in reference to social categories.) In each of these cases, differences in "nutritional, hygienic, disease, and stress experience" contribute to differences in adult stature. Researchers in the field have so far done much more with class differences, national differences, and change over time than with male/female differences.

Still, gender likewise marks distinctive childhood experiences, even when it comes to nutrition. When children in pastoral and agricultural economies begin serious work in their household enterprises, they almost always take on gender-differentiated tasks. That means their daily routines give boys and girls unequal access to food. Most of the time girls get less, and their food is of lower quality. Where men fish or hunt while females till and gather, however, the division of labor often attaches girls and women to the more reliable and continuous sources of calories. Thus in some circumstances females may actually get better nourishment than males.

The fundamental fact, then, is gender differentiation in nutrition, with the usual but not universal condition being inferior nutrition for females. We have enough episodic documentation concerning gender discrimination with respect to health care, feeding, infanticide, and general nurture, as well as slivers of evidence suggesting gender-differential patterns of improvement or decline in nutrition under the influence of broad economic fluctuations, to support hypotheses of widespread unequal treatment of males and females, of inequality in their resulting life chances, hence of a social contribution to gender differences in weight and height as well.

Below a certain threshold of food supply, most households make regular if implicit choices concerning which of their members will have adequate nourishment. Contemporary capitalist countries seem to have risen above that threshold, although we lack reliable evidence concerning nutritional inequality among capitalism's currently increasing share of poor people. But the hungry world as a whole still features gender discrimination in nutrition.

Here Fogel's line of investigation crosses the inquiries of Amartya Sen (Sen 1981, 1982, 1983, 1992). From his analyses of poverty and famine onward, Sen has sniffed out deliberately unequal treatment in the presence of resources that could ensure more general welfare. He recurrently detects gender-differentiated claims on such resources. "There is a lot of indirect evidence," he comments, "of differential treatment of women and men, and particularly of girls *vis-à-vis* boys, in many parts of the world, e.g., among rural families in Asia and North Africa. The observed morbidity and mortality rates frequently reflect differential female deprivation of extraordinary proportions" (Sen 1992, 123). The most dramatic observations concern female infanticide through direct attack or (more often) systematic neglect, which analysts have frequently reported for strongly patrilineal regions of Asia (Johansson and Nygren 1991; Langford and Storey 1993; Lee, Campbell, and Tan 1992; Lee, Feng, and Campbell 1994; Muhuri and Preston 1991; Yi et al. 1993).

People of Western countries have not much practiced selective female infanticide. But Western states have often reinforced gender distinctions in nutrition and nurture, notably by confining military service to males, diverting food stocks from civilian to military use, providing superior health care for troops, and ensuring that soldiers receive better rations than the general population. Florence Nightingale, after all, more or less invented professional nursing as we know it while organizing the health care of British fighting men during the Crimean War. In the absence of powerful drugs and diagnostic instruments, Nightingale's nursing stressed cleanliness, warmth, and nourishment, comforts many women back home in Britain did not then share. If military men at war have historically faced exceptional risks of violent death and disabling disease, in recent centuries they have also typically received three square meals a day when civilians, especially female civilians, were tightening their belts.

Such socially organized differences in well-being illustrate this book's main subject: the causes, uses, structures, and effects of categorical inequality. The book does not ask what causes human inequality in general. Instead it addresses these questions: How, why, and with what consequences do long-lasting, systematic inequalities in life chances distinguish members of different socially defined categories of persons? How do categorical inequalities form, change, and disappear? Since all social relations involve fleeting, fluctuating inequalities, let us concentrate on *durable* inequalities, those that last from one social interaction to the next, with special attention to those that persist over whole careers, lifetimes, and organizational histories.

Let us concentrate, furthermore, on distinctly bounded pairs such as female/male, aristocrat/plebeian, citizen/foreigner, and more complex classifications based on religious affiliation, ethnic origin, or race. We focus on *categories* rather than on continua such as [rich . . . poor], [tall . . . short], [ugly . . . beautiful], and so on. Bounded categories deserve special attention because they provide clearer evidence for the operation of durable inequality, because their boundaries do crucial organizational work, and because categorical differences actually account for much of what ordinary observers take to be results of variation in individual talent or effort.

As Max Weber noted almost a century ago, the creation of what he called "social closure" advances efforts by the powerful to exclude less powerful people from the full benefits of joint enterprises, while facilitating efforts by underdogs to organize for the seizure of benefits denied (Weber 1968, 1:43–46, 1:341–348; Parkin 1979, 44–116). A relationship is likely to be closed, Weber remarked,

> in the following type of situation: a social relationship may provide the parties to it with opportunities for the satisfaction of spiritual or material interests. If the participants expect that the admission of others will lead to an improvement of their situation, an improvement in degree, in kind, in the security or the value of the satisfaction, their interest will be in keeping the relationship open. If, on the other hand, their expectations are of improving their position by monopolistic tactics, their interest is in a closed relationship. (Weber 1968, 1:43)

Organizations such as firms and clans use closure by drawing complete boundaries around themselves and then monitoring flows across those boundaries with care. Contrary to Weber, however, I argue that at a scale larger than a single organization completely bounded categories are rare and difficult to maintain, that most categorical inequality relies on establishment of a partial frontier and defined social relations across that frontier, with much less control in regions distant from the frontier. Yet in other regards my analysis resonates with Weber's discussion. It builds a bridge from Max Weber on social closure to Karl Marx on exploitation, and back. Crossing that bridge repeatedly, this book concerns social mechanisms—recurrent causal sequences of general scope—that actually lock categorical inequality into place. The central argument runs like this: Large, significant inequalities in advantages among human beings correspond mainly to categorical differences such as black / white, male / female, citizen / foreigner, or Muslim / Jew rather than to individual differences in attributes, propensities, or performances. In actual operation, more complex categorical systems involving multiple religions or various races typically resolve into bounded pairs relating just two categories at a time, as when the coexistence of Muslims, Jews, and Christians resolves into the sets Muslim / Jew, Muslim / Christian, and Jew / Christian, with each pair having its own distinct set of boundary relations.

Even where they employ ostensibly biological markers, such categories always depend on extensive social organization, belief, and enforcement. Durable inequality among categories arises because people who

control access to value-producing resources solve pressing organizational problems by means of categorical distinctions. Inadvertently or
otherwise, those people set up systems of social closure, exclusion, and
control. Multiple parties—not all of them powerful, some of them even
victims of exploitation—then acquire stakes in those solutions. Variation
in the form and durability of inequality therefore depends chiefly on the
nature of the resources involved, the previous social locations of the
categories, the character of the organizational problems, and the configurations of interested parties.

Through all these variations, we discover and rediscover paired, recognized, organized, unequal categories such as black/white, male/fe-
male, married/unmarried, and citizen/noncitizen. The dividing line between such categories usually remains incomplete in two regards: first,
some people (persons of mixed race, transsexuals, certified refugees,
and so on) do not fit clearly on one side of the line or the other; and,
second, in many situations the distinction between the members of any
particular pair does not matter. Where they apply, however, paired and
unequal categories do crucial organizational work, producing marked,
durable differences in access to valued resources. Durable inequality depends heavily on the institutionalization of categorical pairs.

ROOTS OF CATEGORICAL INEQUALITY

How and why does the institutionalization of categorical pairs occur?
Since the argument is unfamiliar and complicated, it may help to lay
out its major elements and their causal connections even before defining
crucial terms. The list will serve as a preliminary map of the wilderness
this book will explore:

1.   Paired and unequal categories, consisting of asymmetrical rela-
      tions across a socially recognized (and usually incomplete) divid-
      ing line between interpersonal networks, recur in a wide variety
      of situations, with the usual effect being the unequal exclusion of
      each network from resources controlled by the other.

2.   Two mechanisms we may label *exploitation* and *opportunity hoarding* cause durable inequality when their agents incorporate paired and unequal categories at crucial organizational boundaries.

3.   Two further mechanisms we may title *emulation* and *adaptation* reinforce the effectiveness of categorical distinctions.

4.   Local categorical distinctions gain strength and operate at lower cost when matched with widely available paired and unequal categories.

5.   When many organizations adopt the same categorical distinctions, those distinctions become more pervasive and decisive in social life at large.

6.   Experience within categorically differentiated settings gives participants systematically different and unequal preparation for performance in new organizations.

7.   Much of what observers ordinarily interpret as individual differences that create inequality is actually the consequence of categorical organization.

8.   For these reasons, inequalities by race, gender, ethnicity, class, age, citizenship, educational level, and other apparently contradictory principles of differentiation form through similar social processes and are to an important degree organizationally interchangeable.

Whatever else it accomplishes, the book will make clear what is at issue in such an organizational view of inequality-producing mechanisms. At a minimum, it will challenge other analysts to clarify the causal mechanisms implied by their own preferred explanations of durable inequality and then to search for evidence that those causal mechanisms are actually operating.

Although the word "organization" may call to mind firms, governments, schools, and similar formal, hierarchical structures, I mean the analysis to encompass all sorts of well-bounded clusters of social relations in which occupants of at least one position have the right to commit collective resources to activities reaching across the boundary. Organizations include corporate kin groups, households, religious sects, bands of mercenaries, and many local communities. Durable inequality arises in all of them. All of them at times incorporate categorical distinctions originating in adjacent organizations.

Humans invented categorical inequality millennia ago and have applied it to a wide range of social situations. People establish systems of categorical inequality, however inadvertently, chiefly by means of these two causal mechanisms:

- *Exploitation*, which operates when powerful, connected people command resources from which they draw significantly increased returns by coordinating the effort of outsiders whom they exclude from the full value added by that effort.

- *Opportunity hoarding*, which operates when members of a categorically bounded network acquire access to a resource that is valuable, renewable, subject to monopoly, supportive of network activities, and enhanced by the network's modus operandi.

The two mechanisms obviously parallel each other, but people who lack great power can pursue the second if encouraged, tolerated, or ignored by the powerful. Often the two parties gain complementary, if unequal, benefits from jointly excluding others.

Two further mechanisms cement such arrangements in place: *emulation*, the copying of established organizational models and/or the transplanting of existing social relations from one setting to another; and *adaptation*, the elaboration of daily routines such as mutual aid, political influence, courtship, and information gathering on the basis of categorically unequal structures. Exploitation and opportunity hoarding favor the installation of categorical inequality, while emulation and adaptation generalize its influence.

A certain kind of inequality therefore becomes prevalent over a large population in two complementary ways. Either the categorical pair in question—male/female, legitimate/illegitimate, black/white, citizen/noncitizen, and so on—operates in organizations that control major resources affecting welfare, and its effects spread from there; or the categorical pair repeats in a great many similar organizations, regardless of their power.

In the first case, organizations that produce work and wield coercive power—corporations and states, plantations and mercenary forces, textile mills and drug rings, depending on the context—take pride of place because they ordinarily control the largest concentrations of deployable resources within large populations. In some settings of ideological hegemony, religious organizations and their own categorical distinctions can also have similar effects on inequality around them.

In the second case, households, kin groups, and local communities hold crucial positions for two reasons: within a given population, they form and change according to similar principles, and they strongly influence biological and social reproduction. Gender and age distinctions, for example, do not ordinarily separate lineages from one another, but the repetition of these distinctions in many lineages lends them influence throughout the population. The basic mechanisms that generate inequality operate in a similar fashion over a wide variety of organizational settings as well as over a great range of unequal outcomes: income, wealth, power, deference, fame, privilege, and more.

People who create or sustain categorical inequality by means of the four basic mechanisms rarely set out to manufacture inequality as such. Instead they solve other organizational problems by establishing categorically unequal access to valued outcomes. More than anything else, they seek to secure rewards from sequestered resources. Both exploitation and opportunity hoarding provide a means of doing so. But, once undertaken, exploitation and opportunity hoarding pose their own organizational problems: how to maintain distinctions between insiders and outsiders; how to ensure solidarity, loyalty, control, and succession; how to monopolize knowledge that favors profitable use of sequestered resources. The installation of explicitly categorical boundaries helps to solve such organizational problems, especially if the boundaries in question incorporate forms of inequality that are already well established in the surrounding world. Emulation and adaptation lock such distinctions into place, making them habitual and sometimes even essential to exploiters and exploited alike.

To be sure, widely applicable categories accumulate their own histories and relations to other social structures: male/female distinctions have acquired enormous, slow-moving cultural carapaces yet reappear within almost all social structures of any scale, whereas in the United States the distinction Hispanic/white remains a disputed, politically driven division of uncertain cultural content. Such categorical pairs therefore operate with characteristic differences when imported into new settings. The distinction citizen/foreigner, for instance, does a variety of organizational work—separating temporary from long-term employees, differentiating access to public benefits, managing rights to intervene in political processes, and so on—but everywhere and always its existence and effectiveness depend on the present capacity of a relatively centralized government. The power of a differentiator based on membership or nonmembership in a political party (notable cases being communist parties in state socialist regimes) similarly depends on the existence of a hegemonic party exercising extensive state power and controlling a wide variety of valued resources.

Divisions based on preference for sexual partners—gay, lesbian, straight, and so on—depend far less on governmental structure. As compared to those who differentiate based on citizenship or party membership, those who install sexual preference as a local basis of inequality have less access to governmental backing as well as a lower likelihood of governmental intervention. Sexual preference distinctions, however, do import extensive mythologies, practices, relations, and understandings that significantly affect how the distinctions work within a new setting.

Categorical inequality, in short, has some very general properties. But one of those properties, paradoxically, is to vary in practical operation with the historically accumulated understandings, practices, and social relations already attached to a given set of distinctions.

Consider some quick examples. Josef Stalin knits together an effective political machine by recruiting ethnically identified regional leaders, training them in Moscow, making them regional party bosses, and giving their ethnic identifications priority within semiautonomous political jurisdictions. When the Soviet center later relaxes its grip, political entrepreneurs within regions mobilize followings around those ethnic identities, others mobilize against them, and ostensibly age-old ethnic conflicts flame into civil war.

Again, the founder of a small manufacturing firm, following models already established in the trade, divides the firm's work into clusters of jobs viewed as distinct in character and qualifications and then recruits workers for those jobs within well-marked categories. As turnover occurs and the firm expands, established workers pass word of available jobs among friends and relatives, collaborating with and supporting them once they join the work force. Those new workers therefore prove more reliable and effective than others hired off the street, and all concerned come to associate job with category, so much so that owner and workers come to believe in the superior fitness of that category's members for the particular line of work.

Another case in point. Householders in an urban neighborhood build up a precarious system of trust on the basis of common backgrounds and shared relations to third parties, live with persons and property at risk to that system of trust, and then react violently when newcomers whom they cannot easily integrate into the same networks threaten to occupy part of the territory. In the process, members of the two groups elaborate compelling stories about each other's perfidy and utter incompatibility.

Members of an immigrant stream, finally, peddle craft goods from their home region on big-city streets, and some of them set up businesses as suppliers, manufacturers, or retail merchants. New immigrants find work in the expanding trade, and not only an immigrant niche but an ethnically specific international connection provides exclusive opportunities for the next generation. In all these cases, organizational improvisations lead to durable categorical inequality. In all these cases, but with variable weight, exploitation and opportunity hoarding favor the installation of categorical inequality, while emulation and adaptation generalize its influence.

When it comes to the determinants of durable inequality, are these special cases or the general rule? This book gives reasons for thinking that categorical inequality in general results from varying intersections of exploitation, opportunity hoarding, emulation, and adaptation. It goes farther, claiming that much of the inequality that seems to result from individual or group differences in ability actually stems from the same causes:

- Authoritatively organized categorical differences in current performance (e.g., categorically differentiated cooperation or sabo-
  tage by fellow workers, subordinates, and supervisors)

- Authoritatively organized categorical differences in *rewards* for
  performance (e.g., systematically lower pay for blacks than for
  whites doing similar work)

- Authoritatively organized differences in the acquisition of *capacities* for performance (e.g., categorically segregated and unequal
  schools)

It also argues that the social mechanisms which generate inequality with
respect to a wide range of advantages—wealth, income, esteem, protection, power, and more—are similar. Although historical accumulations
of institutions, social relations, and shared understandings produce differences in the day-to-day operation of various sorts of categories (gender, race, citizenship, and so on) as well as differences in various sorts
of outcomes (e.g., landed wealth versus cash income), ultimately interactions of exploitation, opportunity hoarding, emulation, and adaptation explain them all.

Nutrition turns out to provide a useful general model for categorical
inequality, since in most settings feeding differs with categorical membership, and since in many cases the cumulative effects of feeding elsewhere help to explain categorical differences in performance in the current case. In direct parallel, the information and social ties that
individuals and groups can currently acquire differ categorically, but
previous categorical experience also strongly affects the information and
social ties these individuals and groups already have at their disposal,
not to mention the means they have of acquiring new information and
social ties. Unequal treatment of females and males in a wide range of
social lives creates female/male differences in the qualifications and social ties prospective workers bring to workplaces; those differences interact with (and generally reinforce) gender distinctions built into the
allocation and supervision of work.

Again, categorically differentiated family experience strongly affects
children's school performance and teachers' evaluations of that performance, which in turn channel children into categorically differentiated,

career-shaping educational streams (Hout and Dohan 1996; Taubman 1991). To the extent that teachers, employers, public officials, and other authorities differentiate their responses to performances categorically, they contribute to durable, authoritatively organized categorical differences. More generally, apparent third parties to the inequality in question—state officials, legislatures, owners of firms, and other powerholders—significantly influence the operation of categorical inequality and sometimes take the initiative in creating it. Authorities do, in fact, frequently solve their own organizational problems—how to sort students, whom to hire, what rights to honor—in categorical ways.

Feelings of identity, on one side, and intergroup hostility, on the other, may well accompany, promote, or result from the use of categorical differences to solve organizational problems. But the relative prevalence of such attitudes plays a secondary part in inequality's extent and form. Mistaken beliefs reinforce exploitation, opportunity hoarding, emulation, and adaptation but exercise little independent influence on their initiation—or so I will argue. It follows that the reduction or intensification of racist, sexist, or xenophobic attitudes will have relatively little impact on durable inequality, whereas the introduction of certain new organizational forms—for example, installing different categories or changing the relation between categories and rewards—will have great impact.

If so, the identification of such organizational forms becomes a significant challenge for social scientists. It also follows that similar organizational problems generate parallel solutions in very different settings, in articulation with very different sets of categories. Thus matches of positions with categories, and the justifications for such matches, vary much more than recurrent structural arrangements—for example, when similar clusters of jobs acquire contrasting racial, ethnic, or gender identifications in different labor markets. Causal mechanisms resemble each other greatly, while outcomes differ dramatically, thus inviting very different rationalizations or condemnations after the fact. Social scientists dealing with such durable forms of inequality must hack through dense ideological overgrowth to reach structural roots.

OBSTACLES TO UNDERSTANDING

The essential machete work presents a serious challenge. The literature is vast, evidence mixed, current controversy therefore intense. My personal expertise falls laughably short of sufficing for the effort. Although my ideas about exploitation spring from the Marxist tradition, I have no talent or inclination for the sorts of point-by-point critique and reconstruction of Marxist models that John Roemer, Jon Elster, Samuel Bowles, Herbert Gintis, Howard Botwinick, and Melvin Leiman have undertaken. I cannot hope to provide here a comprehensive review and synthesis of current thinking concerning inequality.

Nor does it seem profitable to proceed chiefly by attacking established models of status attainment, gender inequality, or segmented labor markets, since the critique of each model would require a separate move onto its own terrain, and since I hope to identify the common ground of these ostensibly incompatible accounts of inequality rather than destroying them. My self-appointed task is instead to address the problems that emerge from the crossing of these literatures. Serious trouble begins when we try to synthesize understandings of these different kinds of inequality, when we move from description to explanation, when we search for the actual causal mechanisms that produce, sustain, or alter durable inequality. Trouble comes in four packages labeled *particularism, interaction, transmission,* and *mentalism.*

First, *particularism.* Observers often ground explanations for each form of inequality separately in perennial but peculiar forces. Each one seems sui generis, constituting its own mode of existence. If sexism springs from age-old patriarchy, racism from the heritage of slavery, denigration of noncitizens from xenophobic state traditions, however, it is hard to see why the mechanisms of inclusion and exclusion in all these cases have such striking resemblances. They must have more common causal properties than particularistic accounts suggest.

Our second trouble comes from the weakness of all available explanations for the *interaction* among various forms of categorical inequality. Despite illuminating analyses of ethnic niche formation and variable principles of citizenship taken one at a time, no one has provided a compelling explanation for what actually occurs: simultaneous differentiation of jobs and entrepreneurial niches by gender, race, ethnicity, and citizenship. What intersection of employers' and workers' preferences, for example, could possibly explain sharp segregation in all these regards at once, not to mention the interchangeability of one basis of segregation for another? How do similar sets of jobs end up all-female in one setting, all-black or all-immigrant in another?

Trouble number three concerns the *transmission* of categorical inequality to new members of the related categories. Do instantaneous configurations of interest or impulse that plausibly seem to account for the short-run creation of inequality continue at work from one generation to the next, or do some other mechanisms congeal categories that have unequal relations? Do genes and shared environments so powerfully reproduce individual propensities and capacities? In none of these well-documented fields do we have a convincing explanation of inherited inequality.

Finally, *mentalism*—which relies in the last instance on shared interests, motivations, or attitudes as the bases of inegalitarian institutions— also causes serious trouble. Resort to mental states as fundamental sources of inequality leaves mysterious the cause-effect chains by which these states actually produce the outcomes commonly attributed to them—especially considering how rarely we humans accomplish the precise ends we consciously pursue (Merton 1936, 1989). If collectively a whole population sustains a set of preferences simultaneously ordered by gender, race, ethnicity, and citizenship, whose mental processes contain these preferences, how do they order the preferences, and what translates preferences into a wide range of structural inequalities?

Let us look more closely at the last difficulty, which besets much of today's social science, not just the study of inequality. Most people seeking to explain any sort of social process choose among three ontological foundations; all three presume the existence and centrality of self-propelling essences (individuals, groups, or societies). Two of the ontologies center on the mental processes of such essences. First, *methodological individualism* presumes that social life results chiefly or exclusively from the actions of self-motivated, interest-seeking persons. Second, *phenomenological individualism* posits conscious minds as the ultimate social reality; with sufficient doubt about the possibility of reliable communication among minds, phenomenological individualism becomes solipsism.

The third ontology eschews mentalism, but at the price of other high-risk assumptions about social reality. *Systems theories* impute self-maintaining logics to social structures, from groups, organizations, or institutions to that big, vague structure that analysts refer to as "society." Some theorists, to be sure, combine two of these ontological foundations, as in Emile Durkheim's recurrent image of an individual face to face with a society or Alfred Marshall's representation of a calculating buyer or seller who confronts an impersonal market. But alone or in combination, methodological individualism, phenomenological individualism, and systems theories all nevertheless assume self-sustaining essences, whether individual, collective, or both.

A fourth possibility exists, however, a possibility assuming not essences but bonds: *relational* models of social life beginning with interpersonal transactions or ties. Since Charles Peirce and Georg Simmel, relational models have haunted social science; phenomenological individualists such as George Herbert Mead who wanted to represent the effects of social interaction on consciousness and action have recurrently heard relational voices. The unjustly neglected institutional economist John R. Commons (1934) insisted sixty years ago that economics should begin its analyses with transactions, not individuals. Economists, alas, did not heed him.

More recently, Norbert Elias's "configurations" were largely relational. Although Elias tended to ground his configurations in shared attitudes, he stressed collective connections among the social positions involved. In 1965, for example, Elias and John Scotson published a study of two nearly identical neighborhoods in Winston Parva (a locality near Leicester) whose members had organized hostile, unequal conceptions of each other. In the study's introduction, Elias remarked:

At present the tendency is to discuss the problem of social stigmatisation as if it were simply a question of people showing individually a pronounced dislike of other people as individuals. A well-known way of conceptualising such an observation is to classify it as prejudice. However, that means perceiving only at the individual level something which cannot be understood without perceiving it at the same time at the group level. At present one often fails to distinguish between, and relate to each other, group stigmatisation and individual prejudice. In Winston Parva, as elsewhere, one found members of one group casting a slur on those of another, not because of their qualities as individual people, but because they were members of a group which they considered collectively as different from, and as inferior to, their own group. Thus one misses the key to the problem usually discussed under headings such as "social prejudice," if one looks for it solely in the personality structure of individual people. One can find it only if one considers the figuration formed by the two (or more) groups concerned or, in other words, the nature of their interdependence. (Elias and Scotson 1994, xx)

In Winston Parva, the study shows, the old-timers of one neighborhood had greater cohesion, hence more strategic power, than the newcomers of the other; old-timers collectively translated their organizational advantage into successful stigmatization of the neighboring population. Thus Elias reached at least halfway to a full-fledged relational account.

These days the program of "structural sociology" as variously advocated by such theorists as Mark Granovetter, Alejandro Portes, Pierre Bourdieu, Paul DiMaggio, and Harrison White most aggressively advances relational models (see, e.g., Portes 1995; Powell and DiMaggio 1991; Wellman and Berkowitz 1988). In economics, institutionalists also make allowances, generally more grudging, for relational effects (e.g., Akerlof 1984; Jacoby 1990; Lazonick 1991; North 1991; Osterman 1993; Simon 1991; Williamson 1991). In his *Foundations of Social Theory* (1990), the late James Coleman feinted repeatedly toward relational accounts of norms, commitments, and similar phenomena but pulled his punches as they approached the target. Although his verbal accounts mentioned many agents, monitors, and authorities who influenced individual actions, his mathematical formulations tellingly portrayed a single actor's computations rather than interactions among persons.

Structural and institutional analyses of relations clarify and emphasize the significance of culture in social life. Instead of imagining culture as an autonomous sphere in which ideas change ideas, which then constrain behavior, structural and institutional analyses treat culture as shared understandings and their representations; actors operate within frames of understanding constructed by previous interactions, anticipating one another's responses on the bases of those frames, and modifying their strategies as a consequence of shared experiences. In such a view, culture intertwines unceasingly with social relations; culture and structure are simply two convenient abstractions from the same stream of transactions.

The four ontologies lead characteristically to different ways of accounting for categorical inequality. Following methodological individualism, analysts typically treat inequality by gender, race, ethnicity, or citizenship as a special case of inequality in general, a case in which (1) members of a category come to share attributes (e.g., educational levels) that place them in similar relations to markets and/or (2) other participants in markets build categorically defined preferences (e.g., an aversion to working with foreigners) into the utility schedules guiding their decisions. Methodological individualists who seek to explain social inequality have so far faced an insurmountable obstacle. Their causal mechanisms consist of mental events: decisions. But they have not formulated a plausible theory of how such mental events produce their consequences in the always erratic behavior of human beings, much less in the complexities of social structure.

Phenomenological individualists find it easier to imagine that categories themselves have meaning and that people express their own identities by acting categorically; consumption of commodities and services, for example, becomes a way of broadcasting one's self-conception to the world at large. That sort of phenomenological individualism, however, has produced no coherent account of the interactions among conscious states of different actors or of the processes by which such states produce alterations in social structure.

Systems theorists generally derive categorical distinctions from collective relations between members of categories and some larger social structure—for example, explaining gender differences by their expression of society-wide values or their service to the reproduction of the whole system. It has proved impossible either to identify those relations to larger structures concretely or to assemble convincing evidence for functional explanations of this kind. Despairing of functional explanations, other systems theorists have commonly derived categorical distinctions from a vague, autonomous entity called "culture" or even *the* culture." Such accounts relabel the phenomenon instead of explaining it. For the explanation of durable inequality, systems theories look like a cul-de-sac.

Relational analysis, as we shall see in detail, typically treats categories as problem-solving social inventions and / or by-products of social interaction (Elster 1983, 25–88). Relational analysts characteristically conceive of culture as shared understandings that intertwine closely with social relations, serving as their tools and constraints instead of constituting an autonomous sphere. Strongly relational analysis remains a minority movement in social science as a whole; individualisms and holisms continue to reign. In the choice between essences and bonds, nevertheless, I want to hold high the banner of bonds. I claim that an account of how transactions clump into social ties, social ties concatenate into networks, and existing networks constrain solutions of organizational problems clarifies the creation, maintenance, and change of categorical inequality.

Let me state that claim with care. Since the fading of systems theories a generation ago, methodological individualism and phenomenological individualism have dominated analyses of inequality. Individualistic analyses have in that time accomplished a great deal. They have documented the outcomes (e.g., stark racial differences in income and wealth) that any adequate account of inequality must explain. They have also ruled out all commonly voiced one-cause explanations of inequality—genetic capacity alone, effort alone, educational achievement alone, point-of-hire discrimination alone, and more. They have thereby greatly clarified what any sound theory of inequality must explain. They have, however, relied on obscure, implausible, or insufficient causal mechanisms grounded in individual experience and action. They have centered thinking about inequality on the image of individuals with variable attributes who pass through a screening process that sorts them according to those attributes into positions that give them differential awards. In various explanations, these attributes may include human capital, ambition, educational credentials, gender, race, or even personal connections, but they remain individual properties. The screening processes often considered range from market competition to employers' selection of workers on the basis of prejudice or favoritism, but they always involve selection among individuals as a function of those individuals' attributes.

Take an example of first-rate research on inequality. A University of California group has published a sustained theoretical, methodological, and factual critique of Richard Herrnstein and Charles Murray's well-known 1994 book *The Bell Curve*. The Herrnstein-Murray book argues, among other things, that in the contemporary United States innate intelligence deeply affects success or failure, that inherited class and racial disparities in intelligence account for the major part of differential accomplishment by children born into different classes and races, and that remedial measures such as affirmative action will therefore inevitably fail or will even compound the inequalities they are designed to mitigate. The California group's critique is judicious, skilled, and ultimately devastating for the Herrnstein-Murray argument. In company with abundant material from elsewhere, it deploys the very same body of evidence on which *The Bell Curve* is based to identify errors in the Herrnstein-Murray analysis and to reach distinctly different and better-reasoned conclusions.

The California study makes a powerful contribution to our understanding of American inequality and to the destruction of widely held misunderstandings. But consider the authors' summary of their alternative explanation:

Children *may* start out with different "natural" advantages useful for economic advancement (and such advantages probably include far more than just the sort of narrow intelligence psychometricians dwell on, advantages such as energy and good looks). But children *certainly* do start off with different social advantages, some with more parental resources and better conditions in their communities than others, and some with the advantage of being male. Children in better-off families and better-off places then receive better schooling and develop their cognitive skills further. Having good schooling and skills, added to the original advantages of gender, family, and neighborhood, combines with contemporary circumstances, such as being married and living in an economically booming area, to reduce substantially people's risk of poverty. Young adults who have lost out—in family advantages, in earlier community conditions, in gender, in schooling, or in current community conditions—suffer a heightened risk of poverty. (Fischer et al. 1996, 93)

Every statement in this summary carries conviction. When we examine it more closely, however, the causal links it identifies run something like this:

Community location, household position, and parental resources affect (*a*) individual cognitive skills and (*b*) quality of schooling, which (interacting with gender) jointly affect (*c*) individual educational outcomes and (*d*) certain other unspecified adult characteristics. Educational outcome, gender, and other unspecified adult characteristics affect economic outcomes, notably the likelihood of being poor.

Such an argument derives collective outcomes (e.g., racial differences in poverty) entirely from individual effects. It also fails to specify the causal mechanisms by which community location, household position, parental resources, and gender produce educational outcomes or the other relevant adult characteristics. Nor does it say how and why educational accomplishment, gender, and other characteristics produce their sorting effects. An individualistic framework leads the California authors to slight organizational, relational, and collective processes.

The authors actually say as much:

And yet we have not accounted for most of the inequality in income. Perhaps some of the remaining 63 percent of unexplained variation can be accounted for by other, unmeasured attributes of individuals—energy, looks, charm, whatever—or by other, unmeasured attributes of their social situations—grandparents' legacies, social contacts, the industry they work in, and so on—or, as Christopher Jencks has suggested, by simple luck. But much of that remaining inequality can only be understood by leaving the individual level of analysis and looking at the social structure of inequality. (Fischer et al. 1996, 99)

They then attempt to deal with that deficiency by calling attention to institutional influences on opportunity and mobility: government policies concerning taxation, investment, redistribution, and services; the organization and operation of schools; the activities of unions and employers' associations; residential segregation; categorical hiring and other categorical forms of discrimination. All these factors do, indeed, enter into the production of durable inequality. The questions are how and why.

Those questions—how and why?—drive my inquiry. The crucial causal mechanisms behind categorical inequality, I argue, do not consist of individual mental events, states of consciousness, or self-sustaining actions of social systems. They operate in the domains of collective experience and social interaction. The remainder of this book explicates and defends that claim. For the most part, my analysis accepts the definition of what analysts of inequality must explain that has emerged from a generation of individualistic investigation. But it complements and clarifies the findings of individualistic analyses by looking at the social structure of inequality.

We pay a price for concentrating on well-documented outcomes. Recent students of inequality under capitalism have, unsurprisingly, focused on wages, a topic that lends itself both to measurement and to explanation in individual terms. They have neglected wealth, health, nutrition, power, deference, privilege, security, and other critical zones of inequality that in the long run matter more to well-being than wages do. They have also drawn evidence disproportionately from wage-paying firms, while giving little attention to family enterprises, contracting, the informal economy, and other settings whose categorically differentiated personnel and operations contribute significantly to aggregate differences in well-being. To document such differences, explain them, and relate them to each other remains a major task for analysts. To pursue it here, however, would enormously complicate and lengthen an already dense analysis. Pages to come take up these other forms of inequality when possible, for example, in discussions of South African racial divisions, power within American health care, and nationalism in the contemporary world. Yet on the whole I leave their complexities for later in the hope that the book's analysis will provide a model for their treatment.

Although concern about inequalities in contemporary capitalist countries—especially my own country, the United States—motivates my inquiry, my plan is not to close in immediately on today's inequalities. Instead I am pursuing an indirect strategy, stepping back from current American discussions of comparable worth, white racism, or immigrant/native differentials to place durable categorical inequality in historical, comparative, and theoretical perspective. A relational view identifies common causal mechanisms beneath the bewildering variety of concrete inequalities.

ELEMENTS OF INEQUALITY

Before undertaking the necessary reconstruction, however, let us think about inequality as such. Human inequality in general consists of the uneven distribution of attributes among a set of social units such as individuals, categories, groups, or regions. Social scientists properly concern themselves especially with the uneven distribution of costs and benefits—that is, *goods*, broadly defined. Relevant goods include not only wealth and income but also such various benefits and costs as control of land, exposure to illness, respect from other people, liability to military service, risk of homicide, possession of tools, and availability of sexual partners. Students of social inequality have paid little attention to the uneven distribution of other attributes such as genetic traits and musical tastes except as they correlate with the uneven distribution of goods in this broad sense.

Goods vary in the extent to which they are *autonomous* (observable without reference to outside units, as in accumulations of food) or *relative* (observable only in relation to other units, as in prestige). Wealth, income, and health exemplify autonomous goods, while prestige, power, and clientele exemplify relative goods. (Some analysts prefer to call relative goods "positional," on the grounds that they attach to positions rather than to persons, but that usage draws attention away from their relational character.) On the whole, inequalities with respect to autonomous goods reach greater extremes than inequalities with respect to relative goods.

Analysis of exploitation by the elite, opportunity hoarding by the nonelite, emulation, and adaptation makes it clear that autonomous and relative goods depend intimately on each other. Although people come to value them for their own sakes, relative goods generally occupy a subordinate, derivative position: they serve as a means of creating or maintaining categorical inequality with respect to autonomous goods. Possession of prestige, power, clientele, and status-marking goods then justifies the superior position of favored categories ex post facto, just as the perquisites of favored categories give autonomous goods such as well-built housing, luxurious automobiles, comfortable workspaces, fine foods, good liquor, or rich entertainment the patina of relative goods as well. The chief reversals in the priority of autonomous over relative goods occur in such public displays as potlatch, charitable donations, and ostentatious weddings, where wealthy or powerful people incur great expenditures in the short run to mark their superiority over other people. Even there, successful displays—for example, magnates parading great clienteles in the public rituals of Renaissance Florence—characteristically enhance the longer-run advantages of those who mount them (Paige and Paige 1981; Trexler 1981).

I certainly did not discover the interaction between autonomous and relative goods. Pierre Bourdieu has spent much of his career exploring it, with his analytic division among economic, cultural, and social capitals representing the interdependence of autonomous goods narrowly conceived, valued information, and the social ties that provide differential access to those goods and information (Bourdieu 1979; Bourdieu and Wacquant 1992, 118–119; Buchmann 1989, 31–42). When ever-relational Karl Marx traced back relative goods (not his term!) to origins in relations of production, he likewise portrayed prestige, power, clientele, and possession of status-marking goods as instruments and products of categorically based exploitation. Categorical inequality with respect to autonomous goods gains strength from and generates parallel differences in relative goods.

How can we judge the equality or inequality of two social units—positions, persons, categories, organizations, networks, countries? Estimating the inequality of any set of social units presents three major problems: to identify and bound the units under comparison, to weigh the importance of different goods, and to decide whether the weighted differences are "large" or "small." Generally speaking, all three judgments require a theory of the larger social structures in which the units are embedded.

The difficulty compounds with summary measurement of inequality and its changes among many units—for example, among all households in a national population (as in many analyses of long-term change) or among all the world's states (as in many world-system analyses). In such cases, analysts usually adopt two linked strategies: first choosing a single criterion good (such as current income) that seems to correlate with a number of other inequalities, and then comparing the actual distribution of that good with a standard of absolutely equal distribution. Such widely used devices as the Gini index and the Duncan dissimilarity index illustrate the combined strategy. In this approach, inequality implicitly becomes a one-dimensional phenomenon. Individual units vary in position along the chosen dimension.

Although analysts sometimes apply the term loosely to all sorts of inequality, *stratification* properly designates the rare form of disparity that clusters social units by layers, or *strata*, which are homogeneous with respect to a wide range of goods (both autonomous and relative) and which occupy a single, well-defined rank order. A true system of stratification resembles a pyramidal skyscraper, with its summit and base, its distinct levels, its elevators and stairways for movement from level to level, and its array of multiple graded niches.

One of my own great teachers, I fear, introduced abiding mischief into sociological discussions of inequality and mobility. Pitirim Sorokin's *Social Mobility*, first published in 1927, popularized not only representations of inequality as stratification but also ideas of vertical and horizontal mobility. Sorokin said explicitly that "social stratification means the differentiation of a given population into hierarchically superposed classes" (Sorokin 1959, 11). Stratification implies social strata:

upper, middle, and lower, or some other bounded vertical division. Thus Sorokin committed his followers to the suppositions of continuous, consistent hierarchies transecting whole populations, of discrete individual locations within those hierarchies, and of well-marked boundaries between classes.

Summarizing the causes of stratification, moreover, Sorokin gave them a distinctly individualistic cast:

> First, the very fact of living together; second, innate differences of individuals, due to the differences in the complements of their chromosomes; third, differences in the environment in which individuals are placed since the moment of their conception. (Sorokin 1959, 337)

Although the first cause, the "very fact of living together," sounds groupish, it turns out to consist for Sorokin of an inevitable division between (few) leaders and (many) led. Intergroup and interpersonal processes—of struggle, conquest, or otherwise—play no part.

Sorokin's analysis of vertical and horizontal mobility compounds the difficulty of judging inequality by fostering the illusion of a continuous, homogeneous two-dimensional grid within which individuals and aggregates of individuals occupy specific cells and move along geometric paths. The seductive spatial metaphor misleads analysts to the extent that inequality consists of organized ties among groups, categories, or individuals; that different forms of inequality order the same groups, categories, or individuals differently; that changes in patterns of inequality result from intergroup processes. Since all these conditions actually obtain, sociologists would have benefited if Sorokin had never mentioned vertical and horizontal mobility.

Large organizations such as armies, to be sure, sometimes stratify internally: they create bands of homogeneous rank that reach across the whole organization, establish segregation among ranks, and perform rituals of succession from rank to rank. As a consequence, localities such as company towns and military bases, which depend on large, stratified organizations, likewise fall into ranked strata. But no general population larger than a local community ever maintains a coherent system of stratification in a strong sense of the word; even the so-called caste system of India accommodated great variation in rank orders from village to village. In general, rank orders remain inconsistent, apparent strata contain considerable heterogeneity, and mobility blurs dividing lines. Stratification is therefore a matter of degree.

Inequality is likewise a matter of degree, but for the opposite reason—because it is ubiquitous. Whatever the criterion of equivalence, no two social units ever command precisely equivalent arrays of goods for more than an instant. Possession of different sorts of goods, furthermore, couples loosely enough that the same social unit moves in several directions simultaneously; inequality is always in flux. Any unified, fixed model of inequality—and, *a fortiori*, of stratification—that we impose on social life caricatures a dynamic reality, etches a Gillray portrait of social interaction. As with other useful caricatures, then, the secret is to sketch a model that brings out salient features of its object, but never to confuse model with reality.

Since the late nineteenth century, individualistic models of inequality have crowded out categorical models. From Adam Smith to Karl Marx, classical economists generally analyzed categories and relations among them: chiefly land, labor, and capital for Smith, capital and labor alone for Marx. They examined returns to these factors considered collectively and situated socially rather than returns to individual effort. Discussing returns to labor, for example, Smith reasoned:

> What are the common wages of labour, depends everywhere upon the contract usually made between those two parties, whose interests are by no means the same. The workmen desire to get as much, the masters to give as little as possible. The former are disposed to combine in order to raise, the latter in order to lower the wages of labour. It is not, however, difficult to foresee which of the two parties must, upon all ordinary occasions, have the advantage in the dispute, and force the other into a compliance with their terms. The masters, being fewer in number, can combine much more easily; and the law, besides, authorises, or at least does not prohibit their combinations, while it prohibits those of the workmen. (Smith 1910 [1776], 1:58–59)

Although Smith certainly saw market conditions—in this case, especially rates of growth in demand for labor—as crucial to the advantage of one party or the other, he reasoned about categories, groups, institutions, and ties. Those ties emphatically included collective, categorical, unequal power.

The neoclassical revolution, however, diverted economic attention from categories to individuals and markets. As Suzanne Shanahan and Nancy Tuma remark:

> Theories about allocations among social groups dominated economic and sociological thought in . . . the eighteenth and nineteenth centuries. With growing industrialization and the development of Fordist labor organization in the nineteenth and twentieth centuries, the rise of the individual as the unit of analysis swept through the social sciences—not only psychology and economics, but even sociology, the field that proclaims to study social groups and societies. Whatever the defects in the classical theories of factor distribution, it is telling, we think, that by the middle of the twentieth century, social scientists had almost completely switched their gaze from inter*group* distributions to inter*individual* distributions. (Shanahan and Tuma 1994, 745)

Their switched gaze focused social scientists on situations of choice among relatively well-defined alternatives within known constraints on the basis of clear preference criteria. It meant they acquired little knowledge of the processes by which such choices produced consequences, of indirect and environmentally mediated effects, of situations of choice that did not meet these stipulations, of the influence of shared meanings over action.

On the assumption that the market itself operates impartially, since the late nineteenth century economists and their imitators explaining categorical phenomena have usually tried to reduce them to individual causes and effects. It has become a habit: faced with male/female differences in wages, investigators look for average human-capital differences among the individuals involved. Noticing that school performances of children correlate with the social positions of their parents, researchers attribute those differences in performance to "family background" rather than considering that teachers and school officials may shape those performances by their own categorical responses to parental social positions. Encountering racial differences in job assignments, researchers ask whether members of distinct racial categories are distributed differently by residential location. Uncovering evidence of sharp ethnic differences in industrial concentration, analysts begin to speak of discrimination only when they have factored out individual differences in education, work experience, or productivity.

Familiarity has made these methodological precautions seem natural. Yet few students of social processes would employ logically similar procedures in trying to determine whether or why Jews and Catholics have differing views of divinity, whether some geographic boundary really separates French people from Spaniards, or why white South Africans, on average, enjoy much higher incomes and greater political power than their black fellow citizens. In such cases, we generally assume that category membership and collective ties to nonmembers, rather than individual variation in propensities and capacities, produce group differences. Yet in the world of work and labor markets, the presupposition prevails that inequality results from variation at the individual level. Ruth Milkman and Eleanor Townsley sum up the literature on gender discrimination:

> Typically, a study will examine a variety of factors that might explain wage differences between men and women, such as education, experience, interruptions in work histories, and so forth. The unexplained residual is then attributed to "discrimination," which is implicitly presumed to be a willful act on the employer's part (or sometimes on that of the co-workers, customers, or unions). This approach, while valuable for demonstrating the existence of a serious inequality problem, fails to capture the depth with which gender segregation and the norms associated with it are embedded in the economic order—in fact, they are embedded so deeply that a willful act of discrimination is not really necessary to maintain gender inequality. (Milkman and Townsley 1994, 611)

Similarly, the idea of "statistical discrimination" (Bielby and Baron 1986; Mueser 1989) individualizes a collective process radically: it portrays an employer who avoids hiring members of a whole category on the basis of beliefs or information—however well founded—that on average workers belonging to the category contribute less to productivity than their counterparts from outside the category.

Even as representations of individual decision-making, characteristic models of methodological individualism fall short. "The conventional story about individual behavior" reflects economist Michael Piore on standard economic reasoning, "is built around the notion that human actions are the product of purposive decision making in which the actors make a sharp distinction among means, ends, and the causal models which lead from one to the other." Recent theories based on pragmatic philosophy, hermeneutics, and linguistics, continues Piore, "suggest that these distinctions are at best vague and imprecise, if not completely absent, and that they emerge at all only in practice through the processes in which people first discuss the situation and then eventually act" (Piore 1996, 750; see also Conlisk 1996; Lewin 1996). The century-old move of economics from relational to individualistic accounts simplified analysts' work at the cost of losing verisimilitude.

When they adopted status attainment models of mobility and inequality, sociologists accentuated the shift from collective to individual effects. "In the most brilliant destructive paper in the history of sociology," Arthur Stinchcombe remarked some time ago,

> Otis Dudley Duncan (1966) stopped research into the relation between the labor market in which fathers had attained their status and the labor market in which sons attained theirs. His solution to the difficulties of such analysis was to regard the father's achievement only as a feature of the biography of sons, to be related to other features of that biography (such as later status attainment by the son) by regression analysis or qualitative loglinear models for sons. This tradition has however given a very queer tone to the mobility literature, since it deliberately starts off by talking as if people promoted themselves instead of being promoted by employers, or as if failure and success in self-employment depended on fathers rather than on success in a modern market. (Stinchcombe 1978a, 1)

Duncan's ingenious solution greatly simplified the problem of representing mobility statistically. But the representation of son's present occupational rank as an outcome of father's occupational rank in combination with son's other characteristics—for example, years of school completed—radically individualized the mobility process while obscuring such causes as changes in hiring practices and the formation of job-finding networks by migrants.

In an earlier review of the Christopher Jencks et al. *Inequality* (1972), Stinchcombe had made the essential distinction between two ways of representing inequality among paired persons: first as a difference in the positions of the two individuals with respect to similar variables, second as a characteristic of the relationship between them. "The second kind of analysis," he then pointed out, "requires the comparison of social systems (at the very least, social systems containing the pair), since data on variables describing pairs cannot be derived from data on isolated individuals" (Stinchcombe 1972, 603; for a recent review of status attainment analyses, see Breiger 1995). The Duncan solution stresses comparison of individuals with external standards rather than examining relations among individuals.

Human-capital theory offers a closely related individualistic account of inequality, with the additional twist of radical depersonalization. In strict human-capital models, neither the worker nor the worker's effort earns the rewards of work; instead, previous investments in the quality of workers command current returns. Again Stinchcombe's remark applies: such analyses rule out ties among workers or between bosses and workers as independent causes of inequality. They rely on an almost magical belief in the market's ability to sort out capacities for work.

Still, individualistic analyses of inequality have all the attractions of neoclassical economics: nicely simplified geometric analogies, reassuring references to individual decision-making, insistence on efficiency, avoidance of inconvenient complications such as beliefs, passions, culture, and history. They lend themselves nicely to retroactive rationalization; confronted with unequal outcomes, their user searches the past for individual differences in skill, knowledge, determination, or moral worth that must explain differences in rewards. These analyses fail, however, to the extent that essential causal business takes place not inside individual heads but within social relations among persons and sets of persons. That extent is, I claim, very large. If so, we have no choice but to undertake relational analyses of inequality—whether or not we finally couple them with individualistic elements of relevant decision processes.

Two disclaimers on that very point. First, I consider persons to possess as many identities as the number of social relations they maintain, one identity per relation, and to acquire their individuality through interactions among genetic capabilities and social experiences. Yet I also recognize the existence of sentient individuals whose actions depend mightily on their physiological functioning; all of us perform differently in fatigue than in freshness, in illness than in health, in old age than in childhood. Over the long run, any valid social science must therefore be compatible with known regularities in the operation of individual human organisms—brains, nervous systems, viscera, and all the rest. In the short run, however, our great deficit lies on the interactional side of the individual social ledger. Instead of reducing social behavior to individual decision-making, social scientists urgently need to study the relational constraints within which all individual action takes place.

My second disclaimer is intended chiefly for specialists in the study of inequality. Insiders may find baffling and irritating my tendency to draw heavily from the results of research based on individualistic assumptions and then to trash those assumptions. They may also feel that this book, without attaching specific offenses to any named offender, dismisses status attainment analysts, neoclassical economists, and specialists in wage determination as scoundrels or nitwits. Let me reassure my many friends and collaborators in these fields: I am building gratefully on their work, indeed trying to codify qualifications, objections, findings, anomalies, and hypotheses coming directly from their work.

Analysts of inequality occupy something like the position of seismographers. In the explanation of earthquakes, the recognition that the shifting of great tectonic plates beneath the earth's surface causes much of the heaving and cleaving in that surface has not made small-scale geology irrelevant. On the contrary, it has greatly clarified the causal mechanisms behind the flux of sand, gravel, rock, and soil while also providing partial accounts of such puzzling phenomena as continental drift. In current investigations of deep encounters between Asian plates and those of the Indian subcontinent beneath southern Tibet, for example, seismologists, geologists, and geophysicists are combining evidence from "CMP reflection, wide-angle reflection, broadband earthquake, magnetotelluric and surface geological data" in ways that not only use surface distributions to verify hypotheses concerning tectonic processes but also help to explain those surface distributions (Nelson et al. 1996, 1684). Seismologists draw on these complementary efforts to explain patterns of Tibetan earthquakes but cannot simply reduce those patterns to plate tectonics. Similarly, extension of relational analyses within the study of social inequality does not deny the existence of individuals or individual-level effects. It does, however, place individualistic processes in their organizational context. It does, finally, challenge any ontology that reduces all social processes to the sentient actions of individual persons.

ALTERNATIVES TO INDIVIDUALISM

Over the past few decades, the large body of research based on individualistic assumptions and adopting persons as units of analysis has done a superb job of specifying what analysts of inequality must explain—for example, by showing how much of male/female income differences springs not from unequal pay within the same jobs but from job segregation. My complaint with the literature chiefly concerns available *explanations*. Prevailing accounts of inequality strongly emphasize, first, the one-time decisions of powerholders to allocate rewards in a given manner and, second, the attributes and performances of individuals that attract differential rewards. Drawing clues from existing studies of wage determination, occupational careers, hiring, and labor market segmentation, I hope to show the great importance of cumulative, relational, often unnoticed organizational processes in the actual creation of durable inequality.

No doubt this way of putting it reminds you of the old saw about economics explaining how people's ordered choices produce collective effects and sociology explaining why people have no choices to make. But I urge no such deterministic view; on the contrary, my account of inequality builds relentlessly on counterfactuals, on could-bes and might-have-beens. For social life in general, valid explanations proceed from specifications of possible configurations to specifications of circumstances differentiating those configurations from others that could, in principle, also form.

My central counterfactuals concern organizational problem-solving and collective acquisition of stakes in organizational arrangements. They concern different ways that connected, powerful people draw to their own advantage on the efforts of excluded outsiders and different ways that less powerful people form segregated niches affording them privileged access to more limited but genuine advantages. Such counterfactuals play down the importance of attitudes, prejudices, and mistaken beliefs in unequal arrangements while playing up the significance of convenience, transaction costs, and contingent opportunities. By the same token, they point to organizational innovations—rather than changes in preferences, attitudes, and personal qualifications—as a means of reducing durable inequality.

Although it dovetails with abundant recent work by institutional economists and economic sociologists, my approach, even where it stands on solid logical and empirical ground, will encounter three significant barriers to acceptance. First, as institutional economists themselves have taught us, established solutions generally have the advantage over innovations in the short run because the transaction costs of devising, perfecting, installing, teaching, and integrating new solutions to problems exceed the costs of maintaining old ways, more so to the extent that old ways articulate well with a wide range of adjacent beliefs and practices. As in organizational life, so in social science: the well-developed apparatus of individualistic analysis will not be displaced easily.

Second, and less obvious, the sort of relational analysis I am advocating clashes with the narrative mode in which people ordinarily think and speak about social processes. At least in Western countries, people learn early in life to tell stories in which self-motivating actors firmly located in space and time produce all significant changes in the situation through their own efforts. Actors in narratives need not be rational or efficient, but their own orientations cause their actions. Deliberate individual actions then cause individual reactions, which cause further deliberate individual actions, on to story's end (Bower and Morrow 1990; Somers 1992; Steinmetz 1993; Turner 1996).

Narratives feature essences, not bonds. They therefore favor individualistic analyses, whether rational-choice, phenomenological, or otherwise. The supposition that social processes actually behave as narrative would require motivates (frequent) complaints against social scientists for practicing inferior versions of the novelist's craft and (infrequent) praise of ethnographies because they "read like a novel." By-products of social interaction, tacit constraints, unintended consequences, indirect effects, incremental changes, and causal chains mediated by nonhuman environments play little or no part in customary narratives of social life. Relational analyses of inequality affront narrative common sense by insisting that just such subtle ramifications of social interaction produce and sustain unequal relations among whole categories of persons.

Proximity of social-scientific analysis to moral discourse erects a third barrier to acceptance of relational explanations for inequality. In a narrative mode, social science closely approaches the prevailing discourse of morality. That discourse judges both intentions and actions of self-motivated individuals according to certain criteria of adequacy: goodness, fairness, authenticity, or something else. Every social-scientific narrative invades moral ground, a fact that helps account for the passion such narratives often stir in the hearts of people outside the profession.

Even nonnarrative explanations for inequality, however, touch moral discourse. Doubly so, in fact, both because rejecting self-motivated actors as sufficient causes for social outcomes challenges the standard premises of moral discourse and because relational analyses invoke counterfactuals. Counterfactuals say that other arrangements were, are, or will be possible, hence that present circumstances do not embody the best of all possible worlds. If we assemble known causal links plausibly into previously unknown longer causal chains, we challenge any claims for the inevitability of currently operating chains. If we show that similar causal sequences have in fact operated elsewhere in other eras, we simultaneously strengthen the case for contingency and sharpen the specification of what needs explaining here and now. Thus new worlds of equality or inequality unfold counterfactually from causal analyses of present circumstances.

In principle, the deployment of valid counterfactuals—valid in the sense that they incorporate causal sequences known to be possible—not only advances the work of explanation but also equips social scientists to criticize and compare moral doctrines, political programs, and ideologies very effectively. Every such doctrine includes assertions, implicit or explicit, of possible social conditions; most also include assertions concerning paths from the present state of affairs to those possible conditions. Those assertions invite social-scientific criticism and comparison. If a politician argues that the United States should exclude Asian and Latin American immigrants in order to improve the job prospects of existing U.S. workers, social scientists may of course discuss the value premises of such a recommendation, but they have special expertise in examining the causal reasoning it involves. Is Asian and Latin American immigration actually diminishing the job prospects of American-born workers?

By the same token, we can anticipate heated resistance to causal analyses, however well founded, that contradict the possibility arguments built into cherished doctrines. Here the second and third obstacles combine. Widely accepted American moral, legal, and political doctrines enshrine the individual as a conscious, responsible, efficacious agent of her or his own actions. Here, too, individualism reigns. Anyone who locates efficacious social action in the contract rather than the signers, in the plot rather than the players, in the conversation rather than the speaker invites intuitive rejection on behalf of cherished creeds. This book will succeed if it makes credible and useful a relational account of social inequality. It will succeed doubly if it clarifies what other forms of inequality or equality are possible, and how.

I have undertaken my inquiry because I believe the intensity of capitalist inequality causes unnecessary suffering and because—on the grounds I have just identified—social scientists can help to discover means of alleviating inequality and its attendant suffering. I have written much of the book in egalitarian Sweden, where increasingly confident voices are currently urging reduction of government-guaranteed

benefits on the argument that the logic of free-flowing capital now conflicts with the premises of welfare states, thus sharpening the contradiction between redistribution and economic growth. Historical experience
persuades me that abundance and equality are, on the contrary, compatible, and in some circumstances even complementary. Yet in this book I
do not try to formulate remedies or to persuade readers of their efficacy.
If the book helps produce better understanding of causes, effects, and
crucial questions yet to answer, that will suffice for a preliminary inquiry.

One final warning. A lifetime of densely empirical work based on
large (often obsessively systematic) bodies of evidence bound to particular times and places has given me an irresistible compulsion to illustrate
general points with specific cases. Hardly a page of this book goes by
without irruption of at least one example. Yet the book's handling of
evidence differs from most of my previous work in two crucial ways.
First, it aims not at drawing time- and place-bound generalizations from
careful comparisons of cases but at identifying very general processes
that produce inequality, at singling out causal mechanisms that operate
in an enormous variety of times, places, and social settings. Second, it
introduces illustrations chiefly to clarify theoretical points rather than to
establish their empirical generality. My previous investigations give me
some confidence that the book's main assertions apply widely. Still, for
the moment they stand not as empirically validated generalizations but
as working hypotheses about the interplay of exploitation, opportunity
hoarding, emulation, and adaptation. Those hypotheses invite verifica-
tion, refinement and, no doubt, refutation.

Given the way I have constructed the argument, indeed, skeptics can
challenge it at several different levels:

1. The book describes categorical differences with respect to goods
    and social relations so badly as to undermine its explanations of
    those differences.

2. Its explanations of those categorical differences fail in significant
    ways.

3. Its explanations work for some kinds of categories but not for
    others.

4.   Its argument fails to explain significant differences in the opera-
     tion of various sorts of categories (e.g., gender versus citizenship).

5.   Dimensions of categorical difference that it does not explore exten-
     sively (e.g., in regard to political power or deference) do not be-
     have as the argument implies they should.

6.   Noncategorical inequalities among individuals are larger or
     weightier than the argument claims, and the argument provides
     no means of explaining them.

Objections 1 and 2, if both founded, would destroy the book's credibil-
ity. Objections 3, 4, and 5, if well defended, would point to elaborations
or revisions of its arguments. Objection 6, if sustained, would leave the
main arguments intact but reduce the scope I have claimed for them.
Although I expect all six types of criticism—and suppose that some versions of all six will identify weaknesses in the argument as I have stated
it—I will be disappointed if critics formulate effective combinations of
objections 1 and 2, not surprised to face effective statements of objection
6, and actually encouraged if the book stimulates constructive variants
of all six objections, especially constructive objections that advance relational explanations of inequality. A provisional synthesizer of so vast a
phenomenon as durable inequality, after all, can hope no more than to
push new inquiries in a fruitful direction.

   The book's chapters follow from its program. Chapter 2 lays out the
relational concepts with which the rest of the book works, while Chapter
3 reassembles them into a preliminary analysis of mechanisms generating categorical inequality. Chapters 4, 5, and 6 take up exploitation, opportunity hoarding, emulation, and adaptation in turn before putting
them back together in a general account of how categorically organized
advantage and disadvantage cumulate and endure. Chapter 7 examines
categorical identities and their activation in politics, especially contentious politics. A final chapter treats relations between categorically defined and individual-to-individual inequality and then considers implications of the argument for deliberate intervention to change inequality
and for future varieties of inequality.

2 From Transactions to Structures

Viviana Zelizer identifies a momentous irony in the American federal government's generally successful attempt to monopolize production of legal tender across the United States: the more government action reduced the rights of states, municipalities, and firms to issue legally circulating money, the more ordinary Americans and organizations proliferated private monies in the forms of tokens, symbolic objects, and earmarked official currency (Zelizer 1994b). Americans multiplied monies, Zelizer shows, because they were pursuing serious relational business with their monetary transactions. Symbolically and physically, for example, they segregated money destined for their children, servants, and local merchants. They were not only getting, spending, and saving but also distinguishing different categories of social relations. Disagreeing vigorously with social thinkers who suppose that the monetization of social exchanges inexorably rationalizes these exchanges and thins their contents, Zelizer demonstrates that people reshape monetary

41

transactions to support meaningful, differentiated interpersonal relations.

Zelizer categorizes payments as follows:

- *Gifts*, which are transfers of money at the current possessor's discretion, without a prior stipulation of the recipient's consequent obligations
- *Entitlements*, which are payments due the recipient by contractual right, enforceable by appeal to authoritative third parties
- *Compensation*, which is a monetary exchange for goods and services, based on prior agreement concerning the relation between price and a mix of quality and quantity

Contrary to analysts who assume that ultimately all monetary transfers amount to quid pro quo exchanges, Zelizer argues that gifts, entitlements, and compensation involve contrasting rationales, meanings, and social relations. They rely on characteristically different means of enforcement. To mark them off from each other, people invent segregated currencies and visibly different payment routines.

When people make such distinctions, they embed cultural forms in analyses—usually implicit—of social relations. We watch Mary hand Harry a ten-dollar bill. How can we know whether the monetary transfer is a tip, a bribe, a heartfelt gift, regular compensation for goods or services, fulfillment of an entitlement such as an allowance, or some other sort of payment? We can determine this only by ascertaining the relation between Mary and Harry: apartment dweller and doorman, driver and traffic cop, sister and brother, mother and son, householder and handyman, and so on through a wide variety of possible pairs (Zelizer 1998). To make the discrimination accurately, we require information not only about the categorical connections between Mary and Harry but also about the previous history of their relations (or lack of them) as well as their ties to third parties. The distinction between a tip and a bribe, for example, rests largely on the recipient's obligations to the organization for which he or she works; if Harry's boss has a right to punish the performance for which Mary pays Harry, a tip has become a bribe.

Although gifts, entitlements, and compensation are the primary categories of payments, all three types also vary internally. Gifts, for example, differ in quality as functions of the relative equality between parties to the transaction and the intimacy of the relationship. Even when their gifts are monetary, intimate equals offer each other gifts very differently than distant unequals do. Note the unmistakable contrasts among proper forms for tips, tributes, bribes, allowances, and anniversary presents—all gifts of a sort, but quite distinct in form, meaning, and implied social relation. Where the relation is unclear, contested, or liable to misinterpretation, Zelizer points out, parties commonly adopt dramatic earmarking devices such as wrapping gift money with the same care one might lavish on a personalized object or making sure that banknotes offered as prizes are new, crisp, and uniform.

Larger differences separate gifts, entitlements, and compensation. Although discretion and enforcement may seem incompatible, gift transfers generally rely on the enforcement of obligations that spring from shared commitment to some joint enterprise. Two elements—unspecified future rewards from that enterprise, and immediate satisfaction of solidarity and gratitude—combine to provide incentives for giving. Failure to offer expected gifts therefore signals weakened commitment to the enterprise, an especially damaging sign when the relationship has been intimate and relatively equal. Failure to give when expected also threatens unequal relationships: an inferior's reluctance to offer appropriate gifts signals rebellion, while a superior's neglect signals that the subordinate has declined in favor.

Entitlements stand out from gifts and compensation in relying less on the payer's discretion and the recipient's current performance. Like gifts and compensation, however, entitlements have distinctly different qualities depending on the relevant contract's breadth and equality; a veteran's pension, for example, contrasts sharply with a divorced spouse's payments for child support. Here conceptions of justice and appeals to third-party enforcement figure much more importantly than in the case of gifts. Recipients of entitlements typically use whatever leverage they enjoy with third parties to limit evasion and discretion on the part of payers. Judges, priests, parents, and senior family members all sometimes intervene to enforce entitlements.

Compensation might seem more impervious to variation as a function of social relations, regulated as it often is by bargaining and narrow as market relations can be. Even compensation, however, varies significantly in form depending on the social relations involved. Within the same corporation, compare the compensation packages received by the CEO and the night security guard; they differ in content—daily perquisites, long-term benefits, ownership rights, periodicity of payment, and more—as much as they differ in amount. Or note the enormous difference in form between a one-time settlement with a street vendor and the elaborate monetary exchanges for goods and services inside a family.

Indeed, major legal, domestic, and political struggles formed in the United States over the very question of whether payments from husbands to wives constituted entitlements, gifts, or compensation (Zelizer 1994a). Each position had significantly different implications for the quality of relations between spouses: did the money a woman received from her male companion constitute her rightful share of collective resources, a discretionary gift from a man to a woman, or payment to the woman for her domestic and sexual services? Similarly, donors and recipients of charitable payments have struggled incessantly over the form and status of their monetary transfers: in cash or in earmarked credit, with or without the monitoring of expenditures, and so on. They have implicitly contested whether charitable transfers qualified as entitlements (e.g., family allowances), compensation (e.g., rewards for efforts at self-improvement), or gifts (e.g., the benefaction of a compassionate patron). Precisely because the forms of monetary transfers marked them as gifts, entitlements, or compensation, such transfers characterized the relationships between parties to the transactions. Participants who disagreed over the character of their relationships therefore also fought over the forms.

Similar distinctions and disputes appear in the very heart of market life, within capitalist firms themselves. Forms of payment for work differ systematically as a function of relations among workers as well as between workers and their bosses. Payment in stock options, bonuses, elegant surroundings, wide-ranging perquisites, and ample retirement packages signals a different relation to the bosses and the firm than does straight hourly payment in a weekly check.

Although employees certainly strive to increase their total revenues from the firm that employs them, a surprising share of competition and collective struggle concerns not quantities but forms of payment, hence qualities of social relations within the workplace. The centuries-old arrangement whereby coal-hewers received pay according to amount of coal delivered rather than time or effort expended signaled their position as quasi-independent contractors within their mines; miners' long resistance to standardized time payment revealed their awareness of the change in social relations the new arrangement implied.

Zelizer's analysis nicely illustrates differences between essence and bond accounts of social behavior. Although economists have for a century promoted a picture of monetary payments as solitary acts temporarily connecting individual buyers to impersonal markets, Zelizer shows us that payments are rooted in rich social matrices, their forms and significance varying greatly with the social relations at hand, their modalities (and not just their amounts) objects of heartfelt struggle among the parties. Even when it comes to pecuniary exchanges, we live in a relational world.

Many other human activities that first appear to be quite individual later turn out to have a strong relational component. Consider essence and bond accounts of feeding. This book began by discussing stature and differential nutrition by category. One can, of course, construct essentialist accounts of the matter, focusing on the experiences of individual metabolizing organisms. The superb work of Fogel and associates certainly depends on clear understanding of how individual bodies acquire, accumulate, and expend energy. Yet feeding, the crucial social process, is doubly relational: diets and manners of feeding vary systematically from one social category to the next, marking the boundaries between them. They also depend on relations among members of distinct categories.

Marjorie DeVault's analysis of how American women feed other people in their households, including the men, brings out that relational aspect of nutrition dramatically. DeVault reminds us that, despite rising female employment outside the home, feeding families remains overwhelmingly women's work. In the United States, most women with families—even women who dislike cooking—make serious efforts to do the work competently. In the process they are negotiating definitions of their relations to husbands, children, and other household members. The women that DeVault interviewed described the problem as striking a balance between preference and propriety, being sure that family members got food they enjoyed while receiving nourishment suitable for their positions.

Suitability included not only nutritional adequacy but also symbolic value—what the meal said about the relation between donor and recipient. One women DeVault interviewed had an executive husband who usually ate lunch at work. She worried about what to feed him on the rare occasions when he worked at home, fearing that to share her own usual meal would be demeaning to her husband. When DeVault (indicated here as MD) asked the woman what she might give him, she replied:

> All right. Yesterday, we thought our girls were coming out the night before and I had bought some artichokes for them, so I cooked them anyway. So I scooped out the center and made a tuna salad and put it in the center, on lettuce, tomatoes around. And then, I had made zucchini bread . . . So that was our lunch. If I had to do it every day I would find it difficult.

MD: When you made a distinction between the kind of lunch you would have and what you'd fix for him, what's involved in that? Is it because of what he likes, or what?

> I just feel he should have a really decent meal. He would not like— well, I do terrible things and I know it's fattening. Like I'll sit down with yogurt and drop granola into it and it's great. Well, I can't give him that for lunch.

MD: Why not?

> He doesn't, he wouldn't like it, wouldn't appreciate it. Or peanut butter and jelly, for instance, it's not enough of a lunch to give him. (DeVault 1991, 147–148)

Whatever else a "really decent meal" meant to this woman and her husband, she clearly wanted her food preparation to signify that she understood her proper relationship to him. Commensalism relates people, but it also depends on strongly structured relations among them. Those relations are often categorical: parent/child, wife/husband, servant/ master, boarder/landlord, and so on.

BUILDING BLOCKS

Categorical inequality represents a special case of categorical relations in general. It is a particular but spectacularly potent combination within a small set of network configurations that have reappeared millions of times at different scales, in different settings, throughout human history. Although network analysts have studied some of these configurations repeatedly (see Wasserman and Faust 1994, 17–20), no one has codified our knowledge of how they connect and operate. Provisional nominees for the basic set include the chain, the hierarchy, the triad, the organization, and the categorical pair:

- A *chain* consists of two or more similar and connected ties between social sites (persons, groups, identities, networks, or something else).
- A *hierarchy* is a sort of chain in which the connections are asymmetrical and the sites systematically unequal.
- A *triad* consists of three sites having ties to each other that are similar in content, although not necessarily similar in valence.
- An *organization* is a well-bounded set of ties in which at least one site has the right to establish ties across the boundary that can then bind sites connected by internal ties.
- A *categorical pair* consists of a socially significant boundary and at least one tie between sites on either side of it.

(We might actually reduce the basic set to three, since a hierarchy is simply a special type of chain and, as we shall see, an organization is an overgrown categorical pair. For our purposes, however, it helps to distinguish all five.) Figure 1 schematizes the five elementary forms.

I regard these network configurations as social inventions, perhaps developed incrementally by trial and error, no doubt reinvented independently many times, but, when recognized, more or less deliberately

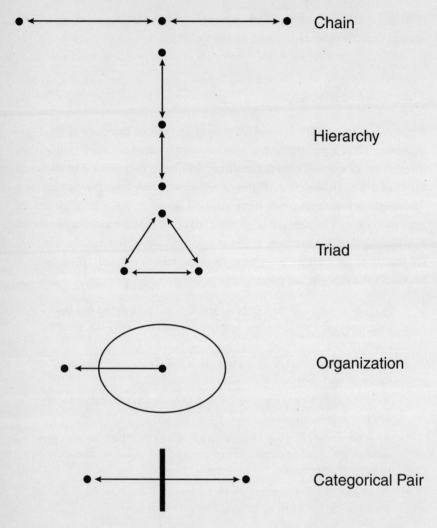

Figure 1.   Basic Social Configurations

installed as a means of coordinating social life. I may be wrong—an alternative line of thought, well represented by Fredrik Barth, regards all existing social structures not as fundamental elements of social life but as variable by-products of generative principles (Barth 1981, 1–118; see also Bunge 1996, 248–253). For Barth, the social structures we identify as kin groups, community networks, and the like resemble instantaneous distributions of vehicles on a stretch of superhighway: coherent, exhibiting recurrent regularities, but not entities in themselves since their structure derives entirely from the actions and interactions of individual drivers.

If Barth's view is correct, my elementary forms could be recurrently emergent outcomes of more elementary social relations. Triads, for example, could emerge simply because stable pairs tend to recruit third parties jointly. Hierarchies could, in principle, simply generalize patterns of asymmetrical interaction. If methodological individualists could specify and validate rules for single-actor decision-making that constitute sufficient conditions for the creation of chains, hierarchies, triads, organizations, and paired categories, they would make strong claims for their favored reductionism. Fortunately, it matters little for purposes of this discussion whether we are dealing with inventions or emergents; once they are in place, people employ them for a wide variety of relational work.

Configurations multiply beyond their elementary forms: chains proliferate into long chains, two-step hierarchies into ten-step hierarchies, triads into dense networks of interconnection, categorical pairs into triplets, and so on. People who work in civil service, for example, become familiar not just with the relation between their own rank and adjacent ranks but also with a whole ladder consisting of asymmetrical connections.

Configurations also compound with each other; many hierarchies, as we shall discover later, incorporate categorical pairs, for instance, when physicians are Caucasian males and the nurses who work for them are Filipinas. An imaginary social structure compounding such configurations appears in Figure 2, which connects hierarchies ABD and ABF, triads BDF and BEF, chain DFG, and categorical pair CD. Also, through command position A, the diagram relates the entire organization (the bounded network) to external site X. In this imaginary case, site A enjoys the right to establish binding contracts between the whole and outside actors.

Whether or not these five network configurations turn out to be the elementary particles of social life, they recur very widely, doing characteristically different forms of social work. Their recurrence poses a triple

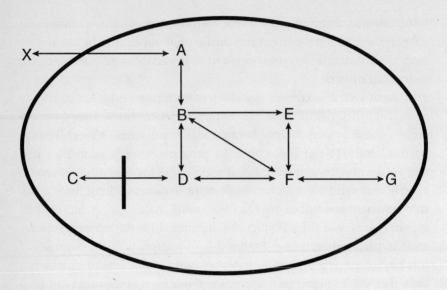

Figure 2.   Combined Configurations in an Imaginary Social Structure

analytic challenge: to detect those characteristic differences among structures, to identify their causal regularities, and to investigate conditions for the structures' concatenation.

First, we must examine characteristic differences among the structures. Chains, hierarchies, triads, organizations, and categorical pairs each have their own operating patterns and consequences. Mark Granovetter's distinction (1985, 1995) between strong ties (those defined by substantial emotion, obligation, range, and durability) and weak ties (more fleeting, neutral, narrow, and discretionary) contrasts two of the basic structures. This distinction gains its importance from the general association of strong ties with small, dense network clumps containing many triads (three-party clusters) and the association of weak ties with long, single-stranded chains. In general, strong ties sustain solidarity, trust, and commitment while circulating a good deal of redundant information. Weak ties break more easily, but they also transmit information from distant sources more efficiently.

Granovetter's famous application concerns job searches, in which weak ties play an exceptional role because they connect job seekers with a much wider range of opportunities, on average, than do strong ones. Although subsequent research has shown that medium-weak ties, with their modicum of commitment, provide better-quality information than very weak ties, the broad distinction between the effects of strong and weak ties has held up well to empirical scrutiny (Erickson 1996; see also Anderson 1974; Campbell, Marsden, and Hurlbert 1986; Campbell and Rosenfeld 1986; Corcoran, Datcher, and Duncan 1980; De Schweinitz 1932; Holzer 1987; Laumann 1973; Lin 1982; Lin and Dumin 1986; Marsden and Hurlbert 1988; Montgomery 1994; Murray, Rankin, and Magill 1981; Simon and Warner 1992). Weak ties occupy important places in all sorts of large-scale coordination. Without weak ties, for example, most people would acquire very little information about current politics, medical innovations, or investment opportunities.

Second, each configuration has its own causal regularities that demand individual attention. In triads, for example, where B and C have a distinctive relation (e.g., they are close friends), stability seems to require that relations AB and AC be similar (e.g., subordination, rivalry, or friendship rather than subordination in one case and friendship in the other). If two relations (AB and AC) are similar, solidary, and symmetrical, furthermore, the third (BC) tends to assume the same form. No doubt such properties help to account for the significance of triads in social structures that promote trust in the face of uncertainty and risk. Behind these apparent regularities lie both mutual learning and responses to the heightened transaction costs of inconsistency.

Third, we must investigate conditions for concatenation of the elementary structures: which ones fit together effectively under what circumstances, whether the presence of one sort of structure promotes the formation of the other, how many of a given kind an organization can contain without starting to collapse. As evidence concerning diminishing returns from large spans of control suggests, for example, very extensive hierarchies seem to negate their coordination advantages by incurring greater transaction costs and to invite subversion, shirking, or rebellion as well. No doubt other structural constraints limit the number of categorical pairs any organization of a given size can maintain, the relations among categories of varying sizes, and the types of viable combinations of categorical pairs with hierarchies (Blau 1977). Categorical boundaries that require the parties on either side of the boundary to mutually avoid each other except for ritualized encounters, for instance, would most likely wreak havoc if installed in the upper reaches of extensive hierarchies.

Such a description of configurations, to be sure, freezes them into ice sculptures when in real life they more closely resemble the recurrent patterns seen in a waterfall. The description summarizes various tendencies that we observers might notice in fast-moving transactions among social sites. In fact, the ties in question shift among configurations, as when actors in a chain invoke or abolish a categorical distinction among themselves (friendly neighbors, for example, forget about or suddenly react to racial barriers that lie between them) or when members of a hierarchy temporarily behave as a fairly equal triad (lieutenant, sergeant, and private, for example, defend each other against the enemy's fire). Any generalizations we make about these configurations necessarily take the form "*Insofar* as ties among sites form triads . . ."

Recall a crucial point about social processes, including those that produce durable inequality. Designed, prescribed, and inherited social structures never work quite as their participants imagine they should or will. People make incessant mistakes; interactions produce unanticipated consequences; and, in many circumstances, if everyone actually followed the ostensible rules, either organizational disaster or an utter standstill would result. A master cabinetmaker once arrived at my home to install a set of handsome bookcases he had built in his shop. With the shelves and hardware, his helper brought in a large sack. I looked in the sack and saw several score small, thin wooden wedges. The conversation continued:

"What are those?"
"Shims."
"What for?"
"Well, it's clear you're not a cabinetmaker. We use shims because there's no such thing as a straight wall or a straight piece of wood. Shims straighten up the connections. Otherwise there'd be gaps all up and down the backs of the bookcases, and they might fall off the wall."

In human interaction, people constantly avert disasters and standstills by inserting social shims in the form of self-corrections, reassurances, clarifications, compensatory actions, and mutual aid. Social processes are worse than bookcases, however: because they keep moving, no social shim stays in place very long. Social structures stick together, more or less, precisely because improvisation never ceases.

SCRIPTING AND LOCAL KNOWLEDGE

Figure 3 captures some of the variability involved. It represents two dimensions along which social transactions differ: the degree of localized common knowledge that participants in a transaction deploy, and the extent of scripting for such a transaction that is already available jointly to the participants. In principle, transactions include events in which one actor changes the state of another actor; the term "transaction costs" describes the energy expended in such interchanges. In practice, we concentrate on distinguishable interactions during which at least one actor exhibits a response to the other. Scripts range from the routines involved in such general configurations as triads and paired categories to the specific formulas people adopt to withdraw money from a bank. Just as pianists recognize and perform not only standard scales but also the intricate figures of a Beethoven sonata, interacting humans engage in routines that range from the virtually universal to those activated by only one social situation.

Similarly, local knowledge extends, for example, from tacit understandings acquired by long-term residents concerning connections among different locations in a city to the memory of previous conversations that frames today's lunch between two old friends. Scripts provide models for participation in particular classes of social relations, while shared local knowledge provides a means of giving variable content to those social relations. Among the four basic mechanisms that generate durable inequality, emulation relies chiefly on scripting, while adaptation relies heavily on accumulation of local knowledge. Actually, however, all four mechanisms—exploitation, opportunity hoarding,

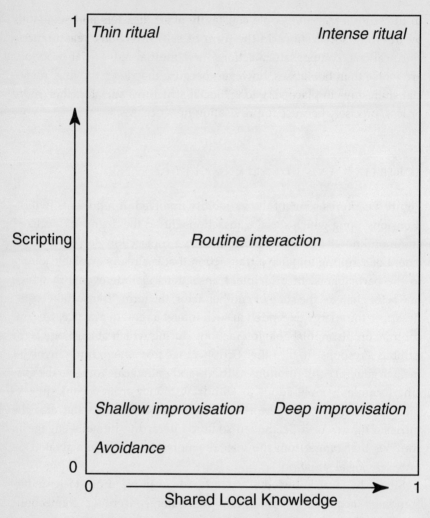

Figure 3.   Scripting and Local Knowledge in Social Ties

emulation, and adaptation—operate through combinations of scripting and local knowledge. Exploitation by means of paired categories, for example, characteristically involves locally constructed variants on widely known differentiations by gender, race, ethnicity, or some other dividing principle.

Sociologists enamored of norms and values have sometimes considered scripts to lie at the center of all durable social processes, with socialization committing newcomers to scripts and sanctions minimizing deviation from them. Such a view involves astonishing confidence in the efficiency and effectiveness of scripting. Because local conditions vary and change incessantly and because social interaction repeatedly involves error, unanticipated consequences, repair, and readjustment, no organization whose members followed scripts to the best of their ability could actually survive. Experienced bureaucrats and artisans, for example, know they can block any effective action in their organizations by following official rules meticulously. Scripts alone promote uniformity, knowledge alone promotes flexibility—and their combination promotes flexibility within established limits.

With little scripting or local knowledge available (the lower lefthand corner of Figure 3), actors either avoid each other or engage in *shallow improvisations* such as the maneuvers that pedestrians on a crowded sidewalk adopt in order to pass each other with a minimum of bumping and blocking. In other cases, scripting can be extensive and common knowledge meager, as when a master of ceremonies directs participants to applaud, rise, sit, and exit; let us call this circumstance *thin ritual.* Here only weak ties obtain. Thin ritual absorbs high transaction costs for the social results that it accomplishes; most people reserve it for very special occasions and escape it when they can.

Where common knowledge is extensive and scripting slight, we enter the *deep improvisation* of professional jazz, intense sociability, competitive soccer, passionate sexual relations, and playful conversation. Extensive common knowledge, strong ties, and frequent improvisation reinforce each other. Participants in deep improvisation often draw on relevant scripts, as when a saxophonist inserts a fragment of "The Star-Spangled Banner" in the midst of a frenetic riff or when old lovers playfully enact the rituals of formal courtship. But in such instances the script becomes part of a private joke recast by local knowledge.

Intense ritual occupies the upper righthand corner of Figure 3—broad common knowledge plus extensive scripting—on the grounds that in rich routines such as weddings, coming-of-age ceremonies, military reviews, and college commencements the participants (however reluctantly) are affirming shared identities and mutual commitments by temporarily abandoning improvisation or (more often) combining public scripting with private improvisation in the form of nudges, winks, grimaces, and *sotto voce* comments. Anyone who imagines that intense ritual always expresses or engenders solidarity, however, should remember this: a funeral that revives old grievances and the impeccable but subtly aggressive performance by veteran dance partners who have grown to detest each other both illustrate the possible cohabitation of intense ritual with hostile interaction.

Routine interaction occurs in the midsection of the diagram, combining some scripting with significant local knowledge. As people carry on their social lives in firms, stores, schools, and neighborhoods, they deploy scripted routines such as greetings, payment procedures, apologies for violating rules, and expressions of personal concern; but they temper such scripts with locally applicable shared knowledge, including the shared knowledge encrusted within the scripts of a common language. Since scripts themselves repeatedly misfire, producing unanticipated consequences and minor disasters, people use local knowledge to repair social interactions as they go. Any representation of social life as consisting solely of following and deviating from norms therefore misses the improvisation that both uses and generates knowledge and makes effective social interaction possible.

Similarly, the common idea that workplaces ordinarily contain two competing sets of rules, practices, or social relations (one "official" or "formal," the other "unofficial" or "informal") misses the point: it contrasts scripts with shared local knowledge rather than seeing that the two necessarily intertwine (Stinchcombe 1990b). Organizations typically herd social interactions toward the middle ground in the scripting/local knowledge space diagrammed in Figure 3, providing enough scripts so that relations have broadly predictable rhythms and consequences but also enough local knowledge so that members can improvise effectively in the face of unexpected threats and opportunities.

Like learning a language, the establishment of new social relations often follows a zigzag pattern within this space: beginning with a rigidly followed but narrow script, accumulating local knowledge, improvising by means of that knowledge, making mistakes and discovering unanticipated consequences, correcting those mistakes and fixing the consequences until a precarious modus vivendi emerges, moving back to acquire new scripts, and then broadening common knowledge until at times the newcomer participates in the intense rituals of solidarity that assume such common knowledge. By that time, any participant who follows the script rigidly—speaks with schoolbook grammar, observes every formality, works by rule—actually disrupts local social relations, unless she or he does so as a recognizable joke or as an understood way of controlling outsiders. Scripting and common knowledge operate dialectically, modifying each other so that each script not only bends under the weight of local knowledge but also limits the sites that share local knowledge.

By no means do all learning processes complete the arc from shallow improvisation through more extensive scripts to deep improvisation. Staying in a strange city among speakers of an unfamiliar tongue, I have often found myself acquiring rudimentary familiarity with map, public transportation, and crucial phrases while working out a simple set of interaction routines for survival through the day, rehearsing the relevant scripts anxiously in anticipation of the next encounter, and then getting by on that combination of a meager script with dangerously restricted local knowledge. Similarly, many immigrants work up just enough involvement with the world outside their immigrant niche to avoid serious trouble when navigating that world. Again, the presence of even one important person who lacks familiarity with local language and practices can drive an entire work group or dinner party into the uncomfortable zone of stilted scripting and cramped improvisation. Because transaction costs absorb considerable resources and entail significant risks, the acquisition of scripts and local knowledge generally occurs in discontinuous increments and often stops somewhere near the lower lefthand corner of our diagram.

As we shall see in detail later, both scripts and common knowledge vary from particular to general, from local to ubiquitous. Gender relations, for example, involve both scripts that transcend any particular organization as well as shared understandings that people transfer unre-flectively from one setting to another. One of the great secrets of categor-ical inequality is this: the routines, understandings, and justifications that organizational participants have acquired in other settings are so readily available for organizational work. Each durable social setting produces some unique scripts and common knowledge, however trivial, that are available only to its habitués; but it also produces some local variations on the scripts and common knowledge that are attached to widely relevant categorical distinctions according to such principles as age, race, ethnicity, class, locality, and gender. Marge Kirk, a concrete-truck driver, summed it up this way:

> It takes a lot of energy just to stand your ground—balancing male egos with your right to survive. I wanted a job, I wanted to be a good truck driver, I wanted to be able to pull my weight as a driver. So years have passed now and somehow I survived. The guys are beginning to see me as a real human, not just a broad with legs and boobs. And the dis-patcher has passed to the point of seeing me as a driver, I think. (Schroedel 1985, 156–157)

Kirk, a woman in an overwhelmingly male job, had worked her way by means of incessant improvisation to a unique combination of scripts and local knowledge.

Our five configurations—chains, hierarchies, triads, organizations, and categorical pairs—provide widely available scripts. They rely on common knowledge, for example, shared understandings of how supe-riors and inferiors signal their relation to each other. They also generate common knowledge as people use them, for example, by relying on third parties in triads to patch up disagreements within any particular pair. Together, familiar scripts and accumulated common knowledge lower the transaction costs of whatever activities an organization carries on. They thereby raise the relative costs of shifting to some other struc-ture of social relations. Managers of organizations ordinarily adopt the five configurations in various combinations as devices for managing so-cial relations within Figure 3's midsection, where some scripting and common knowledge combine.

How configurations work, indeed, depends to a great extent on where in the two-dimensional space they fall. When goldsmiths who have common knowledge of their craft work together for the first time, they may use familiar scripts to establish hierarchies of reward and deference, but they can start to produce golden articles without extensive ritual. New cadets in military academies, however, ordinarily lack familiarity with both organizational structure and local lore; their superiors make up for those deficiencies by intensive scripting and drumming in common knowledge. Only later do superiors let military recruits improvise within the limits set by well-known scripts.

Activating the emulation mechanism, managers of organizations often accomplish their work by importing configurations—particular hierarchies, chains, triads, and categorical pairs—with which new members of the organization already have considerable experience and therefore common knowledge. Organizations build in educational and class differences, with their established patterns of deference; incorporate existing links among people from common ethnic origins; establish triads defined as "teams" recruited from other organizations; and set up categorical pairs such as physician/nurse or professional/client. Such borrowing of categorical pairs, as later chapters of this book explain, plays a crucial part in durable patterns of inequality.

Managers who borrow structure gain the advantage of low startup costs for new chunks of organization. But they also import meanings, relational routines, and external connections whose features and consequences they cannot always control. Many a store manager has hired a few hard-working immigrants for a particular niche only to discover that part of the store has become a patronage network and he or she an unwitting patron. Many a new lawyer has learned that the road to becoming a partner in the firm is closed because a hidden but powerful hierarchy separates graduates of elite law schools from the rest.

Each configuration, and each combination of configurations, no doubt conforms to its own regularities. This book pursues the combination of paired categories with hierarchies on the hypothesis that exploitation, opportunity hoarding, emulation, and adaptation converge to favor such a social arrangement and that its widespread insertion in organizations accounts for a major share of all durable inequality. Regularities peculiar to this pair of configurations include the generation of boundary-maintaining beliefs about differences between actors on either side of the boundary, diversion of some returns from exploitation to boundary maintenance, and many more.

A comprehensive relational sociology requires generalization of this analytic mode. The construction of organizations, for example, entails significant effort: delineating an exclusive perimeter, creating at least one effective center of authority within that perimeter, establishing controls over interactions spanning the perimeter. Ronald Coase spurred a revival of organizational analysis in economics by pointing out that without some significant gains from such bounding and installation of hierarchy, the very existence of firms posed an embarrassing theoretical problem for market-oriented economists (Coase 1992). Hierarchies, in Coase's formulation, reduce the transaction costs of complex interactions.

As Coase did not say, the monopolization of resources underlies organizations. "All organizations," remarks Göran Ahrne, "seem to be founded around a set of collective resources, and access to these resources motivates people to join organizations and to stay with them" (Ahrne 1996, 112–113; see also Ahrne 1994). Ahrne leaves the impression that all clustered resources generate organizations, but that is not the case. The high seas teem with wonderful resources, but their (literal and figurative) fluidity has repeatedly frustrated human efforts to create bounded, exclusive organizations for exploitation of those resources; current struggles over fishing, which threaten the economies of regions as far apart as Newfoundland and Senegal, for example, stem from the ease with which industrial fishing vessels can enter almost all the world's abundant seas (Linard 1996).

Organizers are normally successful at creating a new, fully bounded organization only if they can accomplish three tasks: capturing valuable resources; lowering transaction costs and/or increasing gains in deploying those resources by means of bounded networks; and forming cross-boundary ties to sites that can provide them with the sustaining opportunities and assets that will facilitate the realization of gains from the resources.

In these unusual circumstances, the creation of a complete perimeter, rather than the guarded frontier of categorical pairing, yields significant returns for resource-holders. For a completely bounded organization to survive, those returns must include a margin for the sheer cost of monitoring and sustaining the boundary. Although hierarchies, triads, chains, and even paired categories are often produced inadvertently, no one is likely to create a new sort of organization inadvertently. Most organizations, indeed, come into being modeled directly on other, existing organizations—firms, associations, lineages, states, parties, households, churches, and similar well-established exemplars. Such borrowing lowers the costs of creating new organizations, but it also reduces the structure's conformity to the tasks at hand. Improvisation and the accumulation of shared local knowledge then produce further adjustments to the local situation.

In such circumstances, direct parallels to the opportunity hoarding, emulation, and adaptation that appear in categorical inequality promote the formation of organizations. In fact, another way of thinking about organizations is to see them as extreme forms of categorical inequality: a frontier extended into a complete perimeter separating ins from outs, social relations across the perimeter restricted and coordinated, and a hierarchy concentrating control over social relations in one or a few locations.

In themselves, paired categories do not necessarily feature great inequality. In firms using or selling complex technologies, for example, the line/staff distinction separates command hierarchies from positions providing technical services to members of that hierarchy, but the firm frequently affords ample rewards on the staff side. Managers sometimes encourage competition for better performance by fostering categorical distinctions among largely interchangeable units, as when a military commander pits companies A, B, and C against each other in competition for displays of solidarity, zeal, and effectiveness.

Consider brokers who make their living by mediating between two organizations or populations, equal or not. Such brokers enhance their livelihood by supporting categorical distinctions which ensure that cross-boundary transactions will continue to pass through them instead of knitting together complementary pairs across the boundary. Leaders of ethnic groups often acquire just such an interest in maintaining the distinctions between dominant classes and their own constituencies; they become stronger advocates of bilingual education, distinctive cultural institutions, and installation of legally protected categories than many members of their constituencies (see, e.g., Hofmeyr 1987).

In decentralized rural countries, landlords likewise often set themselves up as interlocutors for their culturally distinct tenants, becoming defenders of that distinctness as they do so without in the least relinquishing their own membership in the cosmopolitan culture (e.g., Rutten 1994). Wherever powerful parties gain from the segregation and coordination of two networks, equal or not, paired categories provide an effective device for realization of that gain.

CATEGORIES REVISITED

We return, then, to categories. Counterintuitively, categories take relational forms. Let us expand the earlier definition. A category consists of a set of actors who share a boundary distinguishing all of them from and relating all of them to at least one set of actors visibly excluded by that boundary. A category simultaneously lumps together actors deemed similar, splits sets of actors considered dissimilar, and defines relations between the two sets (cf. Zerubavel 1996). For obvious examples, consider the following:

Women, a category excluding men

Blacks, a category excluding whites

Slaves, a category excluding masters and other free persons

Muslims, a category generally excluding non-Muslims, but in particular locales excluding Jews, Orthodox Christians, Druse, Baha'i, and others

Other important categorical sets include noble/commoner, citizen/foreigner, professional/client, employer/worker, child/adult, prisoner/guard, and any number of ethnic, religious, or racial pairs. Much more rarely, categorical sets also take the form of rank orders such as Indian castes, gradations among military officers, or ladders of academic titles (instructor, assistant professor, associate professor, professor, and so on).

Categories center on boundaries. What causes the location and shape of boundaries? Let us distinguish among three overlapping origins: invention, borrowing, and by-products of network encounters. At one extreme, powerful actors or clusters of actors deliberately manufacture boundaries and accompanying stories, as when nineteenth-century revolutionary conspirators organized secret societies with their cells, hierarchies, and declared enemies, or when nation-building intellectuals constructed histories for their linguistic group that implied they had occupied their territory before speakers of other languages arrived on the scene. At another extreme, people incorporate into new settings boundaries that already prevail elsewhere. In day-to-day social interaction, most boundary formation occurs through borrowing of this sort. (Borrowing is, of course, simply a special type of emulation. Since emulation, for our purposes, includes the transfer of whole chunks of social structure that do not necessarily contain categorical boundaries, it helps to maintain the distinction between emulation as a general process and borrowing as a special case incorporating categories.)

What about entirely new categories? It looks as though categories form *de novo* chiefly where members of already solidary sets of social relations compete with one or more actors outside their sets: adjacent households contend for living space, connected females encounter predatory males, drinking buddies fight strangers, kin-connected bands claim priority over outsiders within their customary hunting grounds. Such solidary-competitive interactions form fault lines between network clusters. They also generate stories that participants subsequently use to explain and justify their interactions. The stories embody shared understandings of who we are, who they are, what divides us, and what connects us. People create such stories in the context of previously available cultural materials: shared concepts, beliefs, memories, symbols, myths, local knowledge.

Once in place, these stories constrain subsequent interactions across the boundary, modifying only slowly in response to those interactions.

Thus, as combinations of solidary and competitive interactions generate ostensibly racial barriers, they also produce genetically framed stories of each group's origins and attributes. Barriers take on racial rather than ethnic or territorial definitions to the extent that in early encounters members of the two populations use phenotypical markers to distinguish each other and resist forming durable sexual unions. If myths or facts of origin distinguish the populations, on the other hand, ethnic categories emerge from their interaction. Different combinations of encounters, barriers, and stories generate definitions of categories as centering on class, citizenship, age, or locality.

Gender boundaries are at once the most general and the most difficult to explain. Although they map to chromosomally driven anatomical differences, they also conform to deep divisions in childhood relations to mothers and others. They correspond approximately to genetically based variations in physiology, yet they incorporate long historical accumulations of belief and practice. If the solidary-competitive network model explains the emergence of gender boundaries, it must do so on a small scale and within strong limits set by genetic inheritance.

Note the logical parallels between the origins of elementary configurations—chains, hierarchies, triads, organizations, categorical pairs—and the explanations of categorical boundaries. The difference between elementary configurations as one-time inventions that diffuse and as recurrent outcomes of more basic social processes matters enormously for our understanding of social processes in general. It matters much less, however, for my account of exploitation, opportunity hoarding, emulation, and adaptation; any account of origins that allows for negotiation and adaptation of categories in actual use will do. Similarly, general accounts of social differentiation will look very different depending on whether we find that prevailing categorical pairs, their boundaries, and their relations result largely from convention or depend heavily on unavoidably recurrent features of small-scale social life. Yet all but extreme versions of either position will fit with an explanation of durable inequality as an outcome of exploitation, opportunity hoarding, emulation, and adaptation. Some readers will regard that indeterminacy regarding microfoundations to be a weakness of my analysis, others a strength; for my part, I consider it a challenge to further theory and research.

CATEGORIES IN ACTION

The most dramatic forms of categorization involve outright stigma. Robert Jütte summarizes European practice with respect to pariah categories:

> By the late Middle Ages signs and badges had already become a legitimate means of (mostly negative) social distinction and they were also extended to include all marginal groups of the Christian Commonwealth such as public prostitutes, heretics, hangmen, the Jews and even lepers. Jewish women were marked with yellow veils or circles on their costumes. Some cities identified the hangman by either special, flamboyant clothes or a sign depicting a gallow. Heretics were marked with a yellow cross. The bell was a common sign of a leper, but on a prostitute the same sign can be associated with those daughters of Zion whom Isaiah would smite because they walked "with stretched forth necks and wanton eyes, walking and mincing as they go, and making a tinkling sound with their feet" (Isaiah 3: 16–17). In some Italian cities prostitutes were assigned a yellow strip on the shoulder, reminiscent of the yellow circle that Jews had to attach to the clothing of their chest. (Jütte 1994, 160–161)

Such stigmata drew the line between decent citizens and others, but they also defined proper—and improper!—relations across the line. As Erving Goffman insisted long ago, stigmatization uses attributes (sometimes invented or created attributes) to establish relationships (Goffman 1963, 3). The role of stigma in defining relationships becomes even clearer in the badges that Zurich and other European towns issued to their deserving (as distinguished from undeserving) poor, badges that qualified those persons to receive alms from the citizenry as half-gift, half-entitlement (Jütte 1994, 161). In times of famine, Europe's sixteenth-century cities often used the distinction deserving/undeserving or the related distinction native/alien to draw the line between those paupers who would receive food at municipal expense and those who would be sent away to fend for themselves (Geremek 1994, chap. 3).

Despite such extreme cases, a viable category by no means entails a complete perimeter around all actors on one side of the boundary or the other; on the contrary, complete perimeters require a great deal of management and ordinarily cause more trouble than they save. Nor does a viable category require homogeneity among the actors on a given side. You can be more or less a Muslim, even to the point where other Muslims deny your Muslimness, yet at the boundary with Jews you still fall unmistakably into the Muslim category.

Categorical boundaries certainly need not rely on objectively verifiable characteristics. Social control agencies often use grossly inaccurate indicators to stigmatize a suspect segment of the population, as described here:

> In 1993, the Denver police department compiled a roster of suspected gang members based on "clothing choices," "flashing of gang signals," or associating with known gang members. The list included two-thirds of the city's young black men, of whom only a small percentage were actual gang members. (Gans 1995, 66–67)

Similarly, William Chambliss reports his first-hand observations from regular riding with the Rapid Deployment Unit of the Washington D.C. Metropolitan Police:

> The RDU patrols the ghetto continuously looking for cars with young black men in them. They are especially attentive to newer-model cars, Isuzu four-wheel-drive vehicles, BMWs and Honda Accords, based on the belief that these are the favorite cars of drug dealers. During our observations, however, the RDU officers came to the conclusion that drug dealers were leaving their fancy cars at home to avoid vehicular stops. It thus became commonplace for RDU officers to stop any car with young black men in it. (Chambliss 1994, 179)

Categories are not specific sets of people or unmistakable attributes, but standardized, movable social relations.

Complete perimeters and substantial homogeneity are rare limiting cases, contingent social creations achieved and maintained at great effort. Incompletely bounded, heterogeneous categories generally work better, precisely because they demand less socialization, monitoring, and control. For every ACT UP activist seeking to identify gays as a distinct, unified, conscious set of individuals, we find a thousand people who belong to the category of gays in some social ties but spend much of their time tending other categorical boundaries at which gayness is invisible, irrelevant, or denied.

Categorical work always involves imputing distinctive qualities to actors on either side of boundaries; in the crucial case of paired categories, actors on the two sides engage in mutual labeling. Yet categories rarely pervade life so thoroughly as to forbid crosscutting categorical memberships. Many actors occupy multiple categories without great difficulty, as long as the ties defining one category activate at different times, in different places, and/or in different circumstances than do the ties defining other categories. As a broadcaster's off-microphone behavior, a driver's interactions with other nearby drivers while conversing with passengers in the back seat, and our own experiences talking on the telephone while carrying on other local sociability indicate, people are actually quite capable of doing the work of two or more categories simultaneously when they have devices for segregating categorical ties from each other (Goffman 1981, 267).

Remember the distinctions among invention, network interaction, and borrowing as origins of categorical pairs. Some few categories that are new to a given setting result from deliberate design, more result from incremental interaction during which small-scale categorical inventions occur, but most result from incorporation of categorical sets that already operate visibly elsewhere. In extreme cases, members of organizations openly devise categorical pairs and lock them into place. Just as they script some relations by intentionally forming chains, triads, and hierarchies, the creators and managers of organizations often build categories into the organizations. By definition, organizations incorporate categories into their networks; an organization is any well-bounded, categorically defined network in which some actors acquire rights to speak authoritatively for the whole. Everyone who creates a new voluntary association, for example, invents for it a name and criteria for membership, thereby drawing a line between insiders and outsiders.

Powerful figures within organizations, furthermore, often impose an internal distinction on its members: officers versus enlisted in the military, students versus faculty in a university, citizens versus foreigners in a state. These distinctions become interior to the extent that they involve explicit recognition, symbolic representation, and boundary-defining practices. They provide scripts within which local knowledge accumulates.

In addition, exploitation and opportunity hoarding operate incrementally within organizations even when managers resist or ignore them. Ava Baron (1982) has documented the long-successful struggle of America's male printers to exclude women from the more lucrative positions in their trade even as their bosses tried to recruit women. All situations in which nominally subordinate workers possess crucial knowledge or skills that their superiors cannot control or appropriate promote the formation of exclusive categories insulating virtuosi from other organization members; the interactions of football stars, major actresses, leading scientists, or best-selling authors with adjacent functionaries create categorical differences.

More generally, workers who enjoy the advantages of high pay, job security, promotion opportunities, and ready access to management commonly build barriers between themselves and adjacent workers in high-turnover, low-pay positions, whether or not managers mark the differences sharply; that is one reason it usually takes either major organizing efforts or strong off-work connections to promote joint collective action between "skilled" and "unskilled" workers (Hanagan 1980; Hanagan and Tilly 1988). The line between members and nonmembers of professional organizations, craft guilds, or trade unions usually works to the advantage of members, but that advantage depends on enforcement by governments and licensing agencies. Where authorities oppose workers' organizations, the advantage becomes much more contingent. In the anti-union environment of today's Louisiana, Lonnie Shaw (business agent for an International Brotherhood of Electrical Workers local) reports his strategy:

In this state what we have now is a Right to Work law where you can't discriminate. And they've always used it against us union guys. They made us real careful when a non-union guy would come in and apply for work—you better get him a job. Now we are turning it around with "salting." If we send in a union guy to a non-union contractor and he asks "are you a union guy?", he's just violated the law. Or we will intentionally go in with lots of union buttons and T-shirts and he'll say "We are not hiring." So we will let it cool for a day or two and then send in a guy with a bogus resume and the contractor will hire him cause he's not union and they've just violated the law. (Fine and Locke 1996, 18)

Network interaction also creates many categories. Outside of organizations such as firms, governments, parties, and voluntary associations, categories rarely form as deliberate outcomes of planned social action. The most prominent exceptions occur where political entrepreneurs have something to gain by asserting and promoting the existence of a categorical entity that, if recognized, enjoys some sort of collective advantage; claims to speak on behalf of an oppressed, unrecognized, and unorganized nation have this character, as do the demands of social-movement activists to be heard as spokespersons for their unjustly disadvantaged constituencies. Even these instances depend closely on existing organizations, for the political entrepreneurs in action are typically demanding either a special place within a given state or recognition by other states of their sovereign existence as a new state.

Invention and network interaction both produce relational scripts, but they do so in different manners. Organization-based invention of categories begins with scripts and then generates common knowledge that attenuates and enriches the scripts. Thus new military organizations formalize divisions between officers and enlisted personnel, yet senior enlisted men or women (as I remember well from my initiation as a freshly minted disbursing officer in the U.S. Navy) actually play significant parts in socializing new officers to their relations with ostensible subordinates.

In network interaction, however, localized common knowledge and the behavioral regularities it generates form new relational scripts. Members of two migratory streams from the very same village frequently create beliefs, rituals, labels, and exclusive practices that mark the distinction between emerging categories, while socially similar neighbors in a newly constructed housing development immediately set to work creating categories that organize friendships, rivalries, and even enmities. From quite different starting points, organization-imposed and category-related processes therefore end up closer to the middle ground that combines moderate scripting with considerable shared local knowledge.

New categories usually form as by-products of social interaction that simultaneously connects people who share or thereby acquire common traits and also segregates them in some regard from other people with whom they nevertheless maintain significant relations. Thus ostensibly ethnic faction fights often occurred in South Africa's mining compounds during the 1940s, but the actual identities assumed by rival gangs varied with the mix of origins within a compound, the consequent segregation of barracks, and the ethnic divisions of labor within the mine. African "boss boys" who drove underground work gangs frequently stirred up ethnic competition to stimulate production and maintain control. Police from Randfontein reported an April 1940 fight:

> The cause of the trouble originated underground the week before. Two Xosa [sic] boss boys assaulted a Pondo. The Xosas were charged with assault and released on bail . . . The assault caused ill-feeling amongst the Pondos. During the afternoon of 21.4.1940, Xosas, of which one section Bo[m]vanas, visited native huts on Panvlakte. The Bo[m]vanas assaulted 4 Xosas. The Xosas returned to the compound and thereafter attacked the Bo[m]vana section . . . A Pondo took advantage of the turmoil to avenge the assault by the Xosa boss boys on a Pondo the week before and fatally stabbed a Xosa . . . A Pondo was arrested . . . A party of Pondos demanded the release of the prisoner . . . [When this was refused] they replied that they would attack the Xosa unless the prisoner was released. Information was then received that the one affected section of the Xosas . . . of the night before, had joined forces with the Pondos to attack the rest of the Xosas. (Moodie 1994, 183)

Police assumed a major division between "Pondos" (that is, Mpondo) and Xhosas, with the latter divided into Bomvana and others, the

Bomvana unaccountably defecting from their Xhosa category to ally with the Mpondo. In this particular situation, all three sets of miners spoke Xhosa, but the Bomvana, small in number, lived in their own section of a so-called Xhosa block, while the Mpondo lived elsewhere. On other occasions, Mpondo and Bomvana readily fought each other.

What was happening? Mine managers grouped workers and their African straw bosses by linguistic similarity, which then produced boundaries and categories over which young men were willing to kill each other. If we looked farther into the categories Mpondo and Bomvana, furthermore, we would discover that they too designated ties among locally distinguished aggregates rather than irreducible nuclei of solidarity, connection, and common culture. The Transkei migrant whom William Beinart identifies as M became involved in male associations called *indlavini* when he worked on a Natal sugar estate during the late 1930s and then carried that affiliation into Rand gold mines. "In certain contexts, however," reports Beinart,

> M's identity as an *indlavini* could be subsumed in the sense of belonging to a larger Mpondo group. There were, of course, men from many other rural areas in Angelo compound, but they tended to be housed along "ethnic" lines—as perceived by managers and many workers themselves. "There was one wing for Pondos, one for Bhacas, one for Shangaans, one for Zulus." Perhaps he exaggerated when he remembered that "groups like Bhacas and Pondos, Pondos and Zulus never mixed" in their living quarters. "If a Pondo goes to the Zulu side, the Zulus do not know him and they start abusing him and saying all sorts of things. They hit him and when he comes back to the Pondos then the Pondos start arming . . . That was what usually sparked off faction fights." (Beinart 1987, 292–293)

Locally available boundaries defined entire categories much more definitively than did common culture or long-term internal solidarities. Such boundaries took the form of dividing lines rather than complete perimeters. Yet once those boundaries stood in place, participants and observers alike attributed hard, durable, even genetic reality to the categories they inscribed. Wherever they came from, the categories had serious social consequences.

The same holds generally for ethnicity, gender, race, community membership, and other categories sociologists once lumped together as ascribed statuses. They do boundary work, defining ties and locating distinctions between members of different categories more reliably than they create internal solidarity, homogeneity, or connectedness (see, e.g., Smith 1995). They do the work of distinction, more or less as Pierre Bourdieu defines that work. Once any of these categories exists, nevertheless, it lends itself to serious relational work.

Categories support durable inequality when they combine with hierarchies—ties between social sites in which the connections are asymmetrical and the sites systematically unequal. Each reinforces the other, for a relatively impermeable barrier reduces the likelihood that equalizing relations will form across it, while asymmetrical relations based on unequal resources justify the boundary and render it more visible. Racial inequality seems natural precisely to the extent that all transactions across the boundary occur asymmetrically and dramatize the disparity of resources on either side. Only when inconsistencies occur—privileged members of the ostensibly inferior category, disinherited members of the ostensibly superior category, persons straddling the boundary, open competition for the same positions between members of both categories—do vigorous, violent mobilizations from "above" and "below" become likely (Olzak 1992; cf. Patterson 1995).

Institutional economists have indirectly recognized the practical importance of categories by stressing the comparison of markets and hierarchies: markets lending themselves to spot interchanges having low transaction costs, hierarchies facilitating interchanges where high transaction costs prevail. Thus they account for the prevalence of bounded firms, which in idealized markets have no rationale at all.

While acknowledging the advantages of hierarchy in circumstances where coercion rather than shared commitment or direct compensation makes the difference between success and failure, I suggest that the boundary itself has an effect. It contains local knowledge, channels flows of mobility, limits liability, and affords leverage to those who control membership in the organization, hence access to its benefits. A clear boundary greatly facilitates the exercise of collective property rights.

With a well-marked boundary present, not only organization members but also third parties such as governments can adopt low-cost rules of thumb for the reinforcement or denial of claims to deploy an organization's resources or occupy its dedicated space.

Concepts are tools. Their values depend on whether they do the job at hand. Just as a crystal shovel looks lovely but remains useless for digging coal, elaborate concepts sometimes glitter alluringly but break down when put to work. Crystal or steel? The task at hand is to explain the emergence, survival, and change of categorical inequality and then to ascertain how much of what appears to be individual-to-individual inequality actually results from categorically organized differences. Let us see how well the tools discussed here—scripting versus local knowledge; payments as gifts, entitlements, and compensation; a basic set of network configurations including chains, hierarchies, triads, organizations, and categorical pairs; and the four mechanism of exploitation, opportunity hoarding, emulation, and adaptation—can help us do the explanatory job. In a first excavation, they seem to dig deep into inequality's subsoil.

3 How Categories Work

Mary Romero explains how she got involved in research on Chicana domestic workers:

> Before beginning a college teaching post in Texas, I stayed at the home of a colleague who employed a live-in domestic worker. Until then, I had been unaware of the practice of hiring teenage undocumented women as live-in household help. Nor had I had access to the social or "private" space of an employer. I was shocked at the way my colleague and his family treated the 16-year-old domestic whom I will call Juanita. Only recently hired, Juanita was still adjusting to her new environment; her shyness was reinforced by my colleague's constant flirting. I observed many encounters that served to remind Juanita of her subservient role. For example, one evening I walked into the kitchen as the employer's young sons were pointing to dirty dishes on the table and in the sink and yelling "Wash! Clean!" Juanita stood frozen; she was angry and humiliated. Aware of the risks of my reprimanding the boys, I chose instead to suggest that Juanita and I would wash and dry the

dishes, while the boys cleared the table. When my host returned from his meeting and found us cleaning the last pan, his expression told me how shocked he was to find his houseguest and future colleague washing dishes with the maid. His obvious embarrassment confirmed my suspicion that I had violated the normative expectations of class-based behavior within the home. (Romero 1996, 2)

Categorical inequality cuts right into middle-class households and often matches exterior with interior categorical differences. *Interior* categories belong to a particular organization's internally visible structure: staff versus line, enlisted versus officers, faculty versus students, management versus workers, and so on. In these cases, organizational participants devise names for the boundaries and the sets of actors they distinguish; enact rituals recognizing the relevant networks, boundaries, and relations; and represent them by symbolically explicit devices such as uniforms, badges, and organization charts. Interior categories include those that bound the organization itself, separating members from nonmembers.

Exterior categories, in contrast, do not originate in a given organization, but they often install systematic differences in activities, rewards, power, and prospects within that organization; they come from outside. Gender distinctions provide obvious examples: ritualized differences between male and female places in religious organizations, girls' gym classes versus boys' gym classes, distinctions in military service for women and men, sex-typing of occupations.

Householders have commonly recruited domestic help by matching the subordinate interior category of servant with exterior categories of race, ethnicity, gender, and/or class that are widely established in the surrounding population. In the United States of the 1930s, whether domestic servants were Mexican, Indian, Scandinavian, Irish, or (especially) black varied dramatically by region, but by then they were chiefly women and always members of locally disadvantaged categories (Palmer 1989, 67; I recall with a wince the shame I felt as an insecure teenager over the fact that my German-born grandmother supported herself and her disabled husband, my grandfather, by cleaning other people's houses). In the encounter Mary Romero reports, her hosts had matched the exterior categories Chicana and teenager with the interior category servant. They had borrowed the matching from neighbors and colleagues. Matching reinforced the line between full and contingent members of the household.

Similar mechanisms operate in the world of capitalist firms. When Trond Petersen and Laurie Morgan report that "occupation-establishment segregation accounts better for wage differences between men and women than any other set of variables studied in the literature on wage differences" (Petersen and Morgan 1995, 344), they make more precise a finding that sociologists have been turning up in cruder versions for two decades. Inverted, the finding says that sex-typing extends massively not just to broad occupations but to specialized jobs within firms (for qualifications, see Cotter et al. 1995). Sex-typing characterizes jobs not only in big capitalist countries but also in social democracies such as Sweden and socialist regimes such as the former Soviet Union (le Grand 1991; Christenson 1995; Lapidus 1992). The phenomenon has been around long enough for Robert Gray, speaking of British factories between 1845 and 1855, to mention the "male monopoly of such posts as mill mechanics and overlookers (and also of juvenile employment leading to them)" (Gray 1993, 71). Elsewhere and at other times, race-typing, ethnic typing, religion-typing, kinship-typing, and locality-typing have operated just as pervasively and consequentially, sometimes several of them at once.

Matching interior with exterior categories reinforces inequality inside the organization that does the matching. The creation of a well-marked interior boundary itself facilitates exploitation and opportunity hoarding by providing explanations, justifications, and practical routines for unequal distribution of rewards. But matching such an interior boundary with an exterior categorical pair such as white/black or citizen/foreigner imports already established understandings, practices, and relations that lower the cost of maintaining the boundary. It borrows potent scripts and common knowledge. Emulation thereby reinforces exploitation and opportunity hoarding.

The labels "interior" and "exterior" do not identify the content or members of a categorical pair; rather, they indicate the relation of the

	No Exterior Category	Exterior Category
No Interior Category	*Gradient*	*Imported frontier*
Interior Category	*Local frontier*	*Reinforced inequality*

Figure 4. Effects of the Presence or Absence of Interior and Exterior Categories

categories to the organization at hand. The contrast interior/exterior defines endpoints of a continuum from very local to omnipresent. The division between Eagle and Life Scouts, for example, appears in almost all Boy Scout troops, but practically nowhere else; it constitutes a relatively interior categorical pair. Within the United States, the line between college graduates and others cuts across a wide variety of organizations, entering all of them—except perhaps colleges themselves—as a rather exterior categorical pair. Those who run an organization have considerable capacity to redefine its interior categories, but much less power to reshape its exterior categories. A boss who wants to blur the local distinction between college graduates and others must usually work hard to do so.

From the perspective of a particular organization, the major possibilities schematize in as shown in Figure 4. Suppose for a moment that all the social sites we are comparing involve the same amount of inequality among their participants. Given a certain level of inequality among the occupants of a site within the organization, Figure 4 shows the difference made by the presence or absence of boundaries that separate unequal categories, with well-scripted social relations across the boundaries.

This way of looking at the situation immediately suggests a series of plausible hypotheses:

1.   Substantial inequality in the absence of rationalizing boundaries (gradients) generates rivalry, jealousy, and individual sentiments of injustice but provides no basis for categorically based collective action.

2.   Without strong incentives to endure short-term injustice in the expectation of long-term mobility or other rewards, turnover and small-scale conflict make gradients unstable arrangements.

3.   Inequality conforming chiefly to exterior categories (imported frontiers) generates shared resentment, resistance, and collective action. Without extensive controls, it remains unstable.

4.   For the same difference in rewards, inequality that depends on organizationally defined categorical differences alone (local frontiers) is more stable than gradients or imported frontiers, but it requires the expenditure of resources on socialization and commitment while remaining vulnerable to subversion by cross-boundary coalitions based on exterior categories.

5.   Matching interior with exterior categorical boundaries (reinforced inequality) produces a low-cost, stable situation that is chiefly vulnerable to its generation of solidarity, hence of potential resistance and collective action, within categories.

6.   Gradients therefore tend to convert to local frontiers or imported frontiers, while the two sorts of frontiers tend to convert to reinforced inequality.

7.   Reverse movements—from reinforced inequality to local frontiers, imported frontiers, or gradients—occur rarely, mainly when the costs of maintaining the relevant distinctions have risen significantly and visibly.

8.   Where surplus extraction is already operating efficiently by means of gradients or local frontiers, those who control the crucial resources rarely incorporate exterior categories.

These hypotheses guide much of the following inquiry.

How do sites within organizations end up in one or another of Figure 4's four cells? Exterior categorical pairs sometimes play significant parts in organizational life simply because organizational life brings members of the pairs into contact (unequal or not) and because the categories in question pervade social life. Black/white distinctions in South Africa, citizen/foreigner in Kuwait, Muslim/Jew in Israeli-occupied Palestine, male/female almost anywhere on earth provide scripts so pervasive that they modify interactions within all sorts of organizations until and unless the creation of common knowledge mitigates their effects. Whether pervasive or not, exterior categories gain organizational importance when they coincide with interior categories—when, for example, an American steel mill recruits Polish immigrants for its blast furnaces and Irish immigrants for its handling of finished metal. With consequences that organizational managers often cannot foresee or control, such matching of exterior to interior categories builds whatever common knowledge and social relations are already linked with the exterior categorical pairs into the organization itself.

Both interior and exterior categories play significant parts in the organization of work. At the continuum's interior end, the boundaries of firms, professions, trades, and industries come immediately to mind. But within firms organization charts provide cartoons of multiple categories: paired divisions, departments, pay grades, specialized clusters of jobs, and more. The unequal boundaries among them originate in exploitation, in the simultaneous enlistment of the subordinate category's effort and the exclusion of its members from the full value added by their effort.

Most large capitalist firms, for instance, separate job clusters we can designate as *command-and-promotion pools* (whose occupants have opportunities to rise within well-defined hierarchies in which from the start they devote a significant share of their effort to controlling other people's work) from *turnover pools* (in which promotion ladders are short or nonexistent, benefits minimal, and tenure uncertain). The venerable distinction between primary and secondary labor markets rests chiefly on the relative predominance of these two sorts of job clusters. In highly competitive, labor-intensive industries such as garment manufacturing, goes the reasoning, pressure to keep wages low pushes owners toward maintaining a high proportion of turnover jobs. But those owners also maintain small cores of command-and-promotion jobs to drive occupants of the other jobs. Such interior categories facilitate the installation within firms and industries of inequalities with respect to pay, power, autonomy, perquisites, tenure, and deference. These inequalities rest on interior paired categories.

Interior categories likewise figure in work outside the zone of firms, jobs, and labor markets, as in professional boundaries that separate private-practice physicians, psychologists, lawyers, or architects from their clients. Similar ties and distinctions form among owners, tenants, and rental agents in real estate. Outside bureaucratized organizations, however, interior and exterior categories blur into each other, precisely because work embeds so deeply in nonwork networks such as those defined by kinship and ethnicity and therefore builds on the categorical differences they already contain. Family farms, households, ethnic stores, casual prostitution, and punk music intertwine interior and exterior categories so thoroughly that it makes little sense to distinguish one from the other. We might say the same thing another way: such settings typically incorporate the structure of reinforced inequality, the fourth cell in Figure 4. For a given degree of difference in rewards, the matching of interior and exterior categories lowers transaction costs and increases stability.

However they are institutionalized, exterior categories such as race, gender, and ethnicity become interior to the extent that members of organizations create widely recognized names for the boundaries and actors, enact defining rituals, and represent the categories by symbolically explicit devices. Categories become interior, that is, as they move from bare scripts to sites of local knowledge and improvisation. Exterior categories come to loom large within firms in two overlapping ways: first, members of firms ease their organizational work by mapping exterior categories to interior categories; and, second, members of firms employ categorically organized networks outside their firms to carry on important activities.

In the first regard, for example, employers assign female secretaries to male executives, thus importing a powerful distinction and relation directly into the firm in a way that reduces the likelihood of a subordinate becoming the boss's rival. In the second regard, workers organize their searches for employment through segregated networks created or recast by chain migration, employers hire chiefly on recommendations of existing workers, and an ethnically segregated niche forms within the firm. The first case pivots on exploitation, the second on opportunity hoarding.

In both regards, we notice the effects of a condition strongly implied by transaction-cost economics but generally ignored by practitioners of that art: organizational designs and their changes cost a great deal to conceive, test, modify, install, teach, and enforce. The more unfamiliar the design, in general, the greater these costs. In response to such costs, managers and other members of work organizations generally prefer familiar models, including categorical models, for work contracts. They readily incorporate existing social structure—emphatically including exterior categories—into their organizations. Most organizations therefore take shape and change not as efficiency-driven designs but as mosaics of established models and exterior social structure. In the terms used earlier, emulation reproduces familiar clumps of social ties, while adaptation knits them into the webs of connection around them. As a given boundary is set in place, furthermore, the relative cost of shifting to another structure or another pair of categories rises.

For these reasons and others we will encounter later on, organizations that incorporate categorical inequality do not necessarily operate more efficiently than similar organizations (actual or possible) that lack categorical inequality; if they did, we would have little hope of reducing inequality or changing its form. Categorical inequality persists for two main reasons: first, under a wide range of circumstances, it does in fact facilitate exploitation and opportunity hoarding by more favored members of a given organization, who have the means of maintaining their advantage even at the expense of overall inefficiency; and, second, the transaction costs of changing the current circumstances, compounded by the effects of adaptation, pose serious barriers to the deliberate adoption of new organizational models and, when change occurs or new organizations are founded, favor the incorporation of existing models from elsewhere.

According to such an argument, gender, class, ethnicity, race, citizenship, and other pervasive categorical systems do not each operate sui generis but instead share many causal properties. I will not, of course, deny the meanings, memories, social networks, and practices that accumulate separately within each of these containers. Nor will I deny that in much of our world race and class overlap far more than gender and class, with the result that importing a gender boundary line has different consequences than importing racial frontiers. Those distinctive accumulations, indeed, play significant parts in the effectiveness of categorical relations; they save participants the effort of constructing and imposing novel conventions. They provide ready-made scripts and local knowledge.

Although people commonly naturalize pervasive categories by attributing hard genetic edges to them, all such categories depend on a substantial amount of social construction. Take the case of race, where participants at either side of an established boundary regularly assume that inheritance explains much of the behavior on the boundary's other side. When geneticists try to partition human beings into races, however, they discover two crucial facts: (1) genetic differences do not cluster sufficiently to mark well-defined frontiers among human populations; (2) established racial classifications either select one or two genetic characteristics (e.g., skin color) that correlate weakly if at all with other genetic characteristics, or (more often) these classifications correspond to social markers (e.g., categorical membership of ancestors) having no genetic basis whatsoever. As a definitive handbook on the subject summarizes current knowledge:

> The classification into races has proved to be a futile exercise for reasons that were already clear to Darwin. Human races are still extremely unstable entities in the hands of modern taxonomists, who define from 3 to 60 or more races . . . Although there is no doubt that there is only one human species, there are clearly no objective reasons for stopping at any particular level of taxonomic splitting. (Cavalli-Sforza, Menozzi, and Piazza 1994, 19)

In day-to-day social life, most ostensibly racial distinctions have the genetically imprecise and socially negotiated character of the term "black"
in Great Britain after World War I, which "described Africans and West
Indians, South Asians, Arabs, and other colonized people" (Tabili 1996,
167–168). Despite the irony that they had strong claims to the term
"Caucasian," South Asian immigrants to the United States struggled for
decades to escape the category referred to as "Mongoloid" and the restrictions on citizenship attached to it. Categories such as race, age, and
gender build on physical (and partly genetic) characteristics, but they
erect boundaries that rely heavily on socially organized convention and
control.

Some feminist analysts have expressed views of the connection between categorical relationships and exploitation similar to the one
presented here but have insisted on the existence of a single script operating everywhere to the advantage of the same exploiters. Cynthia
Cockburn declares, "Disadvantaged groups are inferiorized on account
of their bodily difference and their cultures so that all are obliged to
aspire to conformity with the white male heterosexual able bodied
norm" (Cockburn 1991, 13). While confirming many of Cockburn's concrete observations, my analysis parts company with hers in asserting
the following:

- Categorical inequality serves many different exploiters and opportunity hoarders—even black female homosexuals at times—depending on their relations to valuable resources.

- Various categorical pairs operate differently and independently
  precisely because they enter organizations as preformed packages
  of scripts and local knowledge.

- Within limits set by available scripts and local knowledge, nevertheless, unequal categorical pairs substitute for each other.

Installing a gender distinction at an otherwise crucial organizational
boundary increases the likelihood of sexual play and predation across
that boundary, while installing a racial distinction at a similar organizational location increases the likelihood of segregated social ties outside
the organization. Where citizenship marks a crucial boundary, appeal to

state authorities becomes more likely as management's way of controlling unruly subordinates. Yet over and above such important differences, categorical inequalities operate and change in similar ways. As a
consequence, the same organization can easily redouble categories (earmarking certain positions, e.g., not just for females but for black females)
or install different categorical pairs (white/black, Puerto Rican/Irish) at
different locations within its perimeter.

CATEGORICAL PAIRS AND THE MECHANISMS
OF INEQUALITY

Let me recapitulate how and why. Humans have devised a limited number of organizational forms that work effectively in a very wide range
of situations. One form is hierarchy, another the network built up of
relatively homogeneous triads, a third the long-stranded network, a
fourth the bounded organization having some concentration of authority. Yet another is the location of paired, unequal categories at a well-
defined boundary.

None of these organizational forms does good or evil in itself; each at
various times does the work of saints, sinners, or the rest of us ordinary
bumblers. But almost all human beings learn to detect, join, connect,
transfer, and even create these forms early in life. All have structurally
predictable yet often unforeseen consequences: unanticipated but frequent encounters among connected people; recurrent myths among occupants of high-ranking positions about occupants of low-ranking positions and vice versa; concentration of intimacy, marriage, and other
relations of trust within triad-dominated networks; exclusion of qualified but unconnected persons from categorically concentrated rewards;
and so on. Categorical inequality results from the institution of a general, powerful, problem-solving organizational form, the asymmetrically related categorical pair, in a location that commands substantial
rewards and/or punishments. Categorical inequality is not necessarily
bad; it can provide benefits by simplifying social life and facilitating the
production of collective goods. It is pernicious, however, to the extent

that it causes harm to the excluded, deprives them of access to what could be collective goods, and produces a net underuse of potentially life-enhancing talent.

What sorts of organizational problems does categorical inequality solve? We enter dangerous terrain where, in the absence of accumulated research, moral indignation and teleological reasoning easily slide us into explanatory quicksand. Within the world of organized work and labor markets alone, many distinguishable processes promote categorical inequality in work's rewards: differences in job qualifications, employer discrimination, differences in job preferences, bounding of various performances as the "same" or "different" jobs, ranking of those jobs, linking of jobs through ease of promotion or transfer, categorical designation of jobs, segregation of networks, and differential distribution of category members among firms and nonfirm worksites.

To encompass categorical inequalities with respect to states, communities, and other organizations, we would only have to lengthen our list. Looking for a single, simple, invariant link between categorical inequality and organizational problems therefore resembles seeking a single explanation for other complex, multiple-use human inventions such as language, cities, and ideology. It makes no sense.

I do not claim, then, that all inequality among members of different categories results from exploitation or that all exploitation entails categorical inequality. I propose instead the following:

- Exploitation rests on unequal distribution of rewards proportionate to value added among participants in the same enterprise.

- Organizationally installed categorical inequality facilitates exploitation.

- Organizations whose survival depends on exploitation therefore tend to adopt categorical inequality.

- Because organizations adopting categorical inequality deliver greater returns to their dominant members and because a portion of those returns goes to organizational maintenance, such organizations tend to crowd out other types of organizations.

- Opportunity hoarding by collaborative agents complements exploitation.

- Opportunity hoarding operates more effectively and at lower cost in conjunction with categorical inequality.

- Emulation and adaptation strengthen the effects of categorical inequality.

- For any given organization, the installation of widely available exterior categories at boundaries defined by exploitation and opportunity hoarding lowers the cost of maintaining categorical inequality.

- In a given population, the more prevalent and/or powerful the organization installing a given pair of unequal categories, the more widespread the overall inequalities in welfare between members of the two categories will become across that population.

- Categorically differentiated experience in a given setting produces differences in individual capacities, propensities, and social relations that transfer into other settings and cause differential performances, hence unequal rewards, in new settings.

- Much of what observers and participants interpret as innate individual differences in capacity actually results from categorically organized experience.

- Seemingly contradictory categorical principles such as age, race, gender, and ethnicity operate in similar ways and can be organizationally combined or substituted within limits set by previously established scripting and local knowledge.

These points summarize the theory behind my entire analysis. At the risk of tedium, let us therefore review and examine in a bit more detail the theory's four central causal mechanisms: exploitation of labor-demanding resources by the elite, sequestering access to resources by the nonelite, diffusion of organizational models, and adaptation of valued social ties to existing divisions.

EXPLOITATION

Exploitation, as earlier defined, is a response to the situation in which some well-connected group of actors controls a valuable, labor-

demanding resource from which they can extract returns only by har-
nessing the effort of others, whom they exclude from the full value
added by that effort. (Let me vault over the crevasse of a fascinating,
important question: how by force, ruse, purchase, inheritance, or legal
device groups of actors acquire control over valuable resources in the
first place.) Here categorical boundaries separate the major beneficiaries—we could label them exploiters, profiteers, or rent-seekers—from
other contributors. This mechanism occupies a central place in Marxist
theory:

> Exploitation occurs when one section of the population produces a sur-
> plus whose use is controlled by another section. Classes in Marxist the-
> ory exist only in relation to each other and that relation turns upon the
> form of exploitation occurring in a given mode of production. It is ex-
> ploitation which gives rise to class conflict. Thus different types of soci-
> ety, the classes within them, and the class conflict which provides the dy-
> namic of any society can all be characterized by the specific way in
> which exploitation occurs. (Bottomore 1983, 157)

Without employing the full apparatus of Marxist theory, my analysis of
exploitation draws directly on that idea of sectionally organized inequality. Note the relational content of the Marxist view: a boundary
coexists with well-defined unequal relations across that boundary; the
boundary and the unequal relations reinforce each other.

Although neoclassical economic doctrine declares that workers generally receive the equivalent of their labor's marginal product, exclusion
from full value added marks the general condition of labor under capitalism. The labor theory of value grew up within eighteenth- and nineteenth-century crafts as a hierarchy of masters, journeymen, and apprentices with significant possibilities of movement upward gave way
to an almost unbridgeable gap between capitalists and workers; organized capitalists excluded workers from full value added, and workers
cast that exclusion in the labor theory of value. During the nineteenth
century, strict wage labor displaced the arrangements of indenture, ap-
prenticeship, slavery, and household incorporation under which most
subordinate workers had previously labored (Steinfeld 1991; Tomlins

1993; Way 1993). In that process, confrontation sharpened between those who owned the means of production and those who contributed to production primarily their own cunning, effort, and collaboration; thus the labor theory of value became even more plausible and urgent. Systems of slavery operate on similar principles of separation between owners and workers, but with even sharper divisions between included and excluded persons. South African racial categorization and the differentiation of American physicians from other specialists in health care, as we shall see in later chapters, likewise conform to the inclusion-exclusion principle.

Citizenship commonly operates in a parallel manner, excluding noncitizens from state-controlled or state-enforced benefits to the advantage of some or all citizens, as in Kuwait, Israel, Germany, the United States, and many other countries. In the United States, sharp distinctions with respect to a wide range of rights and obligations separate citizens, various categories of noncitizen legal residents, and illegal residents. Voting, military service, unemployment compensation, retirement benefits, health care, and much more differ categorically in this multiple system of citizenship and noncitizenship.

Such sharply drawn boundaries between ins and outs facilitate and justify unequal treatment; if the boundary corresponds to one that already prevails in the surrounding population, it costs less to install and maintain. An oligarchy's monopolization of resources becomes easier when a state can draw its revenues and their protection from a patron state or from easily sequestered commodities and activities such as Renaissance Venice's long-distance trade, early twentieth-century Bolivia's tin, and contemporary Saudi Arabia's oil. In such cases, self-reinforcing categorical inequality operates at very low cost to exploiters.

For millennia both mighty emperors and petty tyrants have organized exploitation around categorical distinctions. Long before apartheid, for example, many local southern African populations maintained their own systems of durable inequality, founding exploitation on decisive categorical differences. John and Jean Comaroff describe the nineteenth-century Tshidi population, a southern Tswana group settled in a number of villages near the present Botswana/South Africa border. A first division separated the Tshidi chief from his subjects:

By convention, although all households were domiciled in villages, cattle were tended at distant posts, beasts hunted in the wild, and agriculture conducted at fields to which producers moved for the annual arable cycle. But the regulation of seasonal movement and its associated activities was a prerogative of the ruler. This was the crux of the tension, for its exercise was in the material *dis*interest of the population at large. Yet it was deeply inscribed in the logic of royal power, being an essential aspect of the processes through which the center dominated the domestic periphery and appropriated its surpluses. (Comaroff and Comaroff 1992, 107)

Further sharp divisions appeared within the subject population. Tshidi villages combined agriculture, pastoralism, hunting, and gathering. As is often the case, women did almost all agricultural work and thereby supplied the great bulk of the population's subsistence. But prestigious ritual and exchange activities depended on cattle raising, a male domain in which young boys, poor dependents, and serfs did the routine work. "Female cultivation (and, to a lesser extent, gathering)," remark Comaroff and Comaroff, "actually subsidized male activity in the public domain, establishing a material base on which rested the transactions of agnatic politics" (Comaroff and Comaroff 1992, 107).

Additional categorical systems separated generations, kin groups, and ethnically defined populations. Although Tshidi males hunted intermittently, "those who hunted on a regular basis, Sarwa ('bushmen') serfs, were seen as semi-human creatures; they were allowed into the town only at night to deliver skins, meat, and honey to their masters" (Comaroff and Comaroff 1992, 108). In each case, categorical distinctions did the work of exploitation, enlisting the effort of persons who received less than the value added by their contributions.

In all such circumstances, categorical inequality does not one but two kinds of work for the powerful. It facilitates the extraction of effort from subordinate populations without fully sharing the returns of that effort. But it also permits members of the superior category, which is usually much smaller, to distribute solidarity-generating benefits within their own number, thus ensuring a command structure and orderly succession within an elite. Mancur Olson once denigrated such "distributional coalitions" as barriers to collective efficiency except when they approached coalitions of the whole, but he recognized their value for coalition members (Olson 1982).

I have so far described exploitation as if resource-controlling powerholders organized it free of cost. That initial simplification distorts the world twice. First, every organizational innovation imposes costs for invention, perfection, installation, socialization, and articulation with adjacent elements; most involve hidden and unanticipated costs in the form of impacts on incentives, alteration of existing solidarities, creation of constraining ties outside the organization, and facilitation of resistance.

Second, because no one can entirely control the actions of another, every innovation generates bargaining among organization members; we can label as "struggle" or "contention" the more rambunctious forms of bargaining. Bargaining incorporates local knowledge and modifies standard scripts. Even in Caribbean slave economies, as Arthur Stinchcombe points out, slaveowners varied greatly in the extent of control they exercised over their human chattel; they more often freed slaves, for example, within the same categories they supervised least from day to day. Some slaves therefore lived in "near freedom." Stinchcombe argues persuasively that

> the central determinant of treatment "near freedom" by owners toward slaves was the slaveowner's wanting the slave to be a responsible agent in unsupervised services or work, work involving care, or enthusiasm, or risk to the worker, or requiring loyalty that could be easily betrayed. Thus it was that when the slaveowner wanted trustworthy agency by slaves that he or she treated them as if they were free, as if they had rights, and in the extreme gave them rights. (Stinchcombe 1995, 131)

Despite Stinchcombe's language of intention and calculation, those practices sprang not only from slaveowners' organizational astuteness but also from incremental, implicit, and finally compelling bargains between masters and workers. Any full account of exploitation must include the costs of implementation as well as bargaining—however unequal—among the principals.

As the examples of citizenship, Tshidi social divisions, and slavery indicate, exploitation operates over a broader range than labor processes in any strict sense of the word. It occurs wherever well-connected people control valuable resources from which they extract returns by deploying the effort of others, whom they exclude from the full value added by that effort. The "value" in question may of course be monetary, but it may also take the form of power, deference, perquisites, services, goods, or protections. Categorically organized exploitation plays a part in almost all processes that generate durable inequality.

OPPORTUNITY HOARDING

A second general mechanism promoting categorical inequality, the hoarding of opportunities by the nonelite, complements exploitation. When members of a categorically bounded network acquire access to a resource that is valuable, renewable, subject to monopoly, supportive of network activities, and enhanced by the network's modus operandi, network members regularly hoard their access to the resource, creating beliefs and practices that sustain their control. As in exploitation, a boundary separates beneficiaries from others, while unequal relations across the boundary connect them. In opportunity hoarding, however, beneficiaries do not enlist the efforts of outsiders but instead exclude them from access to the relevant resources. Immigrant niches provide strong examples of this second inequality-promoting mechanism. So, however, do trade diasporas, cults, professions, criminal conspiracies, and homogeneously recruited elite military units.

These last examples point to an important variant on this second type of mechanism. Initially heterogeneous cults, priesthoods, criminal conspiracies, and elite military units sometimes *create* exclusive inequality-sustaining categories in the process of exploiting such valuable resources; and they often enhance commitment to these categories by means of intense socialization and segregation for entering cohorts. Savor the following reflections on the treatment of plebes (first-year military cadets) by a career officer who graduated from the United States Military Academy at West Point and later taught there for years:

West Point breeds restraint deep into a man's soul. A senior cadet can
stand behind a plebe and put his face up close to that man's neck and
tell him to stand straighter, or to recite "Schofield's Definition of Discipline," or to lead his squad mates in a rousing cheer—or he can give
that plebe a series of tasks rapid fire, tasks that would lead most anyone
else to frustration; and the plebe will stand there cool as Napoleon's sev-
enty-fifth maxim demands that he be, and he will take up the tasks one
at a time until he gets them right—or he will suffer the wrath of the up-
perclassman. Take that same plebe to the bayonet course down by the
river and tell him to execute the vertical butt stroke series with his bayo-
netted rifle, and he will rip the sawdust-filled dummy to shreds. A casual observer, on the sidelines of these military spectacles, might think
he's watching homicidal maniacs at work. But he would be wrong. The
cadet is no less human than he, and probably much less prone to random acts of violence. The cadet just happens to be trained in the art of
war. He understands the merits of restraint as well as the application of
force. (Hoy 1996, 64, 66)

Pat Hoy's readers might join me in wondering whether today the larger
threats to human life come from "random acts of violence" or from professionals trained to kill dispassionately, but they will recognize in the
upperclass treatment of plebes at West Point a formidable socialization
process at work. Military academy hazing offers a dramatic illustration
of the process that creates unequal categories, not to mention insight
into why old members and new recruits often conspire to organize categorically segregated recruitment into the elect. This sort of intense socialization will not work unless candidates have prospects of great, last-
ing benefits from survival into membership.

Consider a more benign version of the same arrangements. Rotating
savings and credit associations—*Chit* in India, *Hui* in Taiwan, *Tontines*
in Senegal, *Kye* in Korea (Besley 1995, 170)—all reduce risk by restricting
their membership to carefully screened members of established categories. Because the association's members maintain dense, frequently triadic, relations with one another, monitoring costs fall, and
the costs of exclusion to defaulting members rise. Trade diasporas in
which a handshake with a person of common origin seals a million-
dollar transaction—for example, different specialties within the world

diamond business, most of which belong to particular ethnic net-works—operate on similar principles (Curtin 1984; Greif 1989).

In a situation of fierce competition for scarce resources, such a mecha-nism often comes to involve both exclusion and exploitation. Opportu-nity hoarding turns into exploitation. All it takes is investment of pooled savings and credit in activities that profit disproportionately from the efforts of excluded persons. When members of excluded categories or-ganize to resist—as when South African Zulus attack Asian merchants or New York blacks boycott Korean-owned groceries—they commonly complain that just such a synthesis of exclusion and exploitation is hurt-ing them.

An extreme, often malign, variant of the pattern exists. A threatened elite sometimes tries to create racial divisions, to redefine racial bound-aries, or to racialize boundaries that already exist as a way of reducing an insubordinate population's power. Later we shall see how just such a process worked in South Africa after 1903. But the United States also experienced multiple versions of the process after Emancipation. Given the fact that many people had mixed African and European ancestry, the South's Jim Crow legislation typically not only legislated separate and unequal positions for "black" and "white" citizens but also defined anyone having any known African ancestors as black. Hence great ad-vantages accrued to mixed-race families who could "pass" for white, great anxieties about purity of blood, strenuous efforts at constructing genealogy in support of white claims to superiority.

A similar, often equally pernicious, process unfolds at national and international scales in the creation of ostensible nations whose spokes-persons claim priority within the native territory. Where rewards such as statehood, military aid, or preferential access to land accrue to leaders who assert credibly that they represent unified, distinct, and worthy populations, political entrepreneurs have powerful incentives to create, fortify, and enforce exclusive inequality-sustaining categories while sup-pressing alternative categorizations and denigrating populations that lie across their category-defining boundaries.

Although most such assertions fail, for the past two centuries several hundred of them have succeeded internationally, bringing recognition

of sovereignty to putative nations that previously lacked political autonomy and sovereignty-linked rights to arm, tax, coerce, monitor, and exclude. They acquired independent states. Once, major peace settlements
such as the Treaties of Westphalia (1648) provided the main occasions
on which established states recognized newcomers to their ranks. Since
World War II, great powers have generally delegated to the United Nations the job of certifying successful categorical performances by means
of recognition as an independent state.

Those recurrent processes have built durable categorical inequality
into the international system. Because the stakes are so high, furthermore, members of competing categories within the same polity have
often killed each other over such demands. Disintegration of the Soviet
Union and Yugoslavia after 1989 brought just such fratricide. In fact, the
frequency of genocide and politicide have increased dramatically in the
world as a whole since World War II, precisely as the possibilities and
advantages of a putative nation's controlling its own state and excluding
others from its benefits have risen (Gurr 1994; Gurr and Harff 1994).

These wide-ranging examples establish that a correlation, but not an
equation, exists between elite position and exploitation, between nonelite position and opportunity hoarding. Elites typically become elites
and maintain themselves as elites by controlling valuable resources and
engaging the effort of less-favored others in generating returns from
those resources, whereas nonelites commonly have to settle for the identification of niches not already fully exploited by elites. Yet elite opportunity hoarders thrive in the form of professionals who gain by excluding other potential producers from markets for their services, in the form
of rich individuals who bequeath wealth to their children, and in the
form of powerful persons who enjoy private hunting lodges, beaches,
and similar perquisites. Nonelite exploiters likewise exist in the form of
mafiosi, pimps, and sweatshop operators. We must take care not to fuse
the distinction exploitation/opportunity hoarding with the distinction
elite/nonelite.

Identification of exploitation and opportunity hoarding always relies,
at least implicitly, on a counterfactual hypothesis: with a different sort
of organization—and especially without a categorical division of effort

and reward—people could still produce at least as well as the existing division of labor allows, and a less unequal division of rewards would occur. Although extreme cases such as slavery make hypotheses of this sort plausible, over a wide range of unequal social life they are harder to specify and verify. We must face the counterfactual challenge in the usual ways: empirically by placing observed social arrangements in comparative perspective (what alternative ways of organizing similar activities can we find elsewhere in history, and what governs their relative effectiveness?), theoretically by breaking down complex processes into their elements and showing that in principle those elements can combine differently (using nothing but causal mechanisms and sequences known to have worked elsewhere, can we identify different paths away from the same initial conditions?). Although nowhere will I stage a grand confrontation between theory and evidence, pages to come will repeatedly feature empirical and theoretical discussions along these counterfactual lines.

EMULATION

By extension, the two main mechanisms favoring categorical inequality activate the third mechanism, which I have called emulation, the reproduction of organizational models already operating elsewhere. Emulation works throughout the social world and includes the adoption of egalitarian models of social interaction as well as models applying across a wide range of social relations, from equal to unequal: compounds of chains, triads, organizations, and categorical sets that may or may not articulate with hierarchies. Here we concentrate on the special version of emulation I have called *borrowing,* the transfer of chunks of social structure that happen to include unequal categories. Almost all military organizations install distinctions between officers and enlisted personnel, between those whom the organization entrusts with command or responsibility for its major resources and all others; most of them then assimilate such professionals as physicians, engineers, and chaplains to the officer corps. The dividing line between caballeros (horsemen who owned their own equipment and often brought along their own retainers) and peons (footsoldiers who came to war on foot with little but their own labor power) emerged from Castilian wars against their former Muslim overlords (Powers 1988). Similar historical differences in recruitment of military forces installed such a distinction in European armies.

No functional necessity, it seems, requires all armies to maintain sharp distinctions between officers and enlisted personnel; indeed, most military organizations compromise the boundary by creating warrant officers, high-ranking petty officers, and well-defined channels from enlisted to officer status. Yet any state producing a new military organization reproduces some version of a distinction established by centuries-old ties between landlords and tenants, between nobles and commoners, between knights and retainers.

As long as caste-divided militaries fight no less effectively than egalitarian bands of guerrillas or other forms their enemies may improvise, we can expect each military organization to emulate its predecessors, reproducing the officer/enlisted division. We can reasonably expect emulation because familiar forms transfer more cheaply than unfamiliar forms and ease the process of articulation with other familiar organizational forms such as educational institutions and state bureaucracies. More generally, lower transaction costs favor the reproduction of existing organizational models, whatever their origins.

Emulation duplicates far more than categorical boundaries and relations across those boundaries, to be sure; organization builders emulate chains, hierarchies, triads, and whole organizations as well as unequal categorical sets. Duplication of major organizational segments or even whole organizations, including unequal categorical relations, from one location to another transfers the effects of accumulated adaptations; their familiarity makes them seem natural in the new setting.

Emulated organizational forms are sometimes unique to the organization copied, as when refugees from an established electronics manufacturer create a rival firm by cloning its structure. More often, however, emulation follows general models, including categorical arrangements that encompass any particular class of organizations. New hotels reproduce the ethnic, racial, and gender divisions of labor that are already familiar to their employees from earlier work in other hotels; new universities reproduce the departments, administrative divisions, and hierarchies of payment prevalent in the old universities from which their founders came.

ADAPTATION

A fourth complementary mechanism, adaptation, keeps systems of categorical inequality in place despite playing little part in their creation. Adaptation, like emulation, is an extremely general social mechanism that figures widely outside the realm of inequality. It has two main components: the invention of procedures that ease day-to-day interaction, and the elaboration of valued social relations around existing divisions. In the absence of concerted resistance by members of subordinate categories and exogenous changes in the host organization, all parties build multiple routines around the categorical boundary and thus acquire interests in its maintenance; they alter scripts and accumulate satisfying local knowledge. Assuming the continuity of existing divisions, however much they resent those divisions, office workers elaborate time schedules, evasive practices, mythologies, jokes, epithets, alliances, and conspiracies that actually reinforce the structures within which they grow.

On-the-job sexual harassment and predation by male workers against female co-workers sometimes serve exploitation and opportunity hoarding, as when male artisans drive female competitors off the job. Most of the time, however, it occurs as an adaptation that gives male misogynists additional incentives to maintain the gender boundary without giving female victims the capacity to overturn the practice. Marian Swerdlow's vivid report of her experiences and observations during four years as a rapid-transit conductor affirms that in the absence of a work-based interior boundary corresponding to the gender line, even sexist men eventually tend to recognize the competence of women in the same jobs and to check their harassment as they do so (Swerdlow

1989). Her experience resembles that of Marge Kirk, the concrete-truck driver quoted in Chapter 2. With experience, the relationship shifts from predominantly man/woman to predominantly worker/worker. Accumulated local knowledge actually produces a change of script.

In coping with unequal situations, moreover, victims themselves improvise routines that involve them in the reproduction of inequality. Even slaves acquire interests in the predictability of their masters' behavior, in conformity that will increase their chances of emancipation, and in the segregation that affords them opportunities for mutual aid. Even hard-pressed enlisted personnel collaborate with their officers most of the time; even exploited women form on-the-job friendships with other women that make them reluctant to quit work in protest against their exploitation. As Michael Burawoy points out for industrial workers, "making out" by finding efficient ways to gain extra pay draws producers willy-nilly into local workers' culture and thence into collaboration with at least some management objectives. Burawoy reports his experience as a machinist at Geer:

> It was a matter of three or four months before I began to make out by using a number of angles and by transferring time from one operation to another. Once I knew I had a chance to make out, the rewards of participating in a game in which the outcomes were uncertain absorbed my attention, and I found myself spontaneously cooperating with management in the production of greater surplus value. (Burawoy 1979, 64)

Despite then imagining myself to be some sort of rebel, I remember making exactly the same sorts of accommodations to capital's interests in the factory jobs I held during summers of my high school and college years. Adaptation, in such circumstances, reproduces or even reinforces an exploitative system.

BOUNDARIES OF INEQUALITY

In short, exploitation by an elite, opportunity hoarding by the nonelite, diffusion of organizational models created by one of the first two processes, and adaptation of valued social relations to existing divisions promote the creation and maintenance of categorical inequality. None of these mechanisms requires categories with closed perimeters, equally well-defined from every angle of approach. All they entail is a boundary separating two zones of unequal reward and their occupants, plus stable definitions of ties across the boundary. As I have already insisted ad nauseam, complete perimeters are rare and costly to maintain. They seem to form only in the presence of multiple rivals or enemies and strong pressures for internal control, as in the cases of state-licensed medical professions or internationally recognized states. Neither multiple enemies nor high needs for internal control figure in most cases of categorical inequality. Because most relevant categories consist of boundaries and ties across boundaries rather than closed perimeters, indeed, people often move easily from one unequal system to the next, or even participate simultaneously in more than one, performing as women, workers, and Italians in relation to men, bosses and, say, blacks (quite often different sets of persons) at the same moment (Barnett and Baruch 1987, 123–124). Once we recognize that relevant identities consist not of individual conditions but of relations across boundaries, that multiplicity—admittedly mystifying for any individualistic theory of action and identity—loses its mystery.

Because of its grounding in exploitation, opportunity hoarding, emulation, and adaptation, categorical inequality has a dual relation to change. On one side, in the absence of disturbance it tends to reproduce itself like ivy on a brick wall, conforming to local surfaces and drawing sustenance from its many connections to the surroundings. Yet a shift in the organization, resource base, or social ties of at least one or two major participants can change it rapidly. Witness the alteration of many immigrant niches, the resumption of nonlethal politics after some civil wars, the entry of black workers into American public-sector employment, the tipping of jobs from male to female, the rapid transition of nationalists from "terrorists" to recognized leaders of states, the professionalization of medical specialties, or the rapidity with which race relations started changing in South Africa after the 1990 legalization of the African National Congress. Struggles by members of subordinate categories, furthermore, can obviously promote shifts in their unequal fortunes.

Categories do not in themselves produce deep, durable inequality.

That depends on their combination with a second configuration: hierarchy. Categorical inequality depends on the conjunction of a well-defined boundary separating two sites with a set of asymmetrical social ties connecting actors in the two sites. In such a case, participants equate actors on a given side of the boundary in some regards, without necessarily asserting or enforcing equality in other regards. Citizens, for example, share rights and obligations vis-à-vis their state and in distinction from noncitizens while varying greatly among themselves in race, gender, wealth, and power. They also form mutual representations of the sites on either side of the boundary: labels, attributions, explanations of behavior, stories about difference. Categorical inequality survives, finally, to the extent that sites attach unequally to flows of resources sustaining their interaction. For example, differential access of males and females to food reinforces differences in size, health, and strength that in turn support and provide justifications for differential feeding.

We now need a distinction I have so far suppressed in order to avoid confusion: between direct and indirect effects of unequal categories. *Direct effects* flow from the organization of social relations at the site where the categories themselves are installed—where a division of labor by gender obtains, where residence depends immediately on race, where the line between salaried and hourly workers falls, and so on. Up to this point I have stressed direct effects, arguing that they are much more pervasive than individualistic accounts of inequality allow. But *indirect effects* matter as well. They result ultimately from direct effects accumulated in individual or collective experience. From one situation to another, the effects of differential nutrition, information, education, socialization, belief, and emotional experience carry over as on-the-average categorical differences in performance.

Indirect effects include a variety of attributes that people carry around with them quite individually: personal styles, emotional sensitivities, knowledge, responses to frustration, and more. All of them affect performance outside the settings in which their bearers learn them, and they therefore frequently contribute to categorical differences in rewards for performance. In principle, we can sweep them into the bin of individual human capital. But indirect effects enter relational territory to the extent that they bear on communication and collaboration in a new setting.

In most job settings, for example, any individual's performance—indeed, any individual's apparent skill—depends subtly on communication and collaboration with co-workers, including supervisors. Great dancers need supportive partners; great journalists lean on skilled editors. If co-workers unconsciously or consciously withdraw collaboration and withhold information from categorically different strangers, in general the strangers perform less well. The notorious ability of male craft, military, and protective workers to freeze out women who break into their ranks merely represents an extreme version of a very general practice.

If (as is often the case in professions) workers commonly enhance their performance by relying on off-the-job mentoring and information giving, then previously established networks likewise affect job performance. To the extent that effective work performance depends on collaboration and communication that draws on previously acquired conventions, practices, and social ties, categorical inequality in previous experience produces powerful effects on current performance. Such influences on interaction and performance lie halfway between direct and indirect effects.

Individualistic analysts of human capital (e.g., Taubman 1991) have therefore identified a powerful source of inequality without quite recognizing its significance and generality. The conventional distinction between human-capital effects and discrimination effects captures part of the process but understates its complexity. Human capital (and, for that matter, social capital) consists largely of categorical experience compounded and transmitted. To arrive at a full accounting of categorical inequality's impact, we must examine direct effects, indirect effects, and their interaction. When the books are balanced, I predict that they will assign most individual-to-individual variability in present advantages to categorical effects, either direct or indirect, rather than to genetic capacity, to sheer effort, or to the mysterious concatenation known as chance.

What parts, then, do shared beliefs—racist, sexist, or otherwise—play in the creation and maintenance of categorical inequality? Under competing labels such as prejudice, preference, and xenophobia, many analysts have portrayed shared beliefs as the foundation of categorical inequality. If beliefs lie at inequality's roots, then presumably inequality alters chiefly when processes such as education or sociable contact extirpate, mitigate, or transform these beliefs or substitute new beliefs.

A relational analysis revises that belief-centered account. In a relational view, categorical beliefs result from categorical relations and practices. Beliefs accumulate and change as a consequence of improvisation with social interaction. Once in place, nevertheless, beliefs justify, fortify, and constrain social interaction. Lifetimes of unequal male/female relations inculcate the stories people tell about gender differences, making them seem natural and inevitable. The same holds for race. In the predominantly Jewish and Italian Brooklyn neighborhood of Canarsie, Jonathan Rieder reports the remarks of an Italian worker:

> "All the social classes don't mix. Take the blacks for example. Their culture is different from ours." He recalled the words of a former official: "We got to find a formula to mix two vegetables without making us nauseous," but he rejected that advice. "*I* say, don't put animals in the street without training. I seen what happens, and you don't put the animals with the civilized people. Does a cat and a dog mix? I can't see it. You can't drink milk and scotch. Certain mixes don't mix." (Rieder 1985, 58)

As a left-wing Canarsie man told Rieder, however:

> When the people of Canarsie ran from East New York and Brownsville, they ran from their New Deal concepts of integration. They accepted the concept of civil rights, liberty for all, and freedom of expression until it impinged on them and their basic right to maintain the kind of society which doesn't threaten them. The basic fear of the minority community is participating with them where they live. (Rieder 1985, 57–58)

Thus beliefs and practices shift together under the pressure of collective experience. Especially at the boundaries separating them from members of other categories, people draw on interaction, fear, hope, and imagination to construct boundary-maintaining stories. Such stories strongly limit what people consider to be possible or desirable alternatives to current practices and relations. Once coherent sets of stories, relations, and practices about a given kind of categorical inequality are available, people unthinkingly integrate them into their daily routines and solve organizational problems with them.

When the activities in which people are involved benefit from drawing lines between the included and the excluded, having unequal categories already at hand—whatever the categories—advances those activities handily. Thus shared beliefs play significant parts in the operation of categorical inequality and limit the organizational alternatives that participants consider, fear, or desire. But if the transaction costs of a given system of inequality rise dramatically or the likely benefits of an alternative system increase visibly, shifts in categorical relations occur much more rapidly than any explanation resting on belief alone can account for. The agility of nationalists in shifting from one definition of who they are (and of their relations to others who are not so blessed) to a different definition illustrates the organizational opportunism that regularly moves inequality-sustaining beliefs. So does the quickness with which bosses and workers alter their theories about the inherent talents and deficits of different categories of workers when shifts in labor supply force an alteration in recruitment to particular sets of jobs.

INEQUALITY AT WORK

How can we apply this analysis to the all-important world of work, where so much durable inequality begins and ends? Let us consider work to be any human effort that produces transferable use value. Although plenty of work goes on outside jobs and firms in any strong senses of the two words, let us speak temporarily of jobs and firms. (A *job* is a bundle of work contracts—rights and obligations governing the relations among producers and recipients of transferable use value—attached to a single person; a *firm* is any organization whose internal positions consist chiefly of jobs.)

Even within well-developed capitalist firms and labor markets, we find the causal nexus of categorically organized exploitation, opportunity hoarding, emulation, and adaptation. Where wages vary significantly from job to job and categorical membership strongly affects the allocation of workers to jobs, systematic wage differences by category appear. In all capitalist countries, categorical processes strongly affect the matching of workers with jobs, thereby shaping wage differentials among categories of workers. From initial hiring to career path (if any) through a firm or industry, categorical distinctions—whichever categorical pairs firms and industries have built in—matter profoundly.

Start with the processes that match workers with jobs in the first place. Although of course they merge, we can conveniently distinguish between *recruitment networks,* formed as hiring agents search for potential workers, and *supply networks,* consisting of preexisting ties among potential and actual workers. Even in the contemporary United States, employers commonly start searches for new workers by asking current employees whether they know likely candidates. Employees, furthermore, commonly look within their own firms for information on job openings to benefit potential workers they want to help.

Together, those facts suffice to introduce enormous selectivity into the joining of recruitment and supply networks. Management's initial identification of interior with exterior categories through designating certain jobs as men's work, women's work, Mexicans' work, or something of the sort merely accentuates a process that tends to unfold even without self-conscious managerial incitement.

Why and how does it unfold? Consider the possible components of categorical inequality in regard to the rewards of work. Within firms, only small inequalities in rewards generally appear among occupants of jobs that the organization identifies as the same; most such within-job inequalities result from seniority and similar widely accepted grounds for discrimination. Large differences in rewards usually correspond to separate jobs, distinct bundles of work contracts.

Firms *bound* and *link* jobs—that is, they identify some sets of jobs as belonging to the same category and relate some jobs to each other through linked work contracts, established mobility paths, or both. Skilled machinists may fall within the same organizational boundary and thus enjoy similar systems of reward, while their apprentices occupy jobs linked to their skilled elders by both shared work contracts and prospects for mobility. To the extent that machinists receive distinctive rewards, that recruitment to a position as an apprentice machinist engages categorically segregated supply or recruitment networks, and that a job as a skilled machinist requires promotion from apprentice, categorical inequality separates machinists from other workers in the firm. My earlier distinction between turnover pools and command-and-promotion pools, with their very different packages of rewards, illustrates the same principle. Such large differences typically generate interior categories with well-marked boundaries governing not only forms of payment but also mobility chances, dress, demeanor, sociability, and belief.

Firms also *rank* jobs and categories of jobs with respect to each sort of reward they offer, with different kinds of rewards commonly correlating with each other but not defining identical rank orders. Some jobs give more money, others more autonomy, and so on. We must distinguish ranking from *sorting*, the matching of individuals with jobs. Ranking processes determine how much inequality in rewards appears within a firm, but sorting processes determine to what extent those inequalities coincide with exterior categorical boundaries.

Some sorting certainly corresponds to individual attributes and performances: educational record, demonstrated zeal, acquired familiarity with local procedures, and more. Within the large pools of short-term employees who work in fast-food restaurants, enterprising managers keep their eyes open for workers whose energy, poise, linguistic skills, and sense of responsibility mark them as potential recruits to management. Some self-selection also takes place, as people who enjoy command head for careers in law enforcement rather than social service or human rights advocacy (Sidanius, Pratto, Sinclair, and van Laar 1996). But a large (if still debatable) share of all sorting matches jobs not with individual attributes or performances but with whole categories of people.

Why match interior categories such as turnover pools to exterior categories such as gender, age, race, ethnicity, religion, or social class? The reasons range from the self-conscious to the inadvertent. At the

self-conscious end of the scale, people who build or change organizations save effort by incorporating all sorts of existing social structure—
standard work contracts, linguistic conventions, rhetorical routines, and
much more—directly into organizational structure. Such deliberately
adopted devices often include importation of categories from outside:
gender-typing, ethnic typing, and so on.

At the scale's inadvertent end, however, lie an equally important set
of organizational processes that match exterior to interior categories.
Here members solve various problems and capitalize on various opportunities by drawing on categorically segregated networks. Workers
trust, train, and help each other more fully when they share outside
solidarities and common cultures; employers find new workers through
the contacts of workers already on the job; subcontracting follows the
lines of managers' previous collaborations; and the supply-driven recruitment of people from distinct exterior categories into adjacent interior categories imports externally established relations between the categories into the organization's daily life. Here opportunity hoarding,
emulation, and adaptation intersect to reinforce exploitation.

Let me put it more generally. Seen from the perspective of an entire
labor force, categorical inequality in the rewards of work breaks down
into the effects of eight general factors:

Categorical differences in job qualifications, which may of course result from discrimination in households, neighborhoods, schools, and
other settings or from unequal distribution across such settings

Employer discrimination by category within equivalent jobs

Categorical differences in potential workers' preferences for different
jobs

Bounding of jobs within firms

Ranking of jobs within firms

Linking of jobs within firms, which concerns not only mobility prospects but also access to collaboration, patronage, and on-the-job
training

Categorical designation of jobs

Categorical segregation of recruitment and supply networks by job
and / or firm

In the form of human-capital, discrimination, and queuing theories, standard models of inequality feature the first three factors: categorical differences in job qualifications, employer discrimination, and categorical differences in preferences. These are the factors that lend themselves easily to individualistic interpretations. For all their prominence in the descriptive literature on work and labor markets, the remaining, heavily relational factors—bounding, ranking, linking, categorical designation of jobs, and categorical segregation of networks—have received little theoretical attention.

A ninth, even less visible, factor also helps produce categorical inequality: differential distribution of category members among firms and nonfirm worksites, including sites outside the labor force as customarily defined. To the degree that categories differ in their distribution between sweatshops and other kinds of factories, between formal and informal economy, between work in firms and work at home, those differences contribute to categorical inequality in the rewards of work. Categorical inequality by age makes the strength of such effects clear: people under the age of fifteen or over the age of seventy do plenty of useful work, but they do little of it for wages in jobs, firms, or labor markets; very old and very young workers get much less money per unit of effort than those of other ages. The same sort of unequal distribution across sites of work occurs by gender, race, and national origin.

Without denying the presence of categorical human-capital differences, employer discrimination by category, and categorical variation in job preferences, I claim that organizational processes of the sort I have been describing play a large part in the production, maintenance, and change of categorical inequality. Human-capital differences form largely as indirect effects of categorically segregated experiences in other settings. Employer discrimination operates largely through the installation of organizational boundaries rather than person-by-person differentiation. Workers' preferences conform significantly to built-in boundaries. Even state intervention in the nine inequality-generating factors typically rests on categorical assumptions concerning capacities and propensities for different kinds of work.

Two implications follow: first, that preferences and wage bargains provide too thin a base for explanations of durable inequality at work;

and, second, that a significant portion of that inequality results not from self-conscious discrimination but from efforts to solve other organizational problems by the incorporation, often unintentional, of exterior categories into the structure of work and labor markets. Our job, then, is to investigate how exterior categories are built in, and with what effects.

Exploitation, opportunity hoarding, emulation, and adaptation operate at each node in the processes that allocate differential rewards to members of distinct categories: the acquisition of job qualifications; the distribution of category members over firms, industries, sectors, and work statuses; bounding, ranking, linking, and the categorical designation of jobs; the categorical segregation of recruitment and supply networks; hiring, promotion, and transfer among work positions. In order to explain categorically unequal rewards for work within firms, we must separate two questions that analysts of inequality ordinarily conflate: Why and how do such organizations build unequal categories into their daily operations? Why and how do such interior categories come to incorporate certain widely established exterior categories: gender, race, ethnicity, educational background?

To answer those questions, we must think about the actual organization of firms. Imagine two network X-rays of all the jobs in a firm, the first short-term, the other long-term. The short-term X-ray shows us the day-to-day relations of people occupying various jobs, with thick lines for frequent interaction. It is a current-interaction map. That photograph features some long chains, most of them hierarchical, and many clumps containing multiple triads. The triadic clumps include more people occupying relatively equal positions within the firm than do the chains.

The long-term X-ray, taken over a number of years, registers the persistence of persons in the same positions and the movement of persons from job to job—promotions, demotions, and transfers—as well as firings, layoffs, retirements, and departures from the organization to positions outside. It is a mobility map. It divides even more decisively than the short-term X-ray into long chains (mostly hierarchical) and isolated clumps of relatively equal jobs.

The two X-rays resemble each other. The short-term photograph displays many more lines, since it registers both the relations between subordinates and superiors whose jobs the subordinates can never hope to occupy and the routine interactions, informal and formal, among workers in distinctly different sections of the firm. But held up together against a strong light, the two films reveal similar patterns of connections among jobs. The comparison yields almost unmistakable evidence that the two patterns stem from a common set of causes.

What and how? The organization's history has laid down a mobility map through combinations of innovation, emulation, internal negotiation, and external interaction. With one major exception, that mobility map describes the major fault lines and solidarities within the firm, the actual chunks of social relations around which its work goes on. The exception, however, is crucial: strong collaborative relations, unequal or equal, that form across mobility barriers within small work groups. Examples include secretaries and bosses, surgeons and anesthetists, bricklayers and carpenters. To identify those collaborative relations, we must compare the mobility and current-interaction maps, searching for frequent interactions that deviate from the paths of long-term mobility.

Most organizations therefore incorporate two distinguishable varieties of inequality: within and across mobility systems. Although large disparities of treatment sometimes occur within mobility systems—as in the long chain of positions between an army's second lieutenants and its top generals—the greatest differences in fate separate mobility systems from each other. Enlisted soldier and officer, line and staff, physician and nurse, secretary and executive, chief scientist and laboratory technician often collaborate, share knowledge, and develop solidarity, but the divisions between them constitute major bases of differential treatment. When we map differences within organizations in recruitment procedures, forms of remuneration, physical effort, time scheduling, and control over working conditions, we will find that they vary in clumps rather than as continuous distributions, that they correlate strongly with each other, and that they correspond to distinct mobility systems. Even studies cast in the conventional individual-variation mode (e.g., Birkelund, Goodman, and Rose 1996) regularly describe just such clustering.

Where do categories come in? Members of organizations reify their fault lines and solidarities categorically, labeling the boundary, the positions on either side of the boundary, and the relations between them. The labels show up in annual reports, letterheads, and organization charts, but they also emerge in an organization's informal culture as names for mafias, cabals, connections, cliques, allies, and enemies. The categories both distinguish and relate sets of interconnected workers who have shared stakes in the organization's performance. Each category has a partly independent incentive system.

Figure 5 schematizes the broadest level of variation in that regard. It refines the earlier command/turnover distinction among job pools by differentiating three types of work contracts (the prescribed relations between a given worker and other parties to his or her work). Firms typically bundle work contracts into jobs, the firm-enforced rights and obligations defining the relations of a single worker to all others. Here we see jobs differing significantly with respect to short-term monetization (an eventual share in the firm's profits rates low on monetization, whereas hourly wages paid each day rate high) and time-discipline (the degree to which supervisors prescribe, monitor, and correct the worker's performance continuously). The solitary sculptor who fills a studio with statues in hopes of eventually selling them ranks low on both time-discipline and short-term monetization, whereas the telephone operator who receives hourly pay for closely monitored effort ranks high in both regards.

The diagram differentiates jobs according to their dominant incentive systems. *Task incentive systems* emphasize block payments for goods or services delivered to the firm, as when a company engages a private physician to conduct medical examinations of prospective employees for so much per examination or when a telephone sales agent works at home for straight commission; contingent compensation becomes the dominant incentive. *Drive incentive systems* put the worker's time at the firm's disposition for closely supervised effort; although contingent compensation certainly matters, coercion looms much larger than in task systems. Analysts have often called drive systems "Taylorite" or "Fordist," referring to the routinizing supervisory measures of Frederick W. Taylor and Henry Ford. Owners of American print shops, for example, shifted massively from task to drive systems with the spread of the Li-

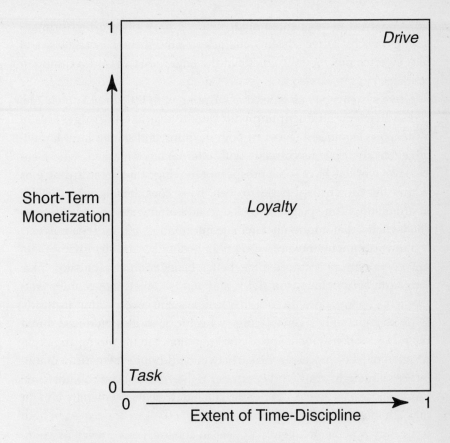

Figure 5. Broad Types of Work Contracts Within Firms

notype around the turn of the twentieth century, substituting hourly pay for payment by the job, sponsoring trade schools that would teach printing outside the shop, challenging craft control over the pace of production, and undermining printers' unions when they could (Baron 1991b, 64–65).

Loyalty systems afford an employee discretion in carrying out job responsibilities, imposing less prescription and monitoring than drive systems but still requiring more continuous performance than task systems. Here commitment (diffuse and long-term guarantees of rewards) figures more prominently among incentives. Loyalty systems mark what analysts of segmented labor markets have often called primary sectors or jobs. Drive systems characterize the secondary sectors, and task systems now operate chiefly at the edges of labor and commodity markets.

Drive systems rely on extensive scripting with little local knowledge, task systems on little scripting with extensive local knowledge, loyalty systems on significant shares of both scripting and shared local knowledge. Loyalty systems correlate with internal labor markets, where entry-level workers have some prospect of moving to more rewarding jobs within the firm if they perform well, have considerable incentive for accumulating firm-specific knowledge, and often enter internal patron-client chains that informally circulate information and exercise power.

Firms commonly reward workers in loyalty systems by giving them higher pay, more secure tenure, better benefits and perquisites, plus long-term accumulations of rights and equity. Nineteenth-century craft workers generally produced under task systems; even within factories, foremen commonly received lump sums for quantities produced, hired their own workers, and enjoyed great autonomy in the timing and organization of labor processes. As early twentieth-century American manufacturers brought craft workers under tighter central control, however, those whose jobs they could not deskill and drive they generally bought off with integration into loyalty systems.

Loyalty systems frequently appear in conjunction with extensive internal labor markets, where the possibility of future promotion provides strong incentives for energetic performance. According to a salary administrator at Indsco, the large multinational studied by Rosabeth Moss Kanter, "Money is not a motivator, anyway. It's just a way for the company to cut its losses by ensuring that people do their job at all. The reward we really control is the ability to promote" (Kanter 1993, 129).

A given firm may, of course, maintain two or more mobility-segregated loyalty systems. A chemical company, for example, might recruit lower-level supervisors chiefly among recent college graduates in chemistry or chemical engineering and then organize an implicit competition among them for promotion into executive ranks. At the same time, the company might create quite a different mobility track for less-educated laboratory technicians who will never have a chance to become executives.

A firm may also create multiple clusters of task incentive or drive incentive jobs, each with its own categorical label; every large hospital, for instance, incorporates several such distinct clusters in food preparation, cleaning, laundry, patient care, and elsewhere. Kanter compares two well-segregated systems within Indsco:

> The great divide in company personnel terms was the exempt/nonexempt distinction. "Nonexempts" were the workers paid weekly and covered by wage-and-hour laws; for example, they must be paid overtime rates for extra hours. In the office and administration side of the company, nonexempts were almost all women, although there were a few nonexempt men at both low and high status, such as mail messengers on the low end or accounting clerks on ladders leading to exempt jobs. "Exempts" were on annual salary; they were the managers, the professionals, and the sales and technical workers, who were still practically all men. (Kanter 1993, 37)

Drive incentives figured more prominently for nonexempts, loyalty incentives for exempts. Mixes of task, loyalty, and drive incentive systems vary drastically from firm to firm and industry to industry, with task work rare or nonexistent in fast-food establishments but predominant in architecture, filmmaking, and commercial art. Television writing, for example, typically operates by the job:

> The employment relation for television writers is closer to the kind of short-term contracting typical of craft administration of production than to the bureaucratically organized internal labor market typical of large firms. Writers are employed for the duration of a project, which might be as short as a few weeks for work on a single telefilm, pilot, or episode of a prime-time series. Most secure (and potentially most lucrative) is employment as a writer-producer on an ongoing prime-time series. Those series last anywhere from a few weeks to a few years, but even on the most enduring series there is considerable turnover among the production staff from season to season. (Bielby and Bielby 1995, 212)

Although drive and loyalty components enter the television writer's contracts, task incentives loom large. Like acting and solo musicianship, television writing operates under incentive systems that are very different from the bureaucratic ladder-climbing of Indsco.

Boundaries of solidarities, mobility clusters, and incentive systems, then, correspond closely to each other. They separate the major inequalities of condition within the organization: relatively equal within, relatively unequal between. Paired categories (in the case of Indsco, exempt/nonexempt) mark those boundaries. The paired categories themselves result in part from deliberate organizational innovation, in part from emulation of other organizations, in part from interaction among workers embedded in the different systems, and in part from intersection of the organization with crosscutting structures such as professions and governmental agencies. That is how an organization's interior categories come into being.

Through processes that the remainder of this book analyzes in detail, then, interior categories often couple with exterior categories of race, gender, class, ethnicity, age, neighborhood, citizenship, and so on. Kanter's observations on gender segregation within Indsco show us just such a coupling of interior (exempt/nonexempt) with exterior (male/female). When those exterior categories pervade a wide range of social life outside organizations and appear in similar form within many organizations, they become the basis of durable inequality across the population at large. How that happens is the major question this book addresses.

Figure 6 summarizes the main causal relationships asserted by this argument. Exploitation and opportunity hoarding cause the installation of categorical boundaries within organizations, while emulation and adaptation reinforce those effects. Within the same organizations, the installation of boundaries directly promotes the categorically unequal distribution of rewards from the organization's activities. Accumulated over time and multiple organizational settings, the operation of categorical boundaries means that members of different categories arrive in new settings with differential capacities and social ties. Those differential capacities and social ties produce different performances, which then generate unequal rewards in the new settings. Because participants in such systems not only emulate and adapt (i.e., ac-

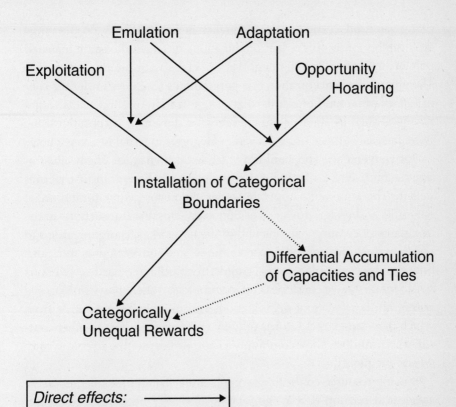

Figure 6. Basic Causal Relationships in Categorical Inequality

quire established scripts and invest in local knowledge) but also create categorically differentiated beliefs, the arrangements perpetuate themselves in the absence of major boundary changes. Thus durable inequality prevails.

From the fundamental network configurations (chain, hierarchy, triad, organization, and categorical pair), a relational view of inequality singles out the conjunction of hierarchy and categories in the unequal categorical pair. Such pairs differ in the extent to which they are exterior or interior to a given organization. Over a whole population, the degree of a given kind of categorical inequality depends heavily on the range and number of resource-rich organizations in which the same matched pair of unequal, exterior categories coincides with interior categories. The greater the concentration of a population's resources under the control of a certain kind of standardized organization or of particular organizations such as states, state churches, or dominant corporations, the more pervasive those organizations' categories in social life as a whole.

For convenience and familiarity, I have drawn most of my illustrations so far from the hierarchical, formal organizations of industrial capitalism. The arguments apply, however, wherever people bound social networks and assign power over boundary-crossing transactions to the occupants of certain positions within the network. The organizations in question include not only corporations and governments but also households, clans, plantations, guilds, revolutionary parties, religious sects, pirate crews, and peasant communes. When powerful people within all these sorts of organizations control valuable resources from which they can extract returns only by enlisting the effort of others outside their number, they commonly create or borrow the forms of categorical inequality.

If many resource-controlling organizations install the same pervasive categorical relation $X > Y$, the relation $X \longleftrightarrow Y$ becomes a dominant basis of inequality over the entire population. The direct effects of categories matter greatly, as powerful sets of actors establish exploitative relationships across readily recognized boundaries. But where certain categorical differences prevail, their indirect effects also contribute greatly to the distribution of advantage and disadvantage in the population at large, as accumulated categorical experience carries over into systematic on-the-average differences in performance. Differences in performance then come to justify, reinforce, even create explicit categorical systems. Thus the spiral of categorical inequality spins on.

4 Modes of Exploitation

Within the space our world now calls South Africa, midway through the seventeenth century Dutch settlers formed a colony on the Cape of Good Hope, long a crucial landfall for voyagers between the Atlantic and Indian oceans. For two centuries, Europeans and their descendants then clung chiefly to South Africa's coasts. The major exceptions were the largely Dutch cattle ranchers who spread into interior regions. At first those mobile pastoralists, like gauchos in Argentina and cowboys in North America, shifted from place to place as opportunity called, battling indigenous Africans for access to grazing land. Later, as their frontier filled and agricultural trade with coastal populations increased, they impressed local Africans as slaves and near-slaves on their large estates. They started a process that eventually produced one of the twentieth century's most spectacular and cruel large-scale systems of categorical inequality.

Discovery of diamonds along the Orange River in 1867 and,

especially, the unearthing of gold on the Witwatersrand in 1886 made the interior much more attractive. Europeans, their weapons, and their capital rushed inland from the sea. Diamonds and gold embittered the struggle for territory between the British, backed by imperial might, and the Dutch-tinged amalgam of other European settlers who had come to be known as Boers, one of those wonderful labels first used in opprobrium for its implications of rusticity and boorishness but eventually worn with pride by its recipients.

British-Boer military struggles began in earnest during the 1790s, continued through the nineteenth century, and culminated in the South African war of 1899 to 1902, known as the Boer War to Britons, the Second War of Freedom to Afrikaners, and a time of troubles for black Africans. Britain's violent victory found a hundred thousand Boer women and children in concentration camps, more than a hundred thousand Africans likewise incarcerated, and Boer farms in smoking ruins. The victors contended with a problem Niccolò Machiavelli had pondered for the benefit of princes four centuries earlier: given a conquest, whether to destroy, co-opt, or transform existing forms of government.

Having already destroyed so much as to disperse and deplete the African labor forces of farms and mines, rulers of the new South African state eventually chose a combination of co-optation and transformation. They first created a partly autonomous Transvaal government and then integrated it into a new Union of South Africa, finally staffing its bureaucracies and coercive forces disproportionately with Boers but deeply reorganizing controls over the non-European population.

The latter process raised what South African and British elites called the "Native Question." That question actually entailed two closely entwined conundrums: first, how to integrate black Africans into the new state while keeping them compliant and subordinate; and, second, how to commit African labor to farms, to urban services, and, above all, to man-devouring diamond and gold mines.

Both conundrums centered on establishing an effective means of exploitation, drawing black workers into work on white-dominated resources while excluding them from the full return of their effort. The first involved maneuvering among missionaries who considered themselves uniquely qualified to define and defend Native welfare, chiefs who claimed competing jurisdictions within predominantly African areas of settlement, and capitalists who already depended heavily on African labor. The second involved ensuring that each year pastoral and agricultural communities would continue to send several hundred thousand able-bodied workers, mostly male, for labor away from home, yet reabsorb them when employment slackened or they lost strength.

South African authorities sought to answer both questions with a series of efforts at category building. The most general categorical cut divided Europeans from Natives, matching to those categories unequal and separate territories, protections, and rights of citizenship. At first, European settlers homogenized the populations on both sides of the line, justifying a system of indirect rule in which co-opted African chiefs spoke for their own territorial segments of a presumably unitary Native population. White rulers justified the division as not only natural but also benign. In 1903 Lord Milner, High Commissioner of South Africa, put it this way:

> The white man must rule because he is elevated by many, many steps above the black man . . . which it will take the latter centuries to climb and which it is quite possible that the vast bulk of the black population may never be able to climb at all . . . One of the strongest arguments why the white man must rule is because that is the only possible means of gradually raising the black man, not to our level of civilisation—which it is doubtful whether he would ever attain—but up to a much higher level than that which he at present occupies. (Marks and Trapido 1987, 7)

The government adopted an unusual approach to enlightenment: it used taxation, deprivation of land, and outright compulsion to drive Natives into labor markets. Economic inequalities paralleled legal inequalities. In the gold mines, where law and standard practice strictly segregated white from black jobs, "white gold miners' annual cash earnings were 11.7 times the cash wages of black gold miners in 1911, and 14.7 times in 1951" (Thompson 1990, 156).

Europeans also segregated themselves, but less rigorously, against Indians descended chiefly from indentured servants (especially Madrasi) and merchants (especially Gujarati) who had arrived between 1860 and World War I. Regional, caste, and religious divisions figured significantly within the Indian population—merchant elites, for example, tended to be Muslim or high-caste Hindu—but little affected the European/Indian division. On the European side, an additional line between British and Afrikaners defined opponents in conflicts that several times approached civil war. A very unequal South African quadrilateral therefore distinguished British, Afrikaners, Indians, and Natives. Natives constituted the vast majority.

On the quadrilateral's Native side, however, South African authorities actually found not neat boxes but a kaleidoscope. Thousands of categories designated and divided different sets of the African population, many of them falling into broadly similar linguistic groupings such as Xhosa, Zulu, and Sotho without their occupants' being much aware of the similarities. Some of these groupings harked back to kingdoms that had dominated various parts of the region before Dutch and British hegemony, but few of them designated sharply bounded populations with long histories of geographic and social segregation.

Although at first British-oriented authorities sought to treat Africans as a homogeneous mass, Boer self-defense within the European population promoted a new view of South Africa as composed of multiple nations. Those presumably distinct nations came to include major segments of the African population. In a remarkable series of direct interventions, the South African state set out to create racial categories that would serve as the basis of unequal rights and rewards. From 1903 to 1981, state-appointed commissions repeatedly enlisted administrators, anthropologists, missionaries, professionals, and capitalists in the work of defining the major categories of Natives, assigning them collective characters, and recommending policies based on those characterizations. They regrouped the thousands of available categories into a handful, attached them to territorial "reserves" little populated by Europeans, categorically differentiated the rights of Africans to work temporarily outside those reserves, and thus produced gradations of citizenship according to officially assigned ethnicity.

During the twentieth century, Boer intellectuals and administrators likewise codified official views of Afrikaner culture, creating not only a unitary, teleological history but also a standardized Afrikaans language to supplant a variety of Dutch-based dialects and creoles (Hofmeyr 1987). South Africa's so-called Ethnos Theory, modeled to some extent on Boer experience, preached that coherent social life depended on the maintenance of distinct cultural groups. Anthropologist W. M. Eiselen, who became permanent secretary for Native Affairs during the initiation of thoroughgoing apartheid in 1948, warned as early as 1929 of threats to the coherence of African cultures:

> There is one factor, and that the most important factor, which I have not yet mentioned. That is the will of a people to stand on guard (*handhaaf*), to remain immortal as a people. If such a will exists, then it can only operate through the medium of a unique ethnic language. From the history of the Boer we learn how a people can retain its identity despite insuperable difficulties and economic disadvantages. (Evans 1990, 26)

The solution would be this: in addition to Afrikaner/English and black/white/Indian segregation, segregation would also be imposed within the African population. Although nineteenth-century regimes had commonly applied the term "coloured" to all non-Europeans, an officially designated category of Coloured people—8 percent of the national population in 1936—now contained the overflow, those nonwhite people who could not be forced into one of the standard categories (Ian Goldin 1987).

Note one telling feature of South Africa's racial categories. Although few large states have ever adopted as explicitly and oppressively racist policies as South Africa, no consistent and durable set of beliefs drove this racial system. Racial distinctions enforced by the state shifted repeatedly over time. Although the African/European line stayed in more or less the same place, other divisions altered as a function of political expediency, practical feasibility, and struggle among the parties. Organizational convenience overrode and transformed prevailing beliefs.

Installation of apartheid from 1948 onward modified and then reinforced the categorical differences that previous administrations had created. It did so with greatly increased intensity: uprooting Africans and

Coloured people from long-established urban residences; herding Africans into small, fragmented, overpopulated "homelands"; even segregating European children into different schools according to the language spoken at home, English or Afrikaans.

The Tomlinson Commission of 1950–1954, a prime architect of apartheid, enshrined ethnographers' distinctions among languages and cultures—Nguni, Sotho, Venda, and Shangaan-Tsonga—on the way to recommending separate lands and statuses for each group. It also asserted that each group divided into lineage-defined tribes, typically headed by a single chief. Thus for a series of South African peoples, including various categories of Europeans and Asians, the Tomlinson Report adopted a model of long-established nations that acquired, or would acquire, their own separate states as they matured (Ashforth 1990, 159). Indeed, the report recommended a kind of ethnic cleansing, exchanging white and black populations until they filled substantial homogeneous regions, with the black-occupied regions further segregated by assigned linguistic-cultural category (Ashforth 1990, 176). Over the next quarter-century, implementation of that policy displaced close to four million people (Marks and Trapido 1987, 22).

South African authorities undertook an immense political and geographic reorganization of the African population. The 1959 Promotion of Bantu Self-Government Act designated ten homelands to house separate "nations": Bophuthatswana for Tswana, Ciskei for Xhosa, Gazankulu for Shangaans and Tsonga, KaNgwane for Swazi, KwaNdebele for Southern Ndebele, KwaZulu for Zulu, Lebowa for Northern Sotho and Northern Ndebele, QwaQwa for Southern Sotho, Transkei for Xhosa, and Venda for Venda (Taylor 1990, 19). Of these, Transkei, Bophuthatswana, Venda, and Ciskei acquired nominal political independence as enclaves within South Africa between 1976 and 1979.

To be sure, white demand for black labor in cities, mines, and farms subverted all plans for total containment of South Africa's populations. Growth of manufacturing and services promoted rapid expansion of the black urban population; by 1945 manufacturing had surpassed mining in its contribution to the South African GDP (Lodge 1996, 188). By 1960 a full 63 percent of the African population lived at least temporarily outside African reserves (Fredrickson 1981, 244). South Africa's rulers had to manage the contradiction between treating Africans as conquest-formed Natives and recognizing them as capitalist-created workers. The contradiction led to costly efforts at segregating residence and sociability while permitting more and more Africans to enter the urban and industrial labor forces. Establishment of tribally defined segregation, furthermore, responded not only to official conceptions of history but also to political convenience:

> The new system provided an expedient opportunity for the NAD [Native Affairs Department] to dilute the influence of chiefs it regarded as uncooperative. The popularly acknowledged Paramount Chief Sabata Dalindyebo, for example, saw his chiefdom arbitrarily split into two regions, Tembuland (later renamed Dalindyebo) and Emigrant Thembuland. In the latter region, Kaizer Mantanzima, a once obscure chief who early showed a genuine interest in the philosophy and practice and soon the material rewards of apartheid, was elevated to paramount chief. (Evans 1990, 44)

Urbanization, industrialization, and political expediency did not keep South African authorities from building racially defined categories deeply into the country's legal and economic structures. Even partial legalization of black unions in 1979 inscribed government-recognized racial divisions into the law. Recipients of this organizational largesse faced an acute dilemma: accept state-endorsed categorization and retain meager claims to land and employment, or reject the categorization and abandon all state-enforced rights whatsoever.

Separatist policies nonetheless had unanticipated consequences. First, they drove Africans, Indians, and Coloureds into a common front as apartheid governments increasingly deprived the latter two categories of the distinctive rights they had previous enjoyed. Second, the apartheid regime's attempt to impose new chiefs and territorial units that would perform the work of indirect rule actually stimulated popular resistance to the authority of chiefs and, beyond it, to governmental control.

Separatist policies finally made government-defined African identities available as bases of political mobilization. "As the South African state in 1990 began to shift away from formal racial exclusion and segregation, toward 'non-racial' democracy," notes Anthony Marx, "racial identity and mobilization has lost some of its salience. In its place, political entrepreneurs have increasingly relied on 'tribal' or 'ethnic' identities as the basis of mobilization, as indicated by Zulu nationalism and 'coloured' fears of African domination under the ANC" (Marx 1995, 169).

Disaggregation occurred at two levels: the nonwhite front cracked, so that by 1996 Coloured voters in the Cape were opting massively for the National Party, former architect of apartheid. But the categories African, Coloured, and Indian also lost unifying force in favor of smaller-scale distinctions. Parallels to recent ethnically defined nationalisms in the former Yugoslavia and the former Soviet Union should give us pause. The Zulu-based and formerly state-subsidized Inkatha movement of M. G. Buthelezi exemplifies the stakes even some Africans acquired in the categories earlier imposed by white South Africans to sustain their domination.

Anthony Marx extends his comparison to the United States and Brazil, pointing out a dialectical relationship: to the degree that a state installs categorical racial distinctions in its laws and institutions, it can use coercive power legally to enforce discrimination. Yet, under changed circumstances, those categories become available as bases of mobilization and demands for rights. In Brazil, where racial inequalities run very deep but lack legal recognition, organizers of black people have little success in mobilizing their constituency and pressing for redress. In parallel reasoning, David Laitin argues that despite large on-the-average differences in wealth and power between Nigerian Christians and Muslims, religion has not become a basis of political mobilization in Nigeria, while attachment to an ancestral city has—the reason being that British colonial authorities built a hierarchy of ancestral cities into their system of indirect rule (Laitin 1985).

The United States, where legal sanctioning of racial distinctions reached much farther than in Brazil but fell far short of the system in South Africa, occupies a middle ground in these regards. Race relations in the United States never constituted a mere attenuated version of South African conditions. As George Fredrickson sums it up, American racial inequality differed from its South African counterpart in these aspects:

- It subordinated a minority, not a majority.
- American blacks and whites shared a wide range of cultural traditions.
- From Emancipation onward, both blacks and whites possessed legal citizenship, with state-supported inequalities maintained by subterfuge and paralegal means.
- On the large scale, whites and blacks never occupied geographically separate territories.

Before Jim Crow legislation locked into place, unofficial lynch mobs enforced racial inequality in the United States, while police and the army defended South Africa's apartheid throughout its history (Fredrickson 1981, 250–252; see also Fredrickson 1995). All these features produced differences in the mobilization of African-origin populations in the two countries. We can conclude that politically enforced categorical inequality sustains widespread discrimination but, with changed political alignments, also offers significant opportunities for collective action on the part of underdogs. Ethnically or racially defined political management strikes back as erstwhile managers falter. Yet the previous character of categorical relations strongly affects the form, content, and intensity of race-based mobilization.

Consider parallels between South African categorical experience and the routine operation of work in capitalist countries as summarized at the end of Chapter 3. Once again we witness powerful people facing an organizational problem—in the South African case, creation and maintenance of a state that will preserve the advantages of a small minority. We see Europeans establishing resource and power differentials within that state in three ways: creating manageable social categories by drawing sharp lines between populations rather than forming coherent entities within them; incorporating established and created social categories directly into state structure; organizing state-fostered inequality around those categories. Mapping the categories into kinship, plus the categorical segregation of residences, schools, jobs, and military service, ensured the transmission of categorical memberships from one generation to the next.

In the long run, South Africa's white rulers blurred the distinction between interior and exterior categories, since vast categorical differences in rewards promoted solidarities and mutual identifications that had previously exerted little or no force. State-promoted racial categories became fundamental facts of life. In the process, multiple parties—including, for example, the nominal rulers of nominally independent homelands—gained investments in the apartheid system. To that extent, opportunity hoarding and adaptation reinforced categorical inequality.

Not that the system worked smoothly or achieved willing assent from the country's nonwhite majority. The contradiction between policies of segregation and demands for black labor guaranteed incessant tension, compromise, and conflict. From 1903 onward, South African authorities repeatedly experimented with reorganizing categories and the inequalities attached to them. Small-scale resistance never ended. Large-scale blockage such as the Soweto uprising of 1976 (which began with black students' refusal to accept Afrikaans as their medium of instruction) recurrently revealed major fissures within the system. By 1989, in the face of popular resistance, growing isolation from the international community, capital flight from South Africa, and widening splits within the white minority, even leaders of the National Party, apartheid's author, recognized that their organizational solution had lost viability.

By no means, then, does all categorical inequality operate with quiet efficiency, drawing happy assent from its various participants. On the contrary, since categorical inequality always leaves members of certain categories visibly disadvantaged, it often occasions discontent and sometimes generates outright rebellion. The big question is whether the disadvantaged have sufficient knowledge, organizational capacity, and leverage to alter the system. In many systems they do not, both because the system delivers them rewards that are less bad than available alternatives and because the very arrangement of unequal categories deprives them of knowledge, organizational capacity, and leverage.

EXPLOITATION IN SOUTH AFRICA AND ELSEWHERE

At the base of the South African system lay exploitation. With state backing, European masters who controlled mines and farms compelled African workers to commit their effort to those enterprises for much less reward than the value their effort added; owners and managers pocketed the difference. But opportunity hoarding also played a crucial part, at four levels:

- First, white workers occupied privileged positions within the labor force, receiving far higher rates of pay for their efforts than African workers and maintaining their categorical monopolies of superior jobs with determination.

- Second, after a period of forced emigration, African villages and households acquired crucial investments in the wages earned by their migrant members. Without those wages, they could not pay taxes or buy externally produced commercial goods.

- Third, members of other categories acquired toeholds in the crevices of apartheid. Asian merchants, for all their subordination to the European population, earned a significant share of their income by selling to an African population practically excluded from larger-scale mercantile activity.

- Finally, some African chiefs and ethnic entrepreneurs found they could enhance their power and wealth by collaborating with the white-dominated regime in the operation of segregated political structures.

To that degree, exploitation and opportunity hoarding dovetailed.

Less visibly, emulation and adaptation cemented the South African system in place. Mining, for example, is a voracious industry that moves incessantly from site to site, exhausting its supplies in one excavation as it searches for new supplies in the next. Once they had put their repressive organizational structure in place, South African mine operators reproduced it over and over, right down to the recruitment of workers and the segregation of their living quarters by imputed ethnicity. Relative uniformity of organization reduced the difficulty of moving the entire operation from an exhausted vein to a fresh one, not to mention the difficulty of expanding to newly discovered deposits of gold or diamonds. The diffusion of management-dominated, segregated mine hostels, in which almost all African mineworkers still lived during the 1980s, provides a striking example of emulation from one site to the next (James 1990, 142).

However reluctantly, all parties also adapted to the evolving system, building routines and social relations that presumed its existence and thereby to some extent reinforced it. Daily, weekly, and annually, the timing of social life in African areas came to depend on the schedules of mines, mills, farms, and state-imposed curfews. Within South African townships, the police practice of patrolling the perimeters of African settlements far more intensively than the interiors encouraged the organization of African self-policing, not to mention the creation of resistance movements within the ghettos. European bosses and their African workers incrementally organized minor deviations and protections from official scripts, building up at least a modicum of loyalty based on shared local knowledge. Although on balance collective resistance to racial oppression grew during the 1980s, it grew in the face of myriad accommodations that had previously taken massive categorical inequality for granted.

The South African state's direct, public involvement in the creation of categorical inequality renders starkly visible those processes that we must usually search out in obscurity; exploiters rarely advertise their work as such. Given our definition of exploitation—powerful, connected people deploying resources from which they draw significantly increased returns by coordinating the effort of outsiders, whom they exclude from the full value added by that effort—any search for exploitation in real life must keep alert for seven elements:

1.   Powerholders (in South Africa, coalitions of state officials and white capitalists)
2.   Their coordinated efforts (in South Africa, the actual cooperation of coalition members)
3.   Deployable resources (in South Africa, mineral deposits and farmland at first, and then the capital of industrial and commercial enterprises)

4.   Command over those resources (in South Africa, state-backed property rights and their exercise by whites)

5.   Returns from those resources (in South Africa, net profits from the sale of goods produced by mines, farms, and capitalist enterprises)

6.   Categorical exclusion (in South Africa of the 1960s, for example, the apparatus of apartheid and labor control, including both boundaries within capitalist enterprises and the division of labor between labor-exporting villages and centers of capitalist enterprise)

7.   Skewed division of returns as compared with effort (in South Africa, a system in which Africans did the great bulk of the work but received only minuscule shares of the proceeds)

Although my capsule history says far too little about coordinating efforts (not to mention ties between government and ruling classes) to make the operation of elements 1 and 2 immediately obvious here, South Africa easily qualifies on all seven counts.

Exploitation worked in South Africa in the same way that it works anywhere: it enlisted African effort in white-run enterprises while giving Africans much less than the equivalent of the value added by their effort. A portion of the return from that profitable arrangement went into organizing repression and buying collaboration from white workers plus a few highly selected African supervisors. The installation of a white/African boundary at the frontier between command structure and laboring masses greatly reduced the cost of such an arrangement, since it called up widely available interracial routines that state agents would, if necessary, back up with force. In company with opportunity hoarding, emulation, and adaptation, South African exploitation constituted a self-sustaining system as long as the white/African boundary remained cheap to maintain. Only in the 1980s did that cost rise visibly. As a result, the system began to crack.

How shall we apply the same style of analysis elsewhere, say, in capitalist firms and labor markets? Let us restrict our attention temporarily to exploitation and direct effects. That means neglecting opportunity hoarding, emulation, and adaptation as well as the effects of categorically unequal experiences outside the immediate setting under examination. We are searching for situations in which exterior categories such as ethnicity, race, and citizenship correspond to interior boundaries of exploitation. We are following the hunch that interior boundaries of unequal return to value added coincide with the organization's mobility map, its segregation of job clusters within which workers move frequently but across whose limits they rarely move. We suspect that distinct incentive systems (drive, loyalty, and task systems and their variants) will characterize the separate clusters. We can use the elements of exploitation—powerholders, coordinated efforts, deployable resources, and so on—as a checklist for thinking through how exploitation promotes inequality in rewards from work.

First, *powerholders*. Who are the relevant powerholders? Certainly owners and managers of firms wield power, although they do not necessarily do so in a unified manner. Anyone who makes decisions at any of the inequality-generating organizational junctions cataloged earlier (recruitment of new employees, wage determination within job categories, bounding of jobs, ranking of jobs, and so on) holds some power over categorical differentials. So frequently do representatives of government and labor unions. To the extent that their livelihoods depend on a firm's profitability, they all have interests in exploitation.

Second, *coordinated efforts*. We must imagine a web of bargained conflict and cooperation among powerholders, with those who most directly control the disposition of the firm's major capital assets generally exercising the greatest influence over the others and within the firm as a whole.

Third, *deployable resources*. Some body of assets, highly variable by industry, ensures the continuance of whatever advantages a firm enjoys with respect both to other firms and to economic actors other than firms. Those assets can include land, location, raw material, industrial plant, technical knowledge, reputation, contacts with suppliers, clients, or officials, and more.

Fourth, *command over resources*. It is one thing to have access to resources, another actually to command them—in particular, to exclude outsiders effectively from their use. No firm can make gains from exploitation if its resources are freely available to everyone outside its perimeter.

Fifth, *returns from those resources.* Capitalist firms generally do not survive long unless they make a profit. That profit depends on effective marshalling of resources. One measure of the effectiveness of a firm's conjunction between deployable resources and coordinated efforts is productivity, the schedule of outputs for various combinations of labor and other inputs. Another is the ratio of the market value of the firm as an integral unit to the market value of its assets sold separately. A firm for which this ratio falls much below 1.0 runs a good chance of disappearing, but one whose ratio rises to 2.0 or more is surely making gains from exploitation. Its high market value represents potential returns to newcomers who could take over its apparatus of exploitation.

Sixth, *categorical exclusion.* We look for categorical exclusion in two places: within a firm and at its perimeter. Within the firm, we detect boundaries between unequal and paired categories in which members of one category benefit from control of sequestered resources and receive returns from the other's output. Around the firm's perimeter, we detect relations between members of the firm and outsiders (e.g., dependent subcontractors) who commit effort to the creation of transferable use value by means of the firm's resources.

Seventh, *skewed division of returns.* This feature will be crucial and often controversial for two reasons: it implies comparison with a counterfactual analysis of likely returns without categorical exclusion, and the effects of exclusion confound easily with returns to land, capital, technology, and other nonhuman inputs into the production of transferable use value. We must handle the counterfactual by the usual methods of nonexperimental disciplines, making comparisons among otherwise similar firms whose systems of exclusion differ significantly, inspecting the extent and character of covariation between exclusion and inequality of rewards, examining what happens as exclusion increases or decreases within particular firms, and breaking into its elements the causal chain connecting returns to effort in order to single out the effects of exclusion. To the extent that discrepancies in rewards within a firm correspond to categorical boundaries and that these discrepancies correspond to differences in control over the firm's central resources, we acquire evidence that categorically organized exploitation is itself generating inequality.

In cases less extreme than South Africa, all seven elements of exploitation elude easy detection. If women generally hold lower-paying jobs than men, for example, how much of the difference results from organized male control over job allocation, as Barbara Reskin (1988) argues? Perhaps all, but the relevant cause-effect chains entangle with the effects of human capital, technology, and other factors that influence output. This, then, sets the challenge: to determine in alleged cases of exploitation whether the seven elements not only exist but concatenate in the manner that my causal story requires.

GENDER AND EXPLOITATION

Consider gender inequality in the rewards to work within capitalist labor markets. Most analysts of the subject—including Barbara Reskin—implicitly adopt an explanatory model in this form:

MALE/FEMALE DIFFERENCES IN REWARDS TO WORK $= M \times$ (DIFFERENCES IN HUMAN CAPITAL $+$ DIFFERENCES IN EFFORT $+$ DISCRIMINATION)

M stands for the mechanisms translating the three inputs into differential rewards. In such a model, the allocator of rewards can be a particular manager, a firm, capitalists in general, male workers, all men, or perhaps society as a whole. Sharp disagreements separate analysts concerning agents, mechanisms, and relative weights among the factors. One set of disputes concerns which agents cause the effects: particular employers, male workers, the market considered as a collective actor, or something else.

The M factor in various formulations specifies the incentives and mechanisms that translate agents' preferences into rewards; theorists disagree rancorously over whether agents are ensuring long-term productivity, minimizing current wage costs, attacking worker solidarity through division, implementing their own preferences and beliefs with respect to workplace personnel and routines, imitating their peers, and so on. Dorothy Sue Cobble summarizes competing views:

> Scholars have analyzed the phenomenon of job segregation by sex from a variety of perspectives. Some view it as a divide-and-conquer strategy adopted by employers wary of a unified working class. Others argue that the creation of female job ghettos characterized by low pay and status is a necessary cornerstone in a patriarchal-capitalist system desirous of and dependent on women's subordinate role in the family. A third approach assumes that the sexual division of labor is the rational result of women's failure to augment their "human capital." (Cobble 1991, 216)

Disagreements among these views pivot chiefly on agents and mechanisms, but they also imply different weights for such elements as human capital. (Cobble herself favors a fourth view, in which struggles of men and women for their own job rights intersect with employer strategies; but her disagreement with her predecessors still concerns agents, mechanisms, and weights within her own version of the formula above.)

Despite disagreements in other regards, analysts of wage inequality generally accept the conventional definition of discrimination as the remainder after taking account of human capital and effort. Open disputes then center on the relative weights and cross-effects of human capital, effort, and discrimination. Neoclassical analysts commonly give strong weight to the interaction of human capital and effort, whereas radical feminists often assign the fundamental causal role to discrimination in one form or another. All sides invoke an essentially individualistic explanation of inequality.

Sophisticated feminist models (e.g., Downs 1995; Reskin and Ross 1995; Tomaskovic-Devey and Johnson 1996) generally stress the centrality of job-level gender segregation; invoke something like Weber's social closure, with males excluding females; and add some notion of queuing to account for changes in the gender composition of jobs. As Donald Tomaskovic-Devey puts it:

> The use of the social closure language is important . . . in that it makes explicit the theoretical explanation that exclusionary practices fostered

by advantaged workers and employers create observed patterns of organizational and job segmentation. Simple notions of unreflective employer discrimination based on prejudices are not sufficient. Social closure arguments are about active practices that produce and preserve
advantages.

The status composition hypothesis is that jobs that are disproportionately female or male become stereotyped, and the work process itself begins to reflect the social value of the master status of typical incumbents.
This is not an argument about discrimination against individuals but
against jobs. The argument is that jobs and organizational structure may
be fundamentally influenced by gender. (Tomaskovic-Devey 1995, 29)

So far, so good. At that point, however, such models enter a dead end.
They lack any principle other than gender composition itself to account
for differential rewards between "male" and "female" jobs or for simultaneous and/or alternative segregation-cum-inequality by race, ethnicity, citizenship, and other ostensibly competing categorical divisions.
In the last analysis, they retreat to gender-specific, if now categorical
rather than individual, discrimination in job allocation and job rewards.

Neoclassical or feminist, such a model will not do. It describes a situation in which a single bargain sets rewards for work. A firm's represen-
tative decides how much to offer a worker on the basis of estimates
(however biased) of that worker's contributions to their shared activity,
and the worker either takes the offer or declines the job. Discrimination
supposedly results from the fact that the hiring agent does one or several of the following things:

Underestimates the likely contributions of certain categories of
workers

Stereotypes the capabilities of certain categories of workers

Foregoes the likely contributions of certain categories of workers in
order (a) to avoid benefiting them, (b) to avoid associating with them,
or (c) to accommodate the preferences of others, such as skilled male
workers

Such situations do occur, but they do not stand at the center of the causal
processes producing categorical inequality. Leaving the formulation
with such an unclear specification of causal mechanisms makes all such
accounts vulnerable to the objection that a better specification of human

capital will explain away gender differences. Indeed, Tony Tam has attacked the argument that workers in female-dominated categories of employment receive lower pay because of their categories' gender composition alone; he shows that specifying human capital not only as years of education but also as years of specialized training required to qualify for a job essentially erases occupational pay differences by gender in the 1988 U.S. Current Population Survey (Tam 1997). Operating within the standard explanatory frame, Tam correctly offers his findings as a challenge to the common explanation of lower wages in predominantly female occupations, the general devaluation of female work. While conceding that gender-specific allocation of jobs might help explain his results, he treats his results as confirmation of human-capital analyses. This book's perspective, however, suggests three other possible interpretations of the evidence: first, that firms install categorical boundaries between jobs requiring more and less occupation-specific training time, offer lower pay on the lesser-training side of the boundaries, and channel women into those jobs whether or not they could actually perform the jobs that require more training; second, that gender sorting begins before or during the acquisition of occupation-specific training; and third, that both of these mechanisms are in operation (as we have already seen).

Categorical inequality in rewards results from sorting not just at the hiring gate or pay table but throughout the job allocation process, from training to recruitment to promotion. And it does far more organizational work than merely satisfying a personnel officer's predilections. Inequality in rewards results from the matching of exploitation boundaries with categorical differences. It rests not on individual-by-individual experience but on organized social relations.

As the story of South African exploitation indicates, no model that lacks explicit representation of continuous interaction among the parties offers much hope of explaining durable, organized, categorically defined inequality in rewards to work effort. Preestablished scripts certainly matter, but they operate effectively through improvisation based on accumulated local knowledge. Exploitation, opportunity hoarding, emulation, and adaptation designate the major sorts of interactions that cumulate into aggregate male/female differences in rewards for work.

Male/female boundaries serve exploitation within firms and labor markets in much the same way that white/African boundaries did in the apartheid economy as a whole. To be sure, in most situations of capitalist employment, gender boundaries mark off life spaces much less completely, occasion less brutality, rely less directly on state-supplied force, and sustain smaller differences in rewards than did ostensibly racial boundaries in South Africa. But analogous mechanisms and outcomes come into play: owner-management control over deployable resources, installation of a categorical boundary separating distinct forms of relationship to the enterprise, matching of that boundary with the exterior categorical pair, enlistment of effort from the subordinate category in producing value from those resources, returning to members of the subordinate category less than the net value that their efforts add to the firm's production.

The crucial cases are not those in which males and females belong to the same organizational categories—e.g., where men and women both deliver mail under similar working conditions—but those that match gender distinctions to significant interior boundaries. Such significant interior boundaries frequently correspond to the limits of loyalty, drive, and task systems of remuneration, with males disproportionately concentrated in zones of loyalty, women disproportionately subject to drive or task controls. Contracts within task and drive spheres deliver fewer rewards, relative to value added, while contracts within loyalty spheres deliver more. Workers in loyalty systems generally enjoy higher pay, more extensive benefits, greater job security, larger opportunities for promotion, and participation in the informal structures of communication and power.

Relevant distinctions, however, often operate more subtly than a simple division among task, drive, and loyalty incentive systems. Among other things, they form filters within internal labor markets. Faced with price competition from new manufacturers, Philadelphia's big Philco radio plant began reorganizing its labor processes and replacing men with lower-paid women in 1937. Consolidating that reorganization, Philco followed a four-month lockout by negotiating a major new labor contract with the United Electrical Workers in 1938:

The union's definitions of equality and fairness built into this rational-ized job structure seemed gender-blind. Workers agreed that favoritism and capriciousness needed to be eliminated and all workers benefited from this aspect of the contract. The new job structure was, however, gender-bound. Since women's and men's jobs were distinctly different, so were their job ladders. The range of women's jobs was much nar-rower and women had no way of moving up to the most skilled, high-est-paying jobs at the top of the male ladder. They could not step onto it, much less climb anywhere. The result was that the possibility of occu-pational mobility was attached to men's rather than women's jobs. (Coo-per 1991, 329–330)

Nor did such segregated job ladders disappear as women's paid em-ployment increased after the 1930s. In a grocery chain described by Bar-bara Reskin and Irene Padavic, men and women alike generally entered a store as low-ranking clerks and then worked their way up. But newly hired women moved disproportionately into the bakery/deli and gen-eral merchandise departments, where the only likely promotion raised them to head of that same department. Store managers came chiefly from grocery departments (where males occupied about half of all clerk positions and well over 80 percent of all supervisory positions) and from produce departments (where 80.9 percent of all clerks and 95.3 percent of all managers were male); entry-level jobs in bakery, delicatessen, gen-eral merchandise, produce, and groceries greatly resembled each other but fell into separate organizational pools (Reskin and Padavic 1994, 88–89). Although Reskin and Padavic do not tell us, we can reasonably speculate that the male-dominated grocery and produce departments constituted the stores' control centers, included more full-time workers, experienced less turnover, and at least to that degree more greatly re-sembled loyalty systems than did the bakery/delicatessen and general merchandise divisions.

Considering all sorts of gender differences in employment and re-wards, Reskin and Padavic distinguish three clusters of explanations: human capital, segregation, and cultural beliefs. They judiciously give weight to each of the three but do not integrate them. In exploitation, however, segregation occupies the central position. The installation of gender boundaries within firms facilitates the distinction of incentive systems and the distinction of returns to value added. To be sure, categorically segregated experiences both off and on the job create differences in human capital, and the matching of interior with exterior categorical pairs carries available cultural baggage.

In such circumstances, members of the organization ordinarily borrow or build up shared beliefs about the appropriateness of such matching between exterior and interior categories, as when my son Chris Tilly's fellow file clerks in a Boston hospital (overwhelmingly female) told him that the job was quintessential women's work because it required dexterity and attention to detail, while later his fellow file clerks in an Oakland, California, hospital (predominantly Filipino male) told him that it was quintessential men's work because of the lifting and hauling it entailed. Thus managers and workers devise or borrow beliefs that support current divisions of labor.

Meanwhile, categorical segregation does the crucial work of exploitation. Skewed returns are difficult to estimate for many of the same reasons that have made it impossible to verify neoclassical claims about wage determination. Do workers tend to receive pay equivalent to the marginal product of their labor? Adjudication of that claim requires disentangling the interactions of capital, technology, organizational form, labor, and accounting conventions. Similarly, alas, we lack effective means for isolating the value added by a single worker or a single category of workers. Study after study reveals that women get lower returns than men for similar increments of human capital and that job segregation plays a central part in the difference (e.g., England and McCreary 1987; England, Reid, and Kilbourne 1996; le Grand 1991; McGuire and Reskin 1993; Tomaskovic-Devey 1993), but such investigations rarely provide much direct evidence on the categorical processes producing unequal rewards.

The exploitation model nevertheless alerts us to a series of indirect indicators for the presence or absence of category-assisted exploitation:

- Scrutiny of a firm's day-to-day operation reveals boundary-maintaining practices, sanctions against persons and actions who violate boundaries, categorically framed public distinctions between essential and nonessential workers, and private contestation of those distinctions.

- Quantities and qualities of rewards within a firm vary discontinuously, with big breaks at categorical boundaries.

- Distinctly different schedules of return to experience and human capital obtain on opposite sides of categorical frontiers, notably where interior and exterior categories coincide.

- For a given pair of categories, schedules of return differ significantly more when a mobility boundary intervenes than when members of the two categories operate within the same mobility system.

- Qualitatively different treatments of incompetence, dereliction, or unscheduled departure exist on either side of categorical lines.

- Barriers in mobility networks correspond closely to category edges—"glass ceilings" and the like.

- Relations between members of the same unequal categories differ significantly at interior boundaries and away from them.

- Categorical differences and taboos operate with respect to control over the firm's central resources.

All these organizational phenomena characterize gender differences in capitalist firms.

Past research on gender inequality, so often implicitly or explicitly individualist rather than organizational in its orientation, has left us less information about boundary work within organizations than we need to trace out the necessary causal connections. Nevertheless, a wide variety of findings concerning gender segregation of jobs and their connections with other jobs point in the expected directions. William Bielby and James Baron's punctilious examination of job segregation in California, for example, yields the following conclusion:

If jobs are almost perfectly segregated by sex, authority hierarchies and career ladders are likely to be segregated as well. Preliminary analyses of our data on job hierarchies show that women in positions of authority almost always supervised other women, though it is also common for women to be supervised by men. Women are much less likely to be in jobs with promotion opportunities, and career ladders are typically longer for men. The few jobs containing men and women are mostly in entry-level slots at the bottom of organizational hierarchies, and typically women's promotion opportunities diminish almost entirely after moving a step or two beyond entry level. (Bielby and Baron 1986, 790)

The Bielby-Baron findings dovetail perfectly with the configuration of jobs and promotion opportunities that Reskin and Padavic found in their grocery chain. Similarly, Sharyn Roach's examination of lawyers working in corporate legal departments describes this situation:

Women were located mainly in financial services and in medium-sized legal departments in lower-paying jobs with fewer opportunities. Men in-house counsel were employed in corporations in the manufacturing sector and in large departments that offered opportunities for career development and lucrative salaries. The different career outcomes of men and women in-house counsel resulted from organizational practices— hiring policies and job-allocation decisions—rather than from individual career choices or preferences. Career development especially appeared to depend on visibility to those in positions to make hiring decisions. (Roach 1990, 209; on similar sorting within law firms, see Rosenberg, Perlstadt, and Phillips 1993; Pierce 1995)

Both current assignments and mobility opportunities, in short, corresponded to gender boundaries within these firms. Similar patterns show up widely outside the world of legal professionals. We can reasonably conclude that whatever contributions male/female human-capital differences, employer preferences, opportunity hoarding, emulation, and adaptation make to gender inequality, exploitation also permeates today's American firms. South Africa is not the only country where exploitation drives categorical inequality.

Widespread coincidence of gender boundaries with exploitation-mobility frontiers within firms has an unexpected, fascinating implication: men should cast women in the conventional roles defined by exterior male/female relations more often *within* exploitation-mobility frontiers than *across* them. Despite greater equality in material rewards, we should find not only more male sexual predation toward females but also more casting of relations as brother-sister, son-mother, or father-daughter where men and women belong to the same crafts, professions, jobs, hierarchies, and mobility systems than where their organizational positions differ sharply. These effects should be exacerbated close to exploitation-mobility boundaries: for females who have recently arrived from across a boundary or in a previously all-male domain; for positions that span boundaries, as in the cases of temporary and probationary workers; for locations along contested and changing boundaries, as in the early phases of affirmative action. Once a gendered mobility boundary settles into place, adaptation occurs, and local knowledge accumulates, both men and women will generally accept the organizational definition of that boundary, will less frequently define relations across it in conventional familial or sexual terms, and will less often establish intimate relations.

Although she does not make the within-across comparison, Rosabeth Kanter identifies four "informal role traps" into which token senior women could easily fall at Indsco: mother; seductress; pet, or kid sister; and iron maiden, or virgin aunt (Kanter 1993, 233). She is talking about female/male relations within the same mobility systems, not across the exempt/nonexempt barrier. Kanter also points out that through sustained performance women sometimes evade the traps, especially if they wield significant power: "power wipes out sex." "On one occasion," she reports,

> a senior Indsco salesman told a long story to colleagues about a problem with a "very, very smart, tough-minded" president of a small company. The president had made good friends among a number of senior Indsco people and therefore managed to get all kinds of concessions. The salesman had to bring this to an end, as well as tell this very powerful client that there would be no credit for the material that had failed when her customers, in turn, used it . . . It took a long time for the audience to this story to realize that the salesman was saying "she." Some even interjected comments using "he." The salesman presented the story with such awe of the powerful customer that sex made no difference. He said later that she was someone he would eagerly work for. (Kanter 1993, 200)

Thus the salesman's colleagues began with standard sexual stereotypes and abandoned them only reluctantly.

Why should such casting occur more widely inside exploitation-mobility frontiers? Both because mobility boundaries encourage taboos on intimacy and because in their absence fellow workers turn to widely available scripts that govern relations between the sexes. Without denying that bosses occasionally seduce their secretaries, that doctors marry nurses more often than chance would predict, that male assembly-line workers sometimes make lewd remarks to passing female clericals, or that American slaveowners sometimes impregnated their female slaves, I speculate that explicitly gendered scripts drawn from routine social life outside a given organizational setting control fewer transactions across exploitation-mobility boundaries than within them. Recent sexual-harassment incidents in the American military appear to follow the expected pattern: male naval officers attacking female naval officers in the Tailhook scandal, male enlisted drill instructors attacking female recruits in the Aberdeen training base affair.

Indeed, a reciprocal effect may well occur: the establishment of strongly gendered relations across an exploitation-mobility barrier may induce the more powerful partner to obscure the barrier, to struggle against it, or to pull the partner across it, as when slaveowners manumit their slave mistresses and children (Stinchcombe 1995, 139). In general, people who erect exploitation-mobility boundaries also limit intimacy and unauthorized gender scripting across those boundaries.

Fear of just such gendered scripting within exploitation-mobility boundaries seems to impel operators of newly coeducational institutions to formulate elaborate counterscripts. When the Citadel military academy in Charleston, South Carolina, finally bowed to legal pressure and prepared to accept women in the fall of 1996, its authorities produced a new code of behavior that, among other things, maintained hazing ("adversative treatment") of newcomers by upperclass cadets but strictly regulated physical contact:

> Female cadets of the fourth class will receive the same adversative treatment as male fourth class cadets.
> An upperclass cadet does not touch a fourth class cadet (male or female) without first asking permission and stating the purpose and specific area(s) that will be touched (i.e. touch hand to correct salute or touch head to correct angle of hat). After receiving permission from the fourth class cadet involved, the upperclass cadet may touch only those

areas that permission was granted to touch. This procedure is to be employed only for the purpose of providing instruction or correcting a uniform or posture discrepancy. Whenever this procedure is used, it will take place on the gallery and in full view of at least one other cadet. (Allen 1996, E7).

Other new regulations govern tucking shirts, showering, entering rooms, and walking or sitting together. More than anything else, the regulations block standard routines of courtship, sexual play, and harassment. What is more, the actual harassment of the four women in the first Citadel class to enter after these regulations were enacted combined the hazing that male workers have commonly given the first female entrants into their trades with the sort of rough treatment sometimes visited by fraternity men on their sorority neighbors: pouring nail polish on the women and setting their clothing afire, "entering the women's rooms in the middle of the night, singing sexually explicit songs and forcing alcoholic beverages on them in the dormitories," and so on (*New York Times* 1996a). Moreover, the men triumphed; two of the four female cadets left the academy in January 1997, declaring that harassment had driven them out (*New York Times* 1997). The academy's authorities had rightly anticipated "adversative treatment" based on exterior male/female categories rather than on the timeless traditions of military discipline.

Does such gendered scripting occur chiefly within rather than across mobility systems? Because previous research into gender relations at work has followed such different assumptions, we lack systematic evidence to confirm or deny this conjecture. Both Jean Reith Schroedel's life histories of women in predominantly male trades and Cynthia Cockburn's study of women's experience in self-consciously egalitarian organizations, nevertheless, indicate that some such process is going on: where they share a common fate, men map women into relations of gender bonding, rough courtship, or family long before they deal with them as asexual fellow workers. Cockburn relates how this happens:

A top woman manager at High Street Retail reported a curious exchange with a senior male colleague who had been staring at her during meetings, behaving in a way she found unsettling. Eventually she asked

him, "What's the matter?" He said, "I'm sorry, but I can't help it. Ev-
erytime I look at you I see my *wife*." She answered curtly, "That's your
problem." But she commented to me on men's confusion in their experience of women in two worlds. "Men do have difficulty in seeing a
woman as anything other than a secretary, a sex object or a wife." (Cockburn 1991, 95)

Still, sometimes men and women in the same mobility systems establish
relations in which performance trumps gender. Elaine Canfield told Jean
Schroedel about how much trouble fellow construction workers had ac-
cepting her and then reported:

> The crew I'm working with now—it's never been better. I'm accepted.
> They kid me like one of the guys. They pay me compliments. They treat
> me like an equal. It has been a real breakthrough. I've had other crews
> that have been really nice, but I know enough now so that I can talk
> business as well as pleasure. Not only am I compatible, but I feel they
> recognize me as a fairly good carpenter. I haven't had that recognition
> before. (Schroedel 1985, 39)

Many of the other women Schroedel interviewed told similar stories.
Exploitation certainly continues to thrive in the construction industry,
but Elaine Canfield is undermining exploitation's coincidence with gender. As "one of the guys," indeed, she is now enjoying the benefits of
the opportunity hoarding practiced by all construction trades. She has
overcome the indirect effects of categorical exploitation in other settings
by acquiring visible job skills few other women have had a chance to
learn. Driven by the imperatives of their craft, her fellow workers have
adapted to her presence, joined with her in the creation of shared local
knowledge, and largely abandoned the standard scripts of gender relations.

Experiences of men in predominantly female occupations seem to
confirm the process illustrated by Elaine Canfield's eventual acceptance.
When men first arrive on the job, women map them into available familial and sexual categories, only later shifting to criteria of competence in
which gender plays little or no part. A fifth-grade science teacher, whom
Jim Allan calls Bill, describes what happened to him:

When I started in elementary education I was the only male teacher, and my reactions were always looked at a little differently, and they were judging me, I think, a little differently because I was a man. They wanted to see how I would handle the young kids' emotions . . . or if I'd be too macho. You know, I've had contact with a number of prejudging teachers as I've entered the field as an elementary teacher . . . People think the reason I'm doing the teaching is because I'm in athletics, and I think I've proven myself, at least in this school system, that my first priority is teaching. (Allan 1993, 118)

Construction worker Elaine Canfield and elementary teacher Bill mark, however, the great exceptions: the vast majority of women workers find themselves separated from the vast majority of men workers by frontiers of exploitation and job mobility.

If we enlarge our view from firms to the entire world of work, furthermore, we begin to see that crucial boundaries of exploitation—as always, in the sense of categorically unequal rewards for value added by pooled effort—often form not within firms but at their edges. With respect to male / female relations, households provide the crucial sites. Whatever else households do, they reproduce the labor power that firms deploy. Despite enormous increases in women's paid employment in firms since World War II throughout the capitalist world, women continue to perform the vast bulk of household labor, the essential work of reproducing labor power through feeding, cleaning, child care, health care, personal service, and emotional support. Where their husbands hold high-ranking occupations, wives commonly perform directly in their spouses' working worlds, regardless of their own commitments, as hostesses, symbols of success, and members of influence networks. Women contribute these efforts for far less material reward than the value they add to the relevant firms' production. Within firms, among firms, and between households and firms, categorical inequality enhances and results from the gains of exploitation.

Nor is gender inequality in rewards for work a peculiarity of capitalist labor markets. Feminist critics of capitalist work are surely right to accent contradictions between declarations of equal opportunity and practices of enduring gender inequality, as well as to pinpoint job segregation as a crucial mechanism producing unequal rewards. But their opponents properly point out how regularly noncapitalist economies have also instituted gender-divided exploitation, with women contributing major efforts to production while getting less than value added as their rewards. The form and degree of gender exploitation have varied greatly, but no economy so far has lived without it.

How, then, does exploitation interact with opportunity hoarding, emulation, and adaptation? Very strongly, as succeeding chapters will show.

5 How To Hoard Opportunities

My friends who make their living from survey research would not have approved. Our rambunctious interview did not conform to professional standards. During the spring of 1988, Pierine Piras, Philippe Videlier, and I sat drinking coffee and nibbling cake in the living room of a modest house in Mamaroneck, New York. Mamaroneck lies on Long Island Sound, about twenty miles north of New York City. We were speaking with a man I'll name Franco Bossi, born in Roccasecca, Italy, not far from Rome, ninety-two years earlier.

Given our standard options of English, French, or Italian for the interview's language (none of us had mastered the dialect of Roccasecca), Mr. Bossi had chosen Italian. Mrs. Bossi, in her eighties, and their daughter Rosa, in her sixties, interrupted frequently to contradict, refresh, complete, or refine Mr. Bossi's recollections when they were not urging him to shift from his rusty Italian to his accented, ungrammatical, but fluent English. Mr. Bossi remembered the Mamaroneck of the World War I era as very Italian:

Tutti qui, sto villagio dove stamo me now, tutti Italiani, Italiani, Italiani! La most part era Roccasecca. Tutte le zone . . . Siciliani . . . Calabresi assai, Calabresi assai . . . Napolitani . . . Down in Mamaroneck they use to call a "Guinea Town" because the Italians they calls the "guinea," it's a nickname.

As of the 1910 census, in fact, only about a sixth of Mamaroneck's population was Italian-born. In Washingtonville, the section of Mamaroneck away from the water on the wrong side of the railroad tracks, about a third of all households then had Italian-born heads. But teenaged Franco Bossi, recently arrived from Roccasecca with his parents, surely lived in a much more Italian world than that.

Not that his parents had come straight from the old country. "I was not born yet, my father left my mother pregnant," reported Mr. Bossi.

He went to Brazil. It was a lot of people that say: "Let's go to Brazil! Let's go to Brazil!" A lot of work over there. So my father went there and all the day he picked coffee, bananas, all this stuff, rice, fruits, but the most were in Brazil for coffee. They must have been in the country, but I don't know the name, but that's where they grew coffee. He only stood one year over there. The heat! *La calor,* ooh! . . . You can't stay there! And the bugs! My father came over here.

Franco Bossi's father came to the United States around 1898, roughly midway through the first important wave of migration from Roccasecca to Mamaroneck and the rest of Westchester County, which lasted from 1890 or so to World War I. He became a construction laborer in Mamaroneck, while Franco himself later found work as a gardener on one of the estates that were springing up along Long Island Sound as the new railroad, and then paved motor roads, made Westchester easily accessible to Manhattan. In a clear example of opportunity hoarding with little or no exploitation, Franco Bossi, his fellow emigrants, and later arrivals concentrated themselves in Westchester's gardening, public works, and connected enterprises, gaining collective advantages by pooling access to jobs and firms.

American restrictions on immigration after World War I greatly slowed the movement of workers from Roccasecca to Mamaroneck and nearby towns. At that point, many more Ciociari (as people from the *paese* including Roccasecca identify themselves) began migrating to France, especially to Lyon's industrial suburbs. But after World War II a new round of migrants took the American road. "My mother and father got married," one fifty-year-old immigrant we can call Anthony Bianco told us, "and went to France because he had three sisters there, one in Saint-Romain-le-Puy and two in Villeurbanne [both towns in the vicinity of Lyon]. My father stayed three years but then he wasn't happy with life there, it was too hot living next to the glassworks, so he went back to Roccasecca. My brother and I had been born in France—my older brother, who now works for the railroad in Rome. My uncle had a motel in Mamaroneck, and we had gotten married, he was there when we got married and said, you were born in France, I can sponsor you, so three months later I came here on my French papers."

Anthony Bianco worked for a year as a gardener and then spent nineteen years in construction before becoming a laborer for the county government. His family now has branches in Italy, France, and the United States, each of them concentrated in a few adjacent locations. Other natives of Roccasecca we met in Mamaroneck had lived in Brazil and Argentina. Some had relatives in Toronto, although (in what may be a testimony to either Toronto's hospitality or the United States immigration controls) we encountered no Roccaseccani who had first emigrated to Toronto only to move on to New York. But a well-established network of kinship and acquaintance link Roccasecca and nearby villages in central Italy, Villeurbanne and adjacent industrial towns in France, São Paulo in Brazil, Buenos Aires in Argentina, Toronto in Canada, and the northern suburbs of New York City.

Fitting fragmentary evidence from Mamaroneck and Lyon into analogies with other migration systems, I conjecture that migration chains connecting Roccasecca with Mamaroneck first took shape in contacts among the village's stonecutters, who went from site to site for construction in Europe, only to return to their farms in the off season. When contractors starting building dams and reservoirs to meet New York City's enormous demands for water late in the nineteenth century, some of them reached out to Italy for their stonecutters. Most of the stonecutters brought laborers with them, I speculate, and most of them returned to Italy when their jobs were done. But others—both stonecutters and their less skilled helpers—liked the opportunities they saw in the New York area and stayed on. Later migrants moved directly into the construction of roads and railways or into gardening on the great estates that lined the nearby Atlantic shore. Many more made their bundles and returned to Italy, but again some stayed on, married, settled their families, and bore children who were Americans. By this speculative account, Anthony Bianco arrived in the United States sixty years or so after those who established the Roccasecca-Mamaroneck link, Franco Bossi and his compatriots.

Piras, Videlier, and I undertook the research on migration between Roccasecca and Mamaroneck because it investigated an imperfect but revealing natural experiment in the creation of durable inequality. From a thousand-person agricultural village, hundreds of emigrants went to Mamaroneck and vicinity, hundreds more to Villeurbanne and vicinity. In Lyon's suburbs, they generally took factory jobs; their children rapidly became working-class French people with Italian names but little other Italian identification. In Westchester, Italians whose families originated in Roccasecca concentrated heavily in landscape gardening, where the current generation enjoys a near-monopoly of the local business; others cluster in construction, public works, and retail trade. Within family firms, a Catholic parish, and ethnic neighborhoods, they have retained a much stronger identification with Italy and small enterprise than have their relatives in France. The situation of ethnic Italians in Mamaroneck clearly illustrates the possibility of opportunity hoarding in the absence of major exploitation: Italians gain modest but secure existences by controlling adjacent economic niches and excluding non-Italians from those niches, but in the process they employ little or no non-Italian labor. More so than their French cousins, they survive by hoarding opportunities.

Anthony Bianco lived a complicated migration history, but not much more intricate than the average. In any case, his history tells us something far more important than how complicated life is. In Roccasecca, Anthony's family and most of their neighbors were peasants. In New

York's suburbs, Mr. Bianco's *paesani* have become shopkeepers and landscape gardeners, while others having essentially the same origins have become French industrial workers, Brazilian businesspeople, or perhaps schoolteachers in Toronto. (My collaborators uncovered a similar range of destinations among closely connected people during their interviews in the region of Lyon.) Transplanted Italians now bear different kinds of names, speak different languages, wear different clothes, follow different politics, do different kinds of work, have different memories and hopes for the future. What caused these divergences? In these cases, we're tempted to answer that it was luck. Ability, determination, and prior wealth or education certainly seem to have mattered little, while the presence of a relative who could provide aid and information mattered a great deal. That presence, however, was not a lucky coincidence but the pivot of an extensive migration system that brought Roccaseccani to Mamaroneck and nearby towns while carrying their close kin and neighbors to Lyon, São Paulo, Buenos Aires, or Toronto. However much the experience of any particular migrant might seem to depend on chance and individual taste, the experience took shape within stringent limits set by preexisting contacts.

Anyone who studies migration and ethnicity has recognized in my rambling account of Mamaroneck's migrants telltale signs of chain migration and niche formation. A well-defined migration chain fed individuals and families into a set of connected economic niches. Mamaroneck's Italian immigrant niches lack the neatness of those Roger Waldinger and Alejandro Portes have identified in New York, Miami, and Los Angeles, but they likewise illustrate how the path by which a given category of people entered the American economy had a strong impact on the opportunities open to subsequent members of that category.

In fact, the Mamaroneck story shows us not the perpetuation but the *creation* of a category—Italian-Americans—by the migration process itself. It also shows us how subsequent generations use the created category: in a classic case of opportunity hoarding, members of a categorically bounded network retain access to a resource—in this case, a set of employers, clients, and jobs—that is valuable, renewable, subject to monopoly, supportive of network activities, and enhanced by the network's modus operandi. Matching the category Italian-American to the business of landscape gardening sequestered opportunities for poor Italian peasants and their descendants, but it also fenced off those opportunities from other people, including the growing number of black residents in Mamaroneck and adjacent Westchester towns. Thus, as compared with Lyon, it reinforced Italian identity as a basis of everyday social relations in Mamaroneck. It sustained dense, bounded networks containing many triads, all three of whose members recognized each other as Italian.

Ciociari who came to Mamaroneck were solving an everyday problem—finding paid work in a strange land—and creating categories more or less inadvertently, but as they did so there took shape a set of social ties in which multiple parties had stakes. Interested parties included kinfolk in Italy and America, fellow Ciociari emigrants, and a variety of local employers. By analogy with other niche builders who tell similar stories today, we can reasonably suppose that they hoarded information about opportunities, shared it chiefly with closely connected others, excluded strangers, and maintained contact with their place of origin through letters, remittances, and occasional visits. Thus their interactions with others created durable categorical inequality.

Consider parallels with steelmaking Johnstown, Pennsylvania. In *For Bread with Butter* (1985) and *Insecure Prosperity* (1996), sociologist-historian Ewa Morawska has chronicled the experiences of various East Central European groups and of East European Jews between 1890 and World War II. Americans of Western European origin dominated Johnstown's industry, real estate, and finance. But immigrants from Poland, Ukraine, Byelorussia, Slovakia, Hungary, and adjacent regions constituted the city's rank and file. Typically beginning as general labor, East European Gentiles gravitated toward well-marked niches in manufacturing. Johnstown's Jews, in contrast, moved overwhelmingly into retail trade. In both cases, chain migration prevailed. To some extent the two populations re-created their European relations, with frequently multilingual Jews providing merchandise, credit, and literate services for their Slavic and Hungarian neighbors. While both groups were integrating into a system of categorical inequality with American capitalists occupying dominant positions, Jews and Gentiles hoarded opportunities in complementary Johnstown niches.

Similarly, in Ciudad Juárez, Mexico, women find work in low-wage *maquiladoras* chiefly through networks connecting them with women already on the job. When researcher María Patricia Fernández-Kelly looked for work in a *maquiladora* by scanning newspaper advertisements, she followed the exceptional path:

> By using newspapers as a source of information for jobs available, I was departing from the common strategy of potential workers in that environment. As my own research would show, the majority of these workers avail themselves of information by word of mouth. They are part of informal networks which include relatives, friends and an occasional acquaintance in the personnel management sector. Most potential workers believe that a personal recommendation from someone already employed at a maquiladora can ease their difficult path.
>
> This belief is well founded. At many plants, managers prefer to hire applicants by direct recommendation of employees who have proven to be dependable and hard-working. For example, at Electro Componentes de Mexico, the subsidiary of General Electric and one of the most stable maquiladoras in Juárez, it is established policy not to hire "outsiders." Only those who are introduced personally to the manager are considered to fill up vacancies. (Fernández-Kelly 1983, 110)

Members of those same networks—often networks of chain migration from rural regions—also supplied child care, lodging, and social support to women workers. Without enormous effectiveness, networks sustained themselves by hoarding access to low-wage employment in American-owned manufacturing plants.

NETWORKS AND OPPORTUNITY HOARDING

Mamaroneck Italians' concentration in landscape gardening excludes other potential workers from the business, but it hardly qualifies as exploitation; neither secure control of a productive resource, incorporation of effort by excluded parties, nor appropriation of a substantial surplus marks the position of these modest people. Rather, the term "opportunity hoarding" describes their generally successful strategy. By sequestering technical knowledge, ties to wealthy households and institutions, reputations for good work, and access to capital within an ethnically defined network, they have fashioned a classic immigrant niche. Similarly, Johnstown's Jews lodged themselves in retail trade without creating a system of exploitation.

In neither Mamaroneck, Johnstown, nor Ciudad Juárez, indeed, do we witness the strong complementarity that often develops between exploitation and opportunity hoarding. It occurs when the effort of a favored minority provides a resource-owning elite with the means to extract surplus from an essential but otherwise unavailable larger population. South Africa showed us extensive complementarity between exploitation by Europeans and opportunity hoarding by collaborating members of subordinate racial categories. In Mamaroneck, Johnstown, and Juárez, we observe opportunity hoarding in a relatively pure, independent form, with crucial resources largely created by the efforts of the hoarding community.

What distinguishes opportunity hoarding from other organizations of effort? If members of a network acquire access to a resource that is valuable, renewable, subject to monopoly, supportive of network activities, and enhanced by the network's modus operandi, network members regularly hoard access to the resource, creating beliefs and practices that sustain their control. If that network is categorically bounded, opportunity hoarding thereby contributes to the creation and maintenance of categorical inequality.

Opportunity hoarding often rests on ethnic categories, members of which reinforce their control over hoarded resources by means of their power to include or exclude other members with respect to language, kinship, courtship, marriage, housing, sociability, religion, ceremonial life, credit, and political patronage. Far-ranging trade diasporas of Gujaratis, Cantonese, Jews, Armenians, Lebanese, and other ethnically homogeneous networks constitute extreme forms of a very general phenomenon.

In all these instances, ethnicity and/or religion supplies the categorical basis of opportunity hoarding. In other circumstances, however, selective migration streams single out community of origin or lineage as the salient categorical principle. Race, gender, schooling, professional training, political affiliation, and sexual preference all, at times, constitute the networks and categorical distinctions on which opportunity hoarding builds.

How? Opportunity hoarding in general brings together these elements:

- A distinctive network
- Valuable resources that are renewable, subject to monopoly, supportive of network activities, and enhanced by the network's modus operandi
- Sequestering of those resources by network members
- Creation of beliefs and practices that sustain network control of the resources

Such a network may take a great variety of forms—large or small, hierarchical or egalitarian, organizational or otherwise—but its monopolizing work depends on explicit monitoring and sanctioning procedures that discourage defection, on the presence of many interdependent triads, or both.

We can make a rough distinction between forms of opportunity hoarding that attach their participants directly to an exploiting organization and those that bear only contingent or indirect relations to exploitation. The creation of immigrant niches within manufacturing firms falls emphatically into the first set, regardless of the extent to which the immigrants themselves benefit or suffer from exploitation. A firm or an alliance of firms that establishes monopoly or oligopoly over production and sale of a given commodity simultaneously practices exploitation within firm boundaries and opportunity hoarding with respect to all other potential producers and sellers.

More contingent and indirect (albeit powerful) relations of opportunity hoarding to exploitation stem from inheritance within households, kin groups, and ethnic categories. Under capitalism, inequality in regard to inherited wealth generally exceeds inequality in regard to monetary income, since the wealthy customarily draw important returns from their wealth in nonmonetary forms and hoard some portion for transmission to heirs. As income inequality has sharpened in the United States during the past two decades, wealth has become even more unequally distributed (Oliver and Shapiro 1997; Wolff 1995). Clever lawyers and a favorable tax regime have made it easy for America's wealthy to retain their property from generation to generation (Drew and Johnston 1996). In this case, beliefs in wealth as property, in the inviolability of property rights, and in the priority of interpersonal ties based on birth and marriage all reinforce the centrality of inheritance as a mode of opportunity hoarding.

Other forms of opportunity hoarding lie between immigrant niches and inheritance. Family farms, family-run stores, and other types of small-scale enterprise often operate with little or no directly exploited labor, but nevertheless gain from the "rents" (to take the economist's term) provided by exclusive use of a site, stock, and clientele (Sørensen 1996). Similarly, members of exclusive crafts such as nineteenth-century glassblowing, printing, and silversmithing characteristically hoarded opportunities by maintaining collective control over production and sale of their commodities without employing more than a few exploited helpers and apprentices. All of these arrangements, and more, gain advantages from combining a distinctive network, a set of valuable resources, and sequestration of the resources as well as beliefs and practices sustaining network control of the resources.

Professions, for example, are organizations among practitioners of some common art who control the licensing of all practitioners of that art within their shared territory; exclude unorthodox, unworthy, unlicensed persons from practicing; and thus secure a monopoly over dispensation of the art's products to nonmembers. Professions typically succeed in establishing their monopolies by enlisting state support for licensing, exclusion, and fee-setting in return for a measure of collective responsibility and self-policing. They typically set up their own institutions for recruitment, training, initiation, and discipline of new members. They engage in quintessential opportunity hoarding without necessarily drawing on exploitation as well. Professions do, however, vary greatly in the extent to which they couple opportunity hoarding with exploitation. Within American health care, for example, physicians who ran hospitals and clinics long combined the two. Nurses, pharmacists, midwives, and members of other such subordinated health professions, in contrast, had to settle mainly for opportunity hoarding.

In capitalist countries, dentists, lawyers, and physicians commonly operate very effective monopolies, while professionally organized architects, scientists, social workers, pharmacists, accountants, nurses, midwives, priests, and engineers all have more trouble excluding competitors from their terrains. But all do what they can to maintain categorical barriers between themselves and nonprofessionals. In France, veterinarians were spectacularly successful at adopting the medical model of practice, organization, ideology, and licensing during the nineteenth century. They followed the classic trajectory of professionalization: establishing schools based on medical science, acquiring recognition from public authorities as experts on such matters as the inspection of meat, excluding rivals such as blacksmiths and butchers from their domains, and finally creating a state-backed monopoly of animal medical practice for graduates of their three official schools (Hubscher 1996). Nevertheless, French veterinarians generally operated on too small a scale to make significant gains from exploitation; they acquired their prestige, power, and income from opportunity hoarding.

Organizationally, licensed trades such as hairdressing typically resemble professions. On the grounds of protecting public health against dangerous practices, they acquire state protection of a monopoly over services in return for subjection to oversight by a state agency. Often they strengthen that position by establishing their own schools and insisting that licensed practitioners pass through those schools successfully. Take the case of cosmetologists, who in most American states must acquire licenses to administer beauty treatments, including hair care. In New York State, cosmetologists have come into competition with braiders, who generally learn how to create African-inspired hairstyles from friends and relatives. In order to sell their services legally, New York's braiders must receive cosmetology licenses:

"If we have to take a minimum of 1,200 curriculum hours and pay up to $10,000 to learn our trade, why shouldn't braiders?" said Barbara G., a black cosmetologist who asked that her full name not be used, expressing concern that her comments might create tension in the mid-town Manhattan salon where she works alongside braiders. (Williams 1997, 4)

Advocates for braiders argue that little of the cosmetology curriculum deals with braiding, that the knowledge involved is distinctive, and that the present arrangement drives braiders into the underground economy. Given the character of opportunity hoarding, New York's braiders will most likely become yet another licensed trade, authorized to operate in a niche just adjacent to those of hairdressers, barbers, and cosmetologists.

Among both professionals and other opportunity hoarders, the valuable resources in question take a wide variety of forms: not only the shared knowledge and access to clients that constitute the major hoarded resources for professions but also ore deposits among miners, reliable suppliers among import-export merchants, well-cultivated friendships among talent scouts, access to government property and officials among Russian ex-apparatchik entrepreneurs, able graduate students among academic departments. Sequestered knowledge that bestows advantages, furthermore, sometimes resides in scripts, local knowledge, and interpersonal ties that members of a network carry over from other experiences, as in the leverage enjoyed by multilingual brokers at the frontiers of distinct but interdependent monolingual populations.

In general, resources that lend themselves well to opportunity hoarding have the characteristics enumerated earlier: they are renewable, subject to monopoly, supportive of network activities, and enhanced by the network's modus operandi. These characteristics apply, to be sure, within specifiable limits; a successful opportunity-hoarding drug ring need only control the supply of its narcotics within its own turf and fight out precise divisions of territory with neighboring rings. A university department that hired all the world's experts in a given specialty might well find outside demand for its expertise declining rather than increasing as a well-behaved monopoly would lead one to expect, since in many academic fields demand depends on having well-placed graduates, clients, and collaborators elsewhere. The value of resources depends on their potential uses outside the circle of hoarders.

Sequestering of resources sometimes takes the form of governmental authorization and licensing favored by organized professions. It often centers on the selective transmission of lore to members of an in-group. But it can also rest chiefly on the withholding of crucial information such as the location of a precious commodity, the formula for an elixir, the means of repairing a complex machine, the turns of hand that virtuoso violinists, surgeons, and potters teach their students and colleagues. Although craft labor markets of printers and glassblowers certainly relied on measures of training and exclusion resembling those of professions, they operated effectively only so long as craft workers themselves knew much more about the manufacturing of the product than their bosses did; beyond that point, bosses generally found less skilled substitutes for stubborn, expensive crafts workers (Jackson 1984; Montgomery 1987; Scott 1974).

Network, valuable resources, and sequestering combine into effective opportunity hoarding when together they yield advantages in relations with actors outside the network. Such advantages do not necessarily depend on or produce categorical inequality. By and large, commercially successful painters hoard access to galleries, critics, and purchasers without drawing sharp lines between themselves and the hoi polloi of painting. Nevertheless, interior categories and their matching with exterior categories lower the cost of hoarding. Within hospitals, the actual work of physicians and nurses overlaps considerably, but the sharp professional line between them reinforces the advantage conferred on physicians by their formal rights to prescribe drugs and courses of treatment. The common matching of that line with gender, ethnic, and class distinctions lowers its enforcement cost. In such circumstances, opportunity hoarding relies on and produces categorical inequality.

Intersection between opportunity hoarding within an organization and categorically segregated sources of supply for new recruits to the relevant network provides a mutually reinforcing system of exceptional power and generality. We discover it recurrently in professional training, residential segregation, aristocratic or caste recruitment of military officers, and a variety of other settings. But in today's capitalist world many of the most dramatic instances take the form of immigrant niches. Hence my concentration here on that very special form of opportunity hoarding.

The admirable literature on immigrant niches and entrepreneurship to which Ivan Light, Roger Waldinger, Alejandro Portes, and their co-workers have made major contributions abounds with evidence concerning the organizational forms and processes involved in opportunity hoarding. Waldinger's study of New York, for example, documents the centrality and persistence of work niches, both job-centered and entre-preneurial, in the varied experiences of major ethnic and racial catego-ries since 1940 (Waldinger 1996; see also Model 1985, 1992, 1996; Wat-kins-Owens 1996). As my own story about Italians in Mamaroneck suggested, even through momentous changes in the overall economy, the migration and employment histories of previous generations cast long shadows over the fates of today's category members.

Waldinger makes many of the same observations I have offered on the basis of his and other people's research: ethnic-racial niches form within limits set by the preferences of owners and established workers, but once established these niches easily reproduce themselves because of their reliance on categorically segregated networks for a wide variety of activities on and off the job. Through long struggles, native black residents of New York formed effective niches in segments of public employment and health care; but in recent decades they have repeatedly been beaten into the expanding areas of private-sector and entrepre-neurial work by immigrant streams whose members formed niches, supplying compliant, low-wage workers and/or gaining access to ethni-cally pooled capital. Waldinger also stresses a consequence I have un-derstated so far:

> Frequent interaction in a highly concentrated niche promotes a sense of group identity. Participation in the niche, one of the salient traits that group members share, helps define who they are. Thus, greater atten-tion is paid to the boundaries that define the niche, and the characteris-tics of those who can and cannot cross those boundaries. The niche, in other words, identifies an "us" and a "them." (Waldinger 1996, 304).

He might have added that it also serves to define the limits of solidarity, trust, and mutual aid. To the extent that collaboration within a niche enhances the quality or efficiency of work, and that denial of collaboration accordingly degrades work performance, an effective niche reinforces its survival by delivering superior results to customers and other segments of the same organizations.

Waldinger takes a deeply historicist view, stressing path-dependency, arguing that each category's coping strategies and relations to opportunities at a given time significantly constrain its available strategies and opportunities in the next round. In that regard, he conforms to recent trends in the history and sociology of American immigration (Morawska 1990, 1994; Portes 1995). A historicist view helps make sense of the connections between migration and durable forms of inequality, especially those forms that people organize as ethnicity—as structured differences according to imputed national or racial origin. It shows the formation of opportunity hoarding not as an instantaneous rational decision but as a struggle-ridden and error-ridden process sometimes extending over a generation.

For a long time, the standard vision of the immigrant portrayed someone who leaves the old country's security, passes through a period of risk and turmoil, and then establishes a definitive equilibrium in the new country. If the immigrant comes to a great city such as New York or Los Angeles, most people find this vision all the easier to accept. Yet actual immigration experiences rarely approximate the classic model. Instead we find people moving back and forth over long distances; relying heavily on colleagues, kin, and Landsmänner as they make their way; maintaining their preexisting personal networks at considerable expense; and generally refusing to become disorganized in the ways that classic theories predict. By now, a whole generation of researchers has documented the dense social ties that commonly accompany long-distance migration and subsequent problem solving.

The old theories required active suppression of knowledge that most of us already have—for many of our own family histories, thoughtfully considered, generally belie all these antitheses of immobility and mobility, order and disorder, contingency and constraint. Our individual and family histories vibrate with movement, with fortuitous connections, with chance meetings, with contingencies having very serious consequences over long periods of time. Yet, seen in perspective, they also embody striking regularities.

Let me illustrate with a personal example. I would not exist—that is, my parents would almost certainly never have met—except for the last-minute decision of my grandfather, a Welsh miner in a time of the mines' decline, not to take an available mining job in South Africa but instead to accept the invitation of his brother, a locomotive driver who had emigrated fifteen years earlier, to join him and his family near Chicago and look for work there. (A disputed family tradition says Uncle Chris, the Chicago brother, sent a telegram skillfully mediating between threat and dire prediction: "If you go to South Africa," he is supposed to have cabled, "I'll never speak to you again.") My grandfather ended up maintaining the machines of an Ovaltine factory in Villa Park, Illinois. His daughters, including my mother, met and married men who lived around Chicago, bore and raised children in the Chicago region. They constructed a tight kinship group consisting chiefly of their family's Chicago branch but ramifying back to Wales and England. Later, I worked summers in the Ovaltine factory to earn money for college . . . and my family often drank Ovaltine.

In one perspective, nothing could be more contingent and individual—a last-minute change of mind about a risky job seals the destiny of an entire family, not to mention their descendants. My grandfather's whim, however, did not cause his brother to leave for Chicago in 1908 or the Rhondda Valley's mines to falter in the 1920s. (Uncle Chris, furthermore, had joined their half-brother Sam, who even earlier had migrated to Chicago to work in retail trade.) My grandfather's apparently arbitrary choice took place within strong limits set by previous actions— his and other people's—and had significant effects on all his later choices. Few moments in most lives pose such fateful alternatives as Hugh Stott's 1925 decision to join his brother in Chicago, but much of long-distance migration brings together similar combinations of contingency and constraint.

CHAIN MIGRATION

Although no one involved at the time would have recognized the term, my mother's family was involved in a system of chain migration. We have already encountered the phenomenon among Italian migrants to Mamaroneck. *Chain migration* is the arrangement in which numerous people leave one well-defined origin serially for another well-defined destination by relying on people from the same origin for aid, information, and encouragement; most chain migrations involve considerable return of migrants to their place of origin.

Many chain migrations begin as *circular* migrations: seasonal, annual, or longer-cycle movement of agricultural workers, craftspersons, or petty merchants from a base to some other well-defined place where temporary work awaits them. Migration from Roccasecca to Mamaroneck probably started with just such circuits of stonecutters. In my mother's family story, the chain was short: from Sam Stott to Chris Stott to Hugh Stott and perhaps a dozen cousins, children, and siblings. Yet it came recognizably from the same sort of process that produces chains spanning multiple generations.

The essence of chain migration was, and is, the existence of continuing contacts between a specific community of origin and a specific community of destination—Roccasecca and Mamaroneck, a Welsh mining village and Chicago, a Polish *shtetl* and Johnstown. It involves frequent moves of persons between the two communities, with help and encouragement from persons at both ends. Even including the forced migration of Africans (who arrived literally, not figuratively, in chains), this sort of continuously connected migration system accounts for the great bulk of immigration to the Americas during the past five centuries. That fact in itself should alert us to the likelihood that what happened to migrants at one point in time, and how they organized their migration, significantly affected the fate of both their descendants and later migrants.

We could stop there. By now we have plenty of evidence showing that the presence or absence of prior contacts has a strong effect on the paths and consequences of long-distance migration. In Toronto, Grace Anderson showed twenty years ago that the initial ties of very similar

Portuguese immigrants to the metropolitan labor market significantly influenced the kinds of jobs with which they began, which in turn made a large difference to their relative success later on; ability and ambition paled in the light of prior social ties. In New York, Suzanne Model has shown that among Jews, Italians, and blacks, employment by members of the same ethnic category, on the average, contributed significantly to better jobs and higher incomes (Model 1985). Model's later work supports those findings with three important qualifications: (1) expanding niches promote such advantages more than fixed or declining niches; (2) as an ethnically segregated migration network saturates a niche, advantages to latecomers decline or even disappear; (3) niche advantages depend on the presence of similarly qualified but excluded populations of potential workers. Roger Waldinger's findings generally confirm Model's conclusion. The mutual employment in question grows up especially as a consequence of collectively organized migration and constitutes a striking case of opportunity hoarding.

Even in the case of solitary migration, migrants commonly drew information, assistance, and financial aid from network members who had already gone to America. The frequency of remittances from emigrants to homefolks and of steamship tickets prepaid by people at the American destination reveals the extent of that mutual aid. After a New Jersey lecture in which I made the same point, however, a second-generation Italian came up to me in indignation, objecting that "mutual aid" hardly described the situation in which relatives in Newark sent his father a steamship ticket, only to reveal on his arrival in America that he would have to work off the passage in their bakery at starvation wages. The day he finished repaying, the father quit his job, left town, and severed connections with his rapacious cousins.

Let no one think, then, that the processes I am describing exclude exploitation, conflict, or antipathy. The tying together of people by mutual aid and obligation often breeds rancor as well as respect. Many immigrants gritted their teeth until they had enough money to go back to their communities of origin or rush off to another destination within their networks. Among streams connecting Mediterranean regions with North America, typically half or more of the immigrants returned home.

The high proportion of Mediterranean migrants who returned after trying their hand in America, or who swung back and forth between the two continents as employment opportunities dictated, superficially a sign of inefficiency in the migration system, actually testifies to the quick, effective flow of information about affairs at both ends of the many chains from the Mediterranean to North America.

In 1906, 435,000 people left Italy for the Americas, but a full 158,000 returned, and many "pendulated" between continents for some time (Harney 1984, 74; see also Harney 1985). Although that sort of evidence tells us nothing about how organized or disorganized the migrants were, it contradicts any notion of the desperate cutting of ties to the old country. From what else we know about Italian migration, it depended heavily on spectacularly long chains between very specific origins and destinations within the continents. *Padroni,* or labor contractors, who recruited Italian workers for construction or agriculture in distant America did exist, but they profited from or emerged out of existing migration chains. In any case, they accounted for only a small minority of Italian immigrants.

For decades, American factories did much of their work through subcontracting, farming out the production of major goods to job bosses or independent entrepreneurs who actually hired their own labor forces and delivered the goods for a price agreed upon in advance. Subcontracting articulates beautifully with chain migration, since the *padrone* has access to an indefinite supply of willing workers and can exercise great control over the fate—and hence over the job performance—of those workers. Where an industry's recruitment and supply networks connect with a migration chain and gain exclusive access to the relevant jobs, an ethnically segregated occupational monopoly appears. Since subcontracting is again actually increasing, as what David Harvey calls "flexible capital accumulation" extends in capitalist countries, we can reasonably predict an increase in the ethnic segregation of work in cities like Chicago, where chain migration still prevails (Harvey 1989, 141–172). Again, opportunity hoarding thrives.

Ethnic entrepreneurship often forms through a very similar process. When I lived in Toronto during the 1960s, my next-door neighbors were

Macedonians. A steady stream of visitors from Macedonia came through their house. One day my neighbor explained, in roughly these terms: "We have short-order restaurants [the day of "fast food" had not yet arrived], and when we need someone to work in one of them, we send back home for a young man. He cleans up and starts cooking as he learns English, then graduates to running the counter. When he's saved up some money and gotten pretty good in English, we try to set him up in his own restaurant. Then he hires newcomers." At that point, as my neighbor didn't say, the new restaurant owner owed plenty of money to his relatives and had to rely on them for help in recruiting his work force; these ties reforged the migration chain. In that way, retail trades often become semi-monopolies of one national group or another—Indian newsstands or Korean groceries in New York, Macedonian short-order restaurants or Italian barbershops in Toronto.

Opportunity hoarding obviously also takes place far outside of immigrant niches. It operates, for example, in the hearts of capitalist firms. Firms combine categories with the special sorts of coercion-containing networks that institutional economists call hierarchies. Firms do a significant part of their organizational work through the creation and operation of interior categories: divisions, departments, ranks, and more. They frequently match those interior categories with exterior categories. With Veblenian irony, for example, Arthur Stinchcombe has identified a relevant puzzle:

> The fundamental generalization about entry into craft and professional jobs (and, as we have argued above, into higher management and top staff jobs in bureaucratic organizations) is *the more democratic control over recruitment into a set of jobs is*—that is, the more entry and training are controlled by workers in that set of jobs—*the fewer women, blacks, Mexican-Americans, or immigrant workers are employed in the group.* (Stinchcombe 1990a, 261)

While we do not usually speak of the problem in terms of democracy, Stinchcombe has it right: given an interior categorization of desirable jobs that afford their occupants considerable collective control over entry, training, tenure, advancement, and separation, participants regularly match interior with exterior categories. They do so because powerful parties to the arrangement—both managers and workers—make substantial organizational gains from the arrangement and because recruitment occurs chiefly through the categorically segregated networks that participants bring to the firm. They do so because in these circumstances exploitation and opportunity hoarding complement each other.

In recent years, a combination of exploitation and opportunity hoarding has contributed to the increasingly perilous position of black men within U.S. labor markets. The relative advance of black women and of better-educated black men in recent decades makes across-the-board racial discrimination a less plausible explanation of black disadvantage. In the light of narrowing black/white educational gaps, furthermore, the mismatch of young black males' skills with available jobs cannot account for their rising unemployment (Grant, Oliver, and James 1996; Wilson 1996a, 1996b). The evaporation of jobs from predominantly black big-city areas and the incarceration of many young black males have surely reduced job prospects for less-educated black men. But something is happening in recruitment to jobs that young black males could, in principle, fill. Estimating (rightly or wrongly) that black job applicants will contribute less to value added than their competitors or will even disrupt production, employers have avoided hiring them.

Philip Moss and Chris Tilly interviewed employment officers in four industries—auto parts manufacturing, retail clothing stores, insurance companies, and the public sector—in the Los Angeles and Detroit metropolitan areas. Interviewees indicate that such firms shy away from hiring young black males not because they lack "hard" skills of literacy and numeracy but because the jobs in question call for "soft" skills:

> We identify two clusters of soft skills that are important to employers in our interviews. The first, *interaction,* regards ability to interact with customers and co-workers, including friendliness, teamwork, ability to fit in, spoken communication skills, and appearance and attire. A second cluster we call *motivation* encompasses characteristics such as enthusiasm, positive work attitude, commitment, dependability, and willingness to learn. (Moss and Tilly 1995a, 361)

Although public-sector employers do regularly require some minimum of education, in general these employment officers stress soft skills more heavily than hard ones. The greater the contact with the public entailed by the job, the more they stress soft skills. The more they stress soft skills, the more often they rely on screening interviews instead of references from existing employees. Moss and Tilly identify two somewhat different modes of recruiting compatible, effective employees: co-optation by existing workers, where worker-to-worker cooperation is central to production (e.g., in auto parts); and screening for personal style, where interaction with superiors and the public is crucial (e.g., in retail sales). Both of them operate categorically, but the first provides more scope for opportunity hoarding by current employees.

In such circumstances, categorical inequality—in this case, black/white inequality in employment—emerges from multiple categorically differentiated experiences. First, segregated housing, schooling, and social life produce distinctive personal styles that promote mutual fear and misunderstanding. Second, white and black job-finding networks remain segregated from each other. Third, both employers and prospective fellow workers screen potential employees on personal style in some combination of personal predilection and predictions about likely performance on the job. All three lend themselves to opportunity hoarding on the part of white workers. In general, black workers have greater opportunities for employment and advancement in large organizations, especially public-sector organizations (Grant, Oliver, and James 1996). That is probably so because large organizations afford less scope to opportunity hoarding: racial inequality becomes more visible on the large scale, governments find it easier (or more politically expedient) to intervene on behalf of affirmative-action laws, civil rights groups have larger incentives and more effective means of exerting pressure directly or via government, and, under pressure, large organizations find it easier to reorganize work in ways that favor integration.

Even in large organizations, nevertheless, opportunity hoarding often couples with exploitation in one of two ways. Either exploiters directly enlist an opportunity-hoarding minority in the exclusion of others from full value added or exploiters and opportunity hoarders attach themselves to adjacent, complementary resources. In the first case, well-rewarded male machinists collaborate in relegating women to lower-paid, sex-segregated production work. In the second case, networks of Indian immigrants acquire exclusive rights to operate lucrative newsstands in and near major business buildings. When either complementarity appears, it reinforces the categorical inequalities in opportunities, capacities, and rewards on which it builds. Thus the two major mechanisms of categorical inequality—exploitation and opportunity hoarding—interlock over a wide range of social processes.

In British nutritional differences, South African apartheid, American manufacturing firms, chain migrants' small enterprises, and many more organizational settings, then, we discover similar self-reproducing patterns of categorical inequality. While each set of categories carries its own historical baggage, recurrent organizational problems lead to parallel structural solutions. Over and over again, exploitation by powerful people and opportunity hoarding by less powerful people articulate to favor the establishment of unequally rewarded categories, while emulation and adaptation fix such categories in place. The creation of interior categories and the matching of interior with exterior categories build durable inequality into organizations and attach them to networks—internal and external—in ways that favor their reproduction, even their transmission to new members of the categories.

6 Emulation, Adaptation, and Inequality

Semezdin Mehmedinovic, a refugee writer from Bosnia, recounts the start of civil war in that tortured land:

> The war started on Sunday. I know this because we always played soccer at Skendirija on Sunday. A guy from my team didn't show up that night but no one paid much attention to it. After the game we went out, as always, for a beer. When it came time for the last trolley, I headed home. It happened to be a short ride because a bunch of guys with stockings over their heads and Kalashnikovs aimed at us stopped the trolley. As I got out, I took a look at this crew and recognized the guy from my soccer team who hadn't shown up. I was so taken by surprise that I had to repeat my question twice: "Sljuka, is that you? Sljuka, is that you?" Embarrassed, he kept quiet behind his stocking. (Mehmedinovic 1996, 29)

Stojan Sljuka was a minor terrorist, but he worked with Radovan Karadzic, the psychiatrist, children's poet, and founder of the Bosnian Green

party who became the pitiless military leader and would-be ruler of a
Serbian Bosnia. Serbian nationalism within Bosnia awarded Sljuka and
Karadzic new political identities. But international promotion of nationalism as a legitimate basis for political action gave them their opportunities to kill.

The Bosnian civil war wrote yet another bloody act in a European
drama two centuries old: the drama of nationalism. As a doctrine, nationalism asserts a series of propositions that had little currency two
hundred years ago but that came to seem like political common sense
during the nineteenth century:

- The whole world's population divides into nations, each of which
  shares a common origin, culture, and sense of destiny.
- Each nation deserves its own state.
- Each state has the right to create its own nation.
- Given a nation's existence, its members have strong obligations to
  serve it and the state that embodies it. Those obligations override
  claims of religion, family, and self-interest.

As claims about how the world works, of course, each of these propositions encounters enormous empirical and normative objections (Anderson 1991; Armstrong 1982; Bjørn, Grant, and Stringer 1994a, 1994b; Brubaker 1996; Comaroff 1991; Fullbrook 1993; Graubard 1993; Greenfeld
1992, 1996; Haas 1986; Hobsbawm 1990, 1994; Jenson 1993; Lerner 1991;
Motyl 1992a, 1992b; Noiriel 1991, 1993; Østergard 1991, 1992; Shell 1993;
Smith 1990; Topalov 1991). But as justifications for social action, they all
gained considerable currency in the Western world after 1789 and then
acquired worldwide scope with the dismantling of empires.

To be more precise and to focus on Europe, nationalist doctrines and
practices took a zigzag course from 1492 to our own time. From 1492
to 1648, schematically, we witness a period in which Western and Central European powers struggled over the alignment between religion
and state power, with outcomes varying: the establishment of state-
dominated Protestant churches in Scandinavia, England, and parts of
Germany; the uneasy and unequal coexistence of multiple religions in

Switzerland and the Dutch republic; the expulsion and forced conversion of Jews and Muslims in Iberia; and the decreasing toleration of a chartered Protestant minority in a France that kept its distance from the pope.

From 1648 to the 1790s, the European state system maintained a rough alignment of official religion with state identity, but the papacy continued to lose secular power, even within nominally Catholic states. The French Revolution and the Napoleonic wars promoted the severing of religion from national identity, with nonreligious or even antireligious definitions of citizenship coming to predominate. It is as if rulers discovered that religion usually encouraged international ties, which in turn subverted their programs of national hegemony. Religion bedded uncomfortably with nationalism.

Although we rarely think of it in these terms, nationalism provides a type case of categorical inequality. It asserts and creates paired and unequal categories, either (a) rival aspirants to nationhood or (b) members of the authentic nation versus others. It embodies claims to prior control over a state, hence to the exclusion of others from that priority. It authorizes agents of the nation to subordinate, segregate, stigmatize, expel, or even exterminate others in the nation's name. In such extreme cases as Napoleonic, Boer, Russian, and Serbian nationalisms, it becomes a warrant for military conquest. When successfully pursued, nationalism commands the support of outsiders in establishing exclusive control over a distinct territory and resources; it thereby solves the organizational problem of acquiring and sustaining political power at national and international scales.

Nationalism creates inequality through exploitation, through opportunity hoarding, or through both at once. To the extent that members of a national category succeed in controlling a state to whose jurisdiction other nonnationals continue to submit (willingly or otherwise), dominant nationalists typically use the state apparatus both to reinforce the prestige of their shared identity and to turn state policy toward their own enrichment. Even though the Ottoman empire stood out among empires for the tolerance and autonomy it granted to recognized and compliant non-Muslim groups, its military and fiscal policies nevertheless concentrated power, wealth, and prestige in its Muslim elite. Other nationalist elites, such as the Tutsi throughout most of Rwanda's postcolonial history, use their control of state agencies, including the army, much more brutally to serve their own advantage, as the Tutsi did against their ethnic cousins the Hutu. Radovan Karadzic and his forces had much to gain from running Bosnia, or at least a Serbian state carved out of Bosnia, just as his ally Slobodan Milosevic gained—at least in the short run—from promoting Serbian nationalism within shattered Yugoslavia.

Nationalist opportunity hoarding also occurs with little or no exploitation along national lines. Opportunity hoarding plays its part when favored but subordinate categories, such as protected religious minorities, acquire rights within their own domains. To the extent that French-speakers in Canada, Tamil-speakers in Sri Lanka, or Basque-speakers in Spain achieve autonomous control of their own regions but not total independence, we can think of them as hoarding opportunities whose continued security depends on their host states' survival. Separatist and autonomist movements such as those of Basques in Spain and Chechens in Russia seek chiefly to control a regional niche and gain outside recognition of their right to do so. If successful, nationalists of this kind benefit from the reinforcement of their collective identities, hence of the social relations that constitute those identities. But they also receive returns from prior or even exclusive access to major resources within the territory. Arab elites of the smaller Middle Eastern oil states commonly profit from a combination of exploitation and opportunity hoarding: they distribute shares of oil revenues to ethnically qualified citizens while employing foreigners who can never become citizens to do a wide range of technical, commercial, administrative, and especially menial work. Precisely because control of a state yields benefits through various forms of exploitation and opportunity hoarding, nationalists who have not yet achieved their goals are pursuing not only pride but material and political interest.

Intense nationalism that mobilizes masses of people is nevertheless a historically recent phenomenon. To understand how it came to occupy such a large place in regional, national, and international politics, we must go beyond exploitation and opportunity hoarding to emulation and adaptation. Emulation—the copying of established, categorically based organizational models and/or the transplanting of existing social relations from one setting to another—lies at the heart of nationalism. Starting in Europe, the world's great powers created standard models of a nation, a state, and their conjunction in a nation-state. Parallel to exported organizational models of market economies, socialism, corporations, democracy, and other Western institutions, sponsors of highly visible models for nation-states promise important rewards to those who install them successfully. Nation building thus becomes a worldwide program.

Adaptation—the elaboration of daily routines such as mutual aid, political influence, courtship, and information gathering on the basis of categorically unequal structures—cements nationalism. Once a categorical distinction separating true members of a nation from others (inside or outside the nation's destined territory) sits firmly in place, people on either side of the boundary have little choice but to organize significant parts of their lives around that distinction. Opportunists who change affiliations or learn languages easily find that they can thrive by working at boundary maintenance.

Let us look more closely at emulation. The creation of standard criteria for "nationness" accomplishes these tasks:

- Encourages the emergence of recognizable public performances one might bill as "We Are a Nation" (for example, patriotic ceremonies and cultural festivals)

- Generates struggles among rival claimants to be or represent the relevant nation

- Promotes the establishment of licensing procedures and agencies such as the assembled parties at a general peace settlement or, eventually, the United Nations

- Couples the top-down programs we can dub "state-led nationalism" with the bottom-up programs we can label "state-seeking nationalism," rendering them mirror images and mortal enemies of each other

- Thereby introduces great uniformity in nationalist beliefs and practices over a highly diverse set of territories

All these processes install standard models of categorical inequality, their boundaries separating valid members of a nation from all others. Emulation exacerbates nationalism.

As political process, nationalism consists of making claims in the name of doctrines which declare both that the state equals the nation and that the nation equals the state. It takes two forms: *state-led* and *state-seeking*. State-led nationalism involves claims by agents of an existing state and their political allies, claims on presumed members of the nation identified with that state, and claims of priority over nonmembers of the nation who happen to occupy its destined territory.

State-led nationalism includes the creation and imposition of a dominant language, an origin myth, symbols, rituals, memberships, educational routines, and obligations by means of histories, literatures, curricula, museums, monuments, public assemblies, electoral procedures, state ceremonies, festivals, military service, and intervention in mass media. It entails the subordination or elimination of competing institutions and practices and, at the extreme, the exercise of control over wide ranges of resources and social life by state agents in the name of the nation's interest.

State-led nationalism has rarely irrupted into human history. Over the roughly ten thousand years that states have existed somewhere in the world, most rulers have settled for assigning priority within their domains to their own cultural definitions and readings of their own interests, and then coexisting more or less comfortably with composite subject populations having distinctive charters, cultures, and social routines. They have relied on opportunity hoarding by regional elites and cultural brokers to sustain systems of indirect rule. Although China and Japan stand as important partial exceptions, state-led nationalism became widely available, or even technically feasible, in most of the world's states only during the nineteenth and twentieth centuries (Ikegami 1995; Ikegami and Tilly 1994; Schram 1985, 1987; Shue 1988; Skinner 1964, 1985; Whitney 1970; Will 1994).

A fortiori for state-seeking nationalism, the mounting of demands for political autonomy and recognition by self-identified representatives of a coherent nation that lacks its own state. Historically, state-seeking nationalism has arisen chiefly in three circumstances:

- When agents of an empire have sought to impose military, fiscal, or (especially) religious obligations on a previously protected minority

- When adjacent powers have attempted to undermine an empire by supporting the rebellion of peripheral populations within the empire

- When rulers of expanding states have undertaken thoroughgoing state-led nationalism in the presence of well-connected populations possessing distinctive cultural, political, and economic institutions

The first two circumstances have rarely stimulated strong assertions of national identity, especially with claims to separate statehood. The third—the encounter of state-led nationalism with well-connected minorities—has frequently done so. As a result, state-seeking nationalism surged during the nineteenth and twentieth centuries.

International relations played a significant part in the development of both varieties of nationalism. Whether initiated by a state's agents or by an antistate minority, the claim to represent a nation could succeed only in relation to other powerholders, especially the rulers of major outside states. At least from the Treaty of Câteau-Cambrésis (1559), settlements of large-scale European wars featured the representation of multiple powers, a muster of those who had valid claims to rule, hence an implicit enumeration of those who *lacked* such claims.

By the time of the Treaties of Westphalia (1648), a ruler's validated claim to represent a nation, at least as connected by a common religious tradition, came to figure among the criteria for recognition by the community of nations. One reason France and Sweden were able to keep Holy Roman Emperor Ferdinand III from representing all his domains as a single power at Westphalia was, precisely, the religious diversity of those scattered territories. By the settlement of the Napoleonic wars, nevertheless, shared religion had lost much of its force as a national political credential, while the concert of nations presumed more than ever before to decide collectively which states enjoyed sovereignty and who was qualified to rule them.

Secularizing French Revolutionary and Napoleonic states set the pattern. They established satellites throughout Western Europe in the guise of liberating oppressed nations, not of establishing religious communities. As they pried away European segments of the predominantly Muslim Ottoman empire such as Greece and Serbia during the nineteenth century, European powers appealed to solidarity with captive nations rather than to the rights of Christendom. The nineteenth-century unifications of Germany and Italy likewise followed principles of secular nationalism. Within the shrunken Austro-Hungarian empire left by those unifications, linguistic divisions (including the hurried codification and imposition of ostensibly national languages in Hungary, Croatia, and elsewhere) predominated in both state-led and state-seeking nationalisms.

Myths of the nation-state thus came to prevail, first in Europe and then throughout the world. As a description of cultural realities, the nation-state remained mythical; after a century of state-led nationalism, even ostensibly homogeneous Norway and Sweden harbor significant Sami minorities, Finnish-speaking regions, and more than one distinguishable version of the national language, to say nothing of recent immigrants. Authorities of tiny Iceland keep struggling against "corruptions" of Icelandic national culture, while such countries as France, the United Kingdom, Belgium, and Switzerland devote important parts of their public effort to dealing with irrepressible diversity.

Yet the mythical idea of the nation-state represents a historical reality: relative to the bulk of human experience, since the year 1800 European states and their imitators elsewhere have accomplished an enormous homogenization of their citizens, thereby establishing an unprecedented justification for imposing a single group's definitions of origins, language, and social practices by means of public institutions. Never before the twentieth century did the world come so close to fencing its entire population into monolingual, monocultural blocks separated by state boundaries.

After World War I, a portentously named League of Nations (promoted by U.S. president Woodrow Wilson but finally boycotted by the United States) inherited some of the victorious powers' authority to certify nations. In World War II's aftermath, the great powers delegated even more certifying power to the United Nations, practically ceding the work of credentialing to that body once massive decolonization began during the 1960s. The more such external authorities insisted on popular elections with widespread suffrage as the means of selecting national regimes, ironically, the greater incentives they gave small, well-connected, geographically concentrated, and culturally bounded populations to demand independence or at least regional autonomy as an alternative to perpetual outnumbering by their larger neighbors; in a sense, democracy stimulated nationalism. Disintegration of the Soviet Union and Yugoslavia both provoked and then fed upon disruption of the credentialing apparatus, as quick if disputed recognition of some fragments (e.g., Slovenia, Croatia, and Ukraine) but not others (e.g., Chechenia and Republika Srpska) incited military action by those who stood to lose political power, livelihood, or even lives as a function of outsiders' confirming others as their rightful rulers.

Increasingly, then, the recognition of who constituted a valid nation entered the process of state formation. It became collective business for some concert of already recognized nation-states, however heterogeneous their own social composition. It also generated international agencies specializing in recognition and its denial and had serious consequences for the relative power of different factions within constituted states. In shattered Yugoslavia today, world powers are trying to contain armed conflict in the face of enormous incentives for conflicting programs of state-seeking nationalism.

As this account suggests, both state-led and state-seeking nationalisms share interesting properties with social movements. Like the claims that activists in social movements make on behalf of themselves and their ostensible constituencies, claims to nationhood always include a measure of mystification in respect to the relevant population's tenure, coherence, and solidarity with its self-identified spokespersons. They almost always incite counterclaims by rivals, enemies, and threatened powerholders.

Identities asserted by nationalists consist crucially of differences from and relations to others rather than actual internal solidarity. Their success rests as least as much on outside recognition as on internal consensus. Disciplined, stereotyped public demonstrations of "nationness," which typically require great internal coordination and repression, play a large part in that recognition. In this case, to be sure, the sheer ability to wield armed force effectively looms much larger than it does in most social movements.

Fredrik Barth provides a sharp summary of a situation bringing together nationalism, social movements, and party politics within the ostensibly homogeneous nation-state of Norway:

> In inner Finnmark in North Norway there lives a Lappish-speaking population, culturally diverse but categorically distinguished from Norwegians. They have tended to be economically impoverished and politically unorganized; through centuries of contact they have accepted cultural loans and accumulated a host of discrepant values. Shame over membership of an underprivileged minority is mingled with strong personal attachment to ethnic identity; a high evaluation of comfort, prosperity, and "the new times" coexists with fear and rejection of urban ways and commitment to traditional values.
>
> In this setting, there emerged after the war a labour politician whose platform was to bring the welfare state to the area. As an enterprise, this gave him profits in the form of political power, social recognition, and economic sustenance; to obtain these, his task was to organize the population and obtain their votes in local elections. The "welfare state" platform was well suited for this: schools, subsidies and loans for development, and other benefits, all highly valued by the local population, could be provided by the state once requests in the proper bureaucratic form were forthcoming. A picture of Finnmark as the underprivileged periphery of a nation state served as the entrepreneur's charter, both in relation to voters and to the center.
>
> But this charter threatened Lappish identity and other values equally held in the population. A contrary current can be noticed which became particularly pronounced in the very community where the same politician was active. Pan-Lappish meetings were held, respect for the Lappish language was demanded. A liberal politician, head of the school board and with an expertise on bilingualism in elementary schools (cultivated through studies of education in Wales, and on American Indian reservations), emerged as a rival political entrepreneur, basing his activity on a charter of respect for ethnic identity, pride in own culture, as well as material welfare. (Barth 1981, 58)

Open competition between the two politicians and their followers ensued, with each claiming to have the true interests of Lappish people at heart. Although neither competitor demanded independence for Finnmark, both played opportunity-hoarding cards within rhetorics of nationalism.

Social movements and nationalism display emulation and adaptation at work. In the case of nationalism, state-led processes created visible, prestigious, transferable models for exploitation and opportunity hoarding precisely as they organized international procedures for recognition of successful claimants to national identity. Managers of new states and leaders of independence movements could see that they would greatly improve their chances of control over surplus-extracting states by disciplining their followers in the myths and practices of unified origins, connections, conditions, and destinies as they denigrated or suppressed competing claims.

Throughout the world, administrative structures, constitutions, and declared commitments of regimes to development, stability, and democracy came to resemble each other far more than did the diversity of their populations, material conditions, and actual accomplishments. That emulation stamped in inequalities between adherents of official cultures and cultural minorities, between citizens and noncitizens, between patriots and dissidents to a degree previously unknown in human history. Because a credible performance at a national scale gained international subvention, support, and recognition, the easily imported national model triumphed.

Adaptation followed. Although state-led nationalism continued to generate intermittent state-seeking nationalism within established states, most citizens adjusted their routines to state requirements. After widespread resistance and painful struggle, most young European men came to accept as an unpleasant or even liberating necessity the military conscription that came with state-led nationalism. However reluctantly, most citizens adjusted to paying national taxes, to conducting their public business in national languages, to attending state-controlled schools, to answering state-appointed census takers, to ordering their affairs in conformity with state-standardized time, to applying for state-issued passports, to obeying and relying on national police, to singing national anthems, to honoring national heroes, to celebrating national holidays, to cursing declared national enemies.

As World War I began, even the great wave of antistate socialist internationalism that had mounted during the later nineteenth century spattered ineffectually against the breakwater of nationalism. In Europe and elsewhere, ordinary people came to take their state for granted, to demand a share of its services, to plan their lives on the assumption that it would remain in place. Their adaptation cemented state-enforced inequalities in place.

Emulation and adaptation, then, commonly reinforce each other; imported organizational forms induce participants to reorganize their personal routines, programs, and social relations, but those and other valued arrangements then come to depend on the organization's persistence in its present configuration. Indeed, emulation and adaptation overlap to the extent that imported organizational forms bring with them associated local knowledge and social relations. Organization of state-seeking nationalist movements draws on preexisting understandings and solidarities, so much so that participants and observers generally (if wrongly) suppose that the movements spring more or less automatically from shared understandings and solidarities. Staffing of ethnic restaurants with new immigrants from the same origins not only multiplies an organizational design but also incorporates previously existing connections among participants directly into restaurant operation. Competition among firms in an industry to hire graduates of a prestigious business school both imports the organizational solutions of that business school and brings in connected young people with their outside networks, distinctive styles, and supporting beliefs. Where importation includes well-defined asymmetrical categories, the convergence of emulation and adaptation reinforces and spreads categorical inequality.

INEQUALITY IN HEALTH CARE

Emulation and adaptation are very general mechanisms; they operate far outside the range of categorical inequality, fixing all sorts of institutional inventions in place. Because observers of nationalism have so rarely thought of it as a relational, categorical phenomenon resting on exploitation and opportunity hoarding, it will probably help to examine emulation and adaptation in a context where exploitation and opportunity hoarding are highly visible. We might return to South African race relations, gender at work, or immigrant niche formation, in all of which emulation and adaptation weigh heavily. But why not try to see whether the explanatory framework helps make sense of quite a different arena, American health care?

Exploitation and opportunity hoarding certainly marked the history of health care in the United States, as various groups of medical practitioners struggled for exclusive rights to provide specified health services but eventually worked out asymmetrical agreements to protect each other's turf. Both through state-licensed professionalization in general and through professionally defined divisions of labor within health care, the installation of categorical inequality solved the problem of guaranteeing medical specialists power and secure livelihoods.

The whole story of American medical professionalization makes a fascinating tale. Here, however, I want to emphasize how regularly an organizational innovation that emerged through local processes of exploitation and opportunity hoarding was then generalized through emulation and modified through local adaptations. Although no one could follow the official scripts of American health care without large inputs of local knowledge, health care organization became astonishingly uniform over a huge country. Then, in recent decades, new uniformities replaced the old: alterations in the general organization of health care both recast categorical divisions within the industry and threatened the advantages physicians had previously drawn from those divisions. Thus the history of health care provides insight into how systems of categorical inequality change, and the part played by emulation and adaptation in such changes.

From the late nineteenth century onward, first physicians, then nurses, and then other specialists struggled more c r less successfully to organize monopolies over training, hiring, dispensation of services, and fee-setting within their own state-protected zones. In so doing, they created unequal but sharply bounded categories. Abetted by state and professional regulatory agencies, doctors' offices, laboratories, hospitals, public health services, and other health care organizations took on standard forms through emulation. In the process, their members and clients fashioned life routines that presumed the organizations' continued existence.

It wasn't easy. With American independence, the country's political fragmentation undermined all legal supports for medical monopolies; during much of the nineteenth century, specialties, doctrines, and forms of practice competed in wonderful profusion. State and local governments generally resisted licensing and restricting medical treatment or the dispensation of drugs. Physicians and surgeons as a group enjoyed little prestige and less income. Their variety nevertheless resembled that of clergy in our own time: just as American clerics run the gamut from Episcopalian bishops to part-time street preachers, medical specialists ranged from Benjamin Rush, signer of the Declaration of Independence and personal physician of George Washington, to itinerant herb-sellers now forgotten by history.

The parallel with clergy extends to doctrine and practice. As Paul Starr describes the American medical situation:

> More than a qualified analogy links religious and medical sects; they often overlap. The Mormons favored Thomsonian medicine and the Millerites hydropathy. The Swedenborgians were inclined toward homeopathic medicine. And the Christian Scientists originated in concerns that were medical as well as religious. In America various religious sects still make active efforts to cure the sick, while the dominant churches are more or less reconciled to the claims of the medical profession and have abandoned healing as part of pastoral care. (Starr 1982, 95)

Various medical persuasions warred with each other for a century. Winners became "the profession" while losers remained "sects."

Intellectual and organizational fragmentation in medicine permitted medical schools to multiply and a great variety of practitioners to hang out their shingles. Elite physicians bemoaned their loss of standing, so much so that Dr. Benjamin Joy Jeffries titled his 1888 annual address to the Massachusetts Medical Society "Re-establishment of the Medical

Profession" (Vogel 1980, 59). The profession's reestablishment took a major political effort, but it occurred. The effort intertwined with importation from Europe of the new "scientific medicine" characterized by antisepsis, bacteriology, X-rays, and the coupling of clinical practice to research. Formation of a medical school at Johns Hopkins in 1893 signaled the new commitment to science and to consolidation of control over medical education. In 1901 the previously ineffectual American Medical Association reorganized with the announced intention to "foster scientific medicine and . . . make the medical profession a power in the social and political life of the republic" (Numbers 1985, 191). The AMA succeeded, with a vengeance.

Notice what happened: however benign their intentions and however great their accomplishments, organized physicians set up a system of exploitation that excluded others from medical practice, enlisted the labor of people who did not share in control over the means of health care, and reaped benefits of income, power, and prestige. Adjacent professions such as nursing hoarded opportunities in partial collaboration with the physicians but gained far fewer benefits. Organized medicine's capture of political influence facilitated the work of emulation by standardizing acceptable models and punishing the unorthodox. Doctors, nurses, other health care specialists, government officials, and patients all adapted, working out a series of understandings and routines that normalized and naturalized a dramatically new organization of health care. Relations among practitioners of health care thus shifted fundamentally.

Only during the early twentieth century did the "orthodox" majority of physicians join with their principal rivals, homeopaths and eclectics (as well as with university administrators, foundation executives, and hospital operators), in state-by-state alliances that licensed medical practice, excluded practitioners from outside their coalition as quacks, and limited the number of medical schools. A famous report on medical education by Abraham Flexner issued in 1910 accelerated and justified the dissolution of the proprietary medical schools that had multiplied with the rising demand for professional health services during the nineteenth century.

The American College of Surgeons (founded in 1910 as the Clinical Congress of Surgeons) established a rating system for hospitals that promoted scientific medicine and physician control. Modeling their organization on hotels rather than prisons or asylums, hospitals managers and their boards turned away from their previous orientation to charity for poor people and began active recruitment of well-off patients who had previously been receiving treatment at home. About the same time, neurologists began (less successfully than their internist cousins) to create "psychopathic hospitals" centered on identification, diagnosis, and treatment of the curable insane by the best scientific means (Rothman 1980, 324–335).

In a similar spirit, the American Medical Association, major drug manufacturers, and the U.S. government eventually worked out standards and agreements giving physicians substantial control over the dispensation of medicines, a set of moves that considerably diminished the autonomy, scope, and authority of American pharmacists. Doctors shouldered their way into the administrations of hospitals where trustees, lay administrators, and superintending nurses had previously held sway; within hospital hierarchies, men displaced women. While chiropractors, psychologists, optometrists, osteopaths, physical therapists, sellers of patent medicine, and a variety of other healers continued to attract patients, a relatively unitary medical establishment, headed by male M.D.'s, came to dominate public policy. The establishment organized opportunity hoarding on a grand and very profitable scale.

Nevertheless, physicians faced a dilemma: how to take advantage of the new facilities without becoming their captives. They repeatedly ran the risk of becoming opportunity hoarders within a system of exploitation from which stockholders, drug manufacturers, insurers, and hospital administrators drew the major benefits. For decades physicians maintained autonomy by means of a triple strategy:

First, the use of doctors in training (interns and residents) in the operation of hospitals; second, the encouragement of a kind of responsible professionalism among the higher ranks of subordinate health workers;

and third, the employment in these auxiliary roles of women who, though professionally trained, would not challenge the authority or economic position of the doctor. (Starr 1982, 220–221)

Mystiques of science and service made it easier for dominant doctors to build loyalty incentive systems integrating would-be professionals and their helpers into the ethos, if not the financial rewards, of the medical profession. Nursing, for example, developed in a dialectic with physicians' hegemony. American nursing professionalized through a system in which students learned their craft in hospital-based schools, thereby supplying the bulk of patients' personal care under intense time-discipline at very low cost; from only 3 in 1873, the number of nurses' training schools in hospitals increased to about 1,600 by World War I (Baer 1990, 462). Graduate nurses then went out to serve, contract by contract, in private homes or, more rarely, as public health employees or private-duty nurses for affluent hospital patients. On graduation, they moved from drive incentive systems to task systems. With the collaboration of a few supervising graduate nurses, hospital administrators thus drew on a cheap, compliant, and committed labor force.

In the course of these changes, physicians became prosperous, doctors turned much more frequently to surgery for internal ailments such as appendicitis and tonsilitis, medical practice capitalized, insurance companies began intervening directly in medical care and policy, and hospitals became central as loci of treatment for the wealthy as well as the poor. Midwives lost their place to medical doctors; having attended roughly half of all American births in 1900, by 1930 midwives accounted for only 15 percent of births and by 1973 for less than 1 percent (Litoff 1978, 27, 58, 114). By that time, a double transformation of childbirth was well under way: not only were physicians taking over the supervision of childbearing, but also women were increasingly giving birth in hospitals.

Until drug companies, equipment manufacturers, hospital administrators, insurers, and government officials developed a common interest in centering medical treatment on heavily capitalized and cost-effective hospitals, laboratories, and clinics rather than doctors' offices, the strategy worked extremely well. It gave American physicians high incomes, extensive autonomy, and formidable political power. Opportunity hoarding paid them large benefits for almost a century.

Even professionalized nurses and technicians, for the most part, found themselves relegated to earning fixed inferior salaries and working under doctors' authority. In few areas of work have official scripts and actual practices differed so much as in relations between physicians and nurses. Officially, physicians design and deliver health care. Practically, nurses do most of the delivery and much of the hour-to-hour design.

Throughout the twentieth century, nurses—not only graduates of hospital nursing schools and university programs but also practical nurses and nurses' aides—have actually provided the bulk of direct commercial health care. Nurses' work centers on ministration to sick bodies: feeding, cleaning, monitoring, administering medicine, managing complaints, offering moral support, and watching death. Despite the rise of paperwork and high-technology treatment, bodywork remains the center of nursing and a major determinant of patients' welfare.

For nurses, the great twentieth-century changes concerned not technology but conditions of employment. First, around World War II, began a major shift of graduate nurses from job-by-job contracts (so-called private duty, whether in homes or hospitals) to direct employment in hospitals. Before that time, nursing students had done the major part of general in-hospital nursing, just as doctors-in-training—interns and residents—did the bulk of in-hospital doctoring. Second, nursing differentiated into multiple levels and specialties, with graduate nurses serving as bosses and intermediaries among patients, physicians, subordinate workers, and hospital managements. Third, nursing work itself incorporated more and more machine-tending and record-keeping. The generality of nursing skills, thus the ability to replace one nurse with another, declined dramatically. The countermovement of relatively autonomous nurse-practitioners constitutes only a minor ripple against a fast-flowing stream.

At a very different scale from nationalism or Italian migration to Mamaroneck, the American health care industry exemplifies the emergence of categorical inequality through the interactive solution of organizational problems by the installation of categories in which multiple parties, however reluctantly, acquired stakes. Against a background of exploitation and opportunity hoarding, emulation and adaptation produced a standardized system with relatively minor local variants. Within health care, orthodox physicians initiated a classic process of professionalization, painfully enlisting state aid in defining their own category, establishing control over membership and practice within that category, creating regular ties to other professionalizing categories such as nurses and pharmacists, stigmatizing rival categories of practitioners, and—for a time—inscribing professional categories with other categorical distinctions of gender, race, and ethnic origin.

Health care has been notorious for connecting job categories with ethnic, racial, and gender categories outside its professional zones: among kitchen help, file clerks, practical nurses, attendants, and many more work force divisions. In those regards, it resembled most other American industries. But health care's professionalized sectors experienced ironies more dramatic than those appearing elsewhere in the industry:

- Physicians' and other professionals' reliance on state support for their monopolies ultimately made them vulnerable to state intervention on behalf of politically mobilized categories that were suffering exclusion from relevant professional training and appointments; under favorable political conditions, state licensing and monitoring gave women, blacks, and members of other excluded categories leverage in opening professional opportunities. Just as the inscription of racial categories into South African and U.S. law in the course of racial oppression before the 1950s later provided bases for black mobilization and redress, the very success of medical practitioners in writing their identities into law early in the twentieth century opened them to political manipulation during the late twentieth century.

- Capitalization, bureaucratization, and government intervention in the provision of health care undermined the economic and decision-making power of those professions that maintained organizational autonomy and fee-for-service prosperity by keeping their distance from big health care organizations. Beyond a certain point, the integration of medical services into capitalist institutions captured the physicians whose predecessors had spearheaded that integration and profited from it.

- The very embedding of categorical inequality (here separating certified members of professions from the uncertified) in adjacent social structure limits the subsequent collective advantages and dis-
  advantages of category members.

Opportunity hoarding almost always carries serious risks for the hoarders: that someone else will take over the opportunities they have so as-
siduously bundled together; that outside authorities on whom they rely
for protection will withdraw their patronage; that competitors will find
ways—legal or illegal—of supplying more attractive or cheaper substitutes for monopoly products; that demand for those products will, for
whatever reasons, fade away. Opportunity hoarders put much of their
collective energy into fending off these risks. Emulation and adaptation
usually serve their purposes, at least in the short run.

FROM EMULATION AND ADAPTATION
TO INEQUALITY

Gender inequality in employment, South African racial classifications,
ethnic niches in urban labor markets, nationalism, incentive systems in
capitalist firms, and changes in American health care's professional
structure have distinctly different histories; no invariant descriptive
scheme of any richness can encompass all of them perfectly. Exploitation
loomed large in the professional transformation of health care, with opportunity hoarding clearly subordinate to the creation of exploitative
relationships by physicians and then secondarily by professions and
trades immediately surrounding physicians. Mamaroneck's Italians emphasized opportunity hoarding, while their stories leave unclear whatever exploitation by more powerful actors occurred in the background.
Yet both health care and Italian experience in Mamaroneck conformed
to similar causal principles. They involved the installation of categories
facilitating inclusion, exclusion, and unequal treatment.

In Mamaroneck, we saw a classic application of these principles
to employment-oriented chain migration and ethnic niche formation.
Both in the public sector and in family firms, Ciociari specialized in

earthwork—landscape gardening and closely related pursuits—which thereby acquired Italian labels and excluded non-Italian workers. In American health care, we witnessed the deliberate creation of interior work categories through professionalization, their installation in such organizations as hospitals, and their frequent reinforcement through matching with exterior categories of gender, race, and ethnicity.

Although categorical stereotypes, enmities, and fears unquestionably welled up in both experiences, we need not attribute to them much autonomous importance in explaining the organizational processes involved. Creation or installation of categorical distinctions does crucial organizational work. Exterior categories usually intersect, and often reinforce, the interior categories put in place by managers and modified by bargaining with existing workers.

Adaptation locks categorical inequality into place. Once exterior categorical distinctions, inadvertent or otherwise, find their way into an organization, they tend to stay in place for the same reasons that other organizational features persist: because they become taken for granted as bases of routine activities within the organization. Routine activities in question include not only the operations that installed exterior categories in the first place—justifying unequal rewards, recruiting new members, establishing authority relations, maintaining connections with outside sources of support, and so on—but also the daily games of organization members: work sharing, flirtation, patronage, snobbery, solidarity, recreation, simply finding their way around the bureaucracy. Categories become crucial chunks of local knowledge, correspondingly expensive to destroy or replace.

Emulation multiplies categorical inequality. Although each set of categories brings its own cultural and organizational baggage (gender distinctions do not operate in exactly the same way as ethnic distinctions), their installation in similar organizations produces striking homologies of form and function. Thus the U.S. Navy, which long barred nonwhites from regular service with whites, nevertheless recruited black and Filipino men as officers' stewards, treating them as the functional equivalent of housemaids and cooks. In replacing newly arrived Korean immigrants with Mexicans at the bottom levels of New York's delicatessens,

Korean entrepreneurs have installed a mobility ceiling in a manner that observers of gender and race find thoroughly familiar. Rosabeth Kanter has long since documented similarities in the positions of token women and other minorities at the higher ranks of large organizations. Organizational forms and processes of categorical inequality repeat themselves in a wide variety of contexts.

With exploitation, opportunity hoarding, emulation, and adaptation properly understood, we have the means of addressing a fundamental question I have so far only brushed in passing: how and why do categorical inequalities persist in a given form despite turnover in the persons and concrete social relations involved? Why do they endure from cohort to cohort, from generation to generation? Each of our four mechanisms has a self-reproducing element, and the four together lock neatly into a self-reproducing complex:

1. Exploitation reproduces itself by supplying resource-controlling elites with surpluses, part of which they use to reward crucial collaborators, another part of which they use to regulate disposition of the resources.

2. Opportunity hoarding feeds rewards selectively into segregated networks, recruiting replacements from less advantaged sites within those networks. Opportunity hoarding emphatically includes the deliberate transmission of wealth and other advantages to children and other recognized heirs.

3. Emulation not only lowers the costs of established organizational divisions below those of their theoretical alternatives but also provides the illusion of ubiquity, therefore of inevitability.

4. Adaptation articulates unequal organizational arrangements with valued adjacent and overlapping social routines so that the costs of moving to theoretically available alternatives rise prohibitively.

Identification of those self-reproducing features, to be sure, helps to specify conditions under which categorical inequality weakens or changes character. If an exploitation-sustaining resource loses its value, if an opportunity-hoarding network exhausts its supply of disadvantaged replacements, if an external authority or a more attractive alternative inhibits adoption of a well-known organizational design, if changes in overlapping or adjacent social arrangements render their articulation with unequal categories less secure or more costly, a given system of categorical inequality loses force.

Existing social arrangements have enduring advantages because their theoretical alternatives always entail the costs of movement away from the present situation; change therefore occurs under conditions that reduce returns from existing arrangements, raise their current operating costs, lower the costs of transition to alternative arrangements, or (much more rarely) increase expected returns from alternatives sufficiently to overcome the transition costs. "Costs" and "returns," of course, include not just easily monetized goods and services but the whole range of valued transactions we have been examining.

These conclusions are obvious but not trivial. In South Africa, we see the European/African boundary wavering as the economy moved away from the farms and mines in which the boundary previously worked so effectively. In the American health care system, we see physicians losing their autonomy as hospital administrators and insurance executives acquire control over medicine's basic resources. Kinship and neighborhood networks of New York's Korean merchants stop supplying young, poor, eager immigrants, so Koreans start turning to disposable, low-wage Hispanic helpers.

Each of our principles has implications for the likely effects of different sorts of deliberate intervention to reduce inequality. None of them suggests that educational and hortatory efforts to reduce prejudice and increase good feeling will have more than marginal effects on categorical inequality. They imply instead that effective equalizing programs will include some combination of these elements: redistribution of returns from monopolized resources; redistribution of control over monopolized resources; recasting of organizational structure; provision of easily adopted and effective alternative organizational models; and reduction of the transition costs to more egalitarian structures. The controversial character of any such intervention draws us immediately into the politics of inequality.

7 The Politics of Inequality

In the presence of an effective government, politics as usual involves both exploitation and opportunity hoarding. Since generations of anarchists and libertarians have railed against it, the exploitative side of government comes easily into view. Ruling classes use government-controlled means and resources to extract surplus value from the efforts of categorically excluded subject populations, redirecting at least some of the surplus to activities from which the subject population does not benefit, although the ruling classes do. Taxes and conscription represent two obvious forms of extraction, colonial wars and promotion of ruling-class businesses two obvious forms of diverted resources. The big question is not whether exploitation happens, but who belongs to the ruling classes and how they dispose of surplus value: on their own private enterprises, on their own creature comforts, on war, on public goods.

In general, democrats prefer democracy because large parts of the citizenry join the ruling classes and because, consequently, decision makers are inclined to invest extracted surplus in public goods. On the whole, democracies enforce distinctions between inclusion and exclusion with as much energy as autocracies; recent moves by Western democracies to exclude noncitizens from public benefits illustrate just such exclusiveness. As compared with tyrannies and oligarchies, nevertheless, democracies include far more of their populations in the ruling classes and provide more regular channels for movement from exclusion to inclusion.

Categorically organized opportunity hoarding likewise occurs widely in politics, but less visibly than exploitation. Consider only two examples: state enforcement of class-specific property rights and creation of regional autonomies on the basis of ethnic distinctness. In the first case, most historical states have given preference to the property rights of landlords over those of peasants, herders, hunters, and gatherers who live from the same land. In the second, systems of indirect rule such as the Ottoman empire and Stalin's nationalities policy generally give priority and state backing to one declared ethnicity within each subunit. Under these circumstances, to be sure, at a regional scale opportunity hoarding edges easily over into exploitation.

Some exploitative states, indeed, have made a business of promoting opportunity hoarding for a consideration. The seventeenth- and eighteenth-century French state pushed to an extreme the sale of privileges: revenue-generating public offices, craft monopolies, powers to control (and therefore to draw income from) musical performances, municipal charters, mining rights, and much more. (See Henshall 1992; Kettering 1993; for the promotion of opportunity hoarding in other European states, see, e.g., Adams 1994; Samuel Clark 1995; Gustafsson 1994a, 1994b.) Holding a state-sold public office, for example, commonly entitled the officeholder not only to collect a stipend from some stream of state revenues but also to charge large fees for state-mandated services, not to mention under-the-table *pots de vin*—gifts, tips commissions, or bribes, depending on your perspective. In these cases, the state treasury typically collected a cash payment from the beneficiary as the privilege began and loaned state power when necessary to exclude unauthorized persons from competitive activities.

Under Louis XIV, the great regional administrators, the Intendants, put significant shares of their effort into enticing, persuading, or coercing rich men to buy such privileges. They also frequently forced less rich members of guilds and municipal governments to make collective payments for maintenance of their exclusive rights to govern, to gather customary fees, or to exercise their trades. Coerced or not, privilege-holders drew benefits from their state-backed exclusive access to circumscribed sets of opportunities. In the process, state authorities reinforced or created categorical inequality, most visibly by attaching noble status to a wide range of purchased offices.

Even where they do not draw major revenues from the activity, all contemporary states engage in some promotion of opportunity hoarding. Licensing of professions always entails state-backed exclusion of uncertified persons from the practice of those professions, while selective recruitment of military veterans into certain occupational niches has a similar effect. In the name of public health, public safety, promotion of enterprise, and protection of property, states repeatedly help favored networks to establish exclusive control over valued resources.

Emulation and adaptation, in their turn, usually sustain government-supported categorical inequality. Governments imitate other governments' forms, including their forms of inequality. Citizens then adapt, fashioning routines that facilitate their own individual and collective projects. Since they set up routines that secure their survival, however contingently, many citizens then start to condemn other citizens who escape common obligations, even obligations to a recognizably exploitative state. Only under great pressures such as those endured by the South African state during the 1980s do those supports for the routine politics of inequality begin to tremble.

Inequality's politics, then, simply constitutes a special case of inequality's general operation. The special case consists of those situations in which one of the parties is a government—that is, an organization controlling the principal concentrated means of coercion within some substantial territory. (As the earlier discussion of nationalism suggests, a government is a state if it does not clearly fall under the jurisdiction of another government and if it receives recognition from other relatively autonomous governments.) The politics of inequality concerns the involvement of governments in inequality-generating social processes. But it also concerns the impact of inequality on governmental processes and struggles for power over governments. That includes situations in which contenders explicitly struggle over issues of inequality.

Four distinguishable questions therefore confront us:

- When one of the parties is a government, how do exploitation, opportunity hoarding, emulation, and adaptation operate in the creation, installation, maintenance, transformation, and destruction of paired and unequal categories?

- How do the character and extent of categorical inequality in an organization or population affect its basic political processes?

- Under what conditions, how, and with what possible consequences does inequality itself become an object of political struggle?

- Under what conditions do political struggle and/or governmental action produce significant changes in prevailing patterns of inequality?

I make no pretense of providing comprehensive answers to such large questions here. I hope only to show that the framework slowly constructed in previous chapters offers fresh perspectives on each of them.

Inequality-generating processes operate similarly whether or not one of the parties is a government. Critical differences spring chiefly from two defining features of governments: their *organizational priority* within a defined territory, and their control of concentrated *coercive means*. Organizational priority helps to explain why governmental agents frequently intervene, or at least hover, as third parties in nonstate relations of exploitation or opportunity hoarding. Control of coercive means helps to explain why the intervention of governmental agents often makes a large difference to inequality and why people so regularly struggle over state control of major resources. Governmental actions guarantee or threaten a wide range of rights, including categorically differentiated property rights.

Since their emergence as distinct forms of social organization some ten thousand years ago, states have always intervened in patterns of inequality across the territories their rulers have controlled. Most of the time, their agents have tried to maintain and reproduce existing inequalities, notably those guaranteeing the dominance of their ruling classes and sustaining supplies of essential state resources: money, weapons, soldiers, food, transport, communications. Tax and tribute policies, military conscription and requisitioning, and defense of the state's central resource base—trade, for city-states and city-empires; agricultural property, for agrarian empires; flocks and grazing land, for states based on pastoral economies; manufacturing and transport facilities, for states of industrial capitalism—have generally assumed and reinforced existing relations of inequality. In their armies, hospitals, and bureaucracies, states have provided models for exploitation and opportunity hoarding in nongovernmental organizations.

As they enact laws, states commonly create paired categories or put their weight behind existing categorical pairs. Marriage licenses underscore the line between married and unmarried; birth certificates, the division between legitimate and illegitimate; government-issued identity cards, the separation between citizens and noncitizens; military discharge papers, the border between veterans and nonveterans. On either side of such a categorical partition, rights and duties differ significantly. In most cases, the incorporation of categorical distinctions into law reinforces existing structures of power and inequality.

Although states have often provided meager aid to their "deserving" poor, have frequently attacked regional populations that resisted central rule, have occasionally dispossessed churches and other wealthy institutions in times of crisis, and have sometimes inadvertently undermined their own supporters through military and fiscal policies, only under mass democracy, with its pitting of numbers against other resources, have many states deliberately sought to redistribute income, wealth, or goods in ways that might alter existing relations of inequality. States, then, significantly affect durable inequality, chiefly by reproducing its existing forms.

States also serve as sites and instruments of exploitation and opportunity hoarding. Every government sustains a *polity*, a set of relations among actors who have routine, low-cost access to governmental agents. Collectively, if unequally, polity members exercise control over the government's resources. A thin version of polity membership consists of citizenship: a publicly established set of mutual rights and obligations linking the entire category of native-born and naturalized persons to government agents. Observers customarily think of citizenship as the affair of states, but exactly parallel phenomena of inclusion and obligation appeared in European municipalities and other local units long before any substantial national citizenships formed (Cerutti, Descimon, and Prak 1995; Gustafsson 1994a, 1994b). Even today all but the most centralized states tolerate (or even insist on) some forms of citizenship below the national level. Almost all citizens of federal states such as Switzerland, the United States, and Germany, for example, also belong to at least one of their country's component units.

In addition to broad rights of protection from agents of outside states, citizenship frequently entails obligations such as military service and rights such as health benefits. Citizenship commonly occurs in multiple degrees—all states having elections, for example, exclude small children and some certified incompetents from voting. In forty-six states of the contemporary United States, for example, a felony conviction disfranchises the convict for his or her prison term, and in thirty-one states disfranchisement extends to the period of parole or probation; because black men receive felony convictions at much higher rates than the rest of the American population, a full 14 percent of them currently lack the right to vote (Butterfield 1997, 12). The larger categorical system to which citizenship belongs typically includes further distinctions such as native-born citizen/naturalized citizen/legal resident/illegal resident/ legal visitor/excluded foreigner. Such systems always include formal procedures to transfer persons from one category to another.

Thicker versions of polity membership crosscut categories of citizenship; they create standing for collective actors either in the form of licensed organizations (the American Medical Association, the AFL-CIO) or institutionalized categories (the medical profession, organized labor). Much political struggle centers on establishing, challenging, maintaining, or exercising the claims of such categorically defined collective actors. When those struggles gain ground, indeed, we frequently witness corresponding alterations in the state's own structure, as when cabinet-level departments of labor, women's affairs, environmental problems, or health form to deal with the claims raised by their counterparts among the polity members.

Since every inclusion entails some exclusion, these processes incorporate categorical inequality into public affairs. Where polity members succeed in directing state-controlled resources to their own exclusive activities and in using government power to commit other people's effort to the extraction of return from those resources, state-backed exploitation and opportunity hoarding occur. Veterans get pensions that nonveterans pay for, well-organized ranchers get cheap access to public lands, recognized Indian tribes get rights to operate tax-exempt casinos. Once such government-validated scripts come into play, however, the advantages they confer typically stir widespread emulation, for example, in the demands of previously unorganized Indian tribes to be recognized as full-fledged Native American entities, entitled to the same fiscal exemptions as their established cousins.

In the United States, exclusion has operated especially along racial lines, excluding Americans who have known African forebears from full citizenship through much of the country's history, excluding Chinese in the nineteenth century, actually interning Japanese Americans during World War II. Black exclusion has varied dramatically by region within the United States, with states of the old Cotton South more often using legal means to exclude black people from voting, public facilities, benefits, and employment. For Louisiana, Virginia Domínguez documents how the term "Creole" long referred to all the native-born population regardless of genetic or national ancestry. In the black/white politicization of Reconstruction, however, the term became an instrument by which whites of French or Spanish background not only claimed domination over anyone with detectable African ancestry but also excluded from rule other whites who lacked their colonial ancestry (Domínguez 1986). A contradictory situation emerged:

> Two types of Louisianians consequently identify themselves today as Creole. One is socially and legally white; the other, socially and legally colored. The white side by definition cannot accept the existence of colored Creoles; the colored side, by definition, cannot accept the white

conception of *Creole*. The problem is encapsulated in the use of the terms *Cajun Creole* and *Creole Cajun*. These expressions make no sense at all to white Creoles. A Creole in their estimation is a purely white descendant of French or Spanish settlers in colonial Louisiana; a Cajun is a purely white descendant of Acadian colonial settlers in southern Louisiana. (Domínguez 1986, 149)

Although the term has changed meaning several times, although genetically the Louisiana population is amply mixed, and although socially defined people of color have their own version of the categories involved, in the twentieth century the "white" version of Creole/other became a basis of claims for political control. Within the socially defined nonwhite population, the term also became politicized, first serving to distinguish the elite (especially the light-skinned elite) of mixed African and European descent from the rest and then becoming controversial and losing favor as civil rights activists led the move toward defining everyone having some known African ancestry as black.

By the 1930s, most of the American South had installed systems of racial domination based on the white/black line. Theda Skocpol points out a paradoxical result of New Deal legislation, which allocated great discretionary power to the states:

> Southern authorities feared that even small public assistance grants to nonworkers would cause entire black families to stay out of the cotton fields. They prevented this by excluding blacks altogether or by suspending assistance payments during harvest. Even when grants were given, moreover, "although discrimination was illegal, southern states were allowed to pay blacks lower grants than whites by using different criteria for determining need, and by paying Confederate veterans and their dependents the maximum grant." In broad historical perspective, it is amazing that southern states were able to use federal subsidies after 1934 to enrich assistance to Confederate veterans and survivors, the very persons who had been excluded altogether from the federal Civil War pensions of the nineteenth century! (Skocpol 1995, 143)

Even in the face of formal federal prohibitions, individual states and local administrators managed to build categorical racial inequality into the very rights of citizens.

Similar processes operate at an international scale. We have already examined the creation of new states in response to state-seeking nationalism as a categorical process. International institutions, interstate compacts, and transnational organizations likewise involve themselves in support of categorical distinctions within existing states. The category of refugee, for example, relates a set of residents juridically, economically, and socially to inhabitants of at least two territories: the one they have fled and the one in which they currently live. Liisa Malkki has worked with Hutu refugees from Burundi, a group whose core fled to Tanzania in response to 1972 mass killings by the Tutsi-dominated Burundian army. The majority who settled in internationally certified refugee camps (such as Mishamo, where Malkki concentrated her effort) differed little at the start from the smaller number who found toeholds in and around Kigoma township. By the mid-1980s, however, the two populations occupied very different positions:

> The most relevant contrast in the present context is that the social status of being a refugee had a very pronounced salience in the camp refugees' life-worlds, while in town it generally did not. In Mishamo it was indispensable to understand something of the social and political meaning given collectively to refugeeness and to exile by the camp inhabitants. In contrast, for the people I have called the town refugees, refugee status was generally not a collectively heroized or positively valued aspect of one's social person. Insofar as it was considered relevant at all, it was more often a liability than a protective or positive status. (Malkki 1996, 379–380)

Like small-scale nationalists and internationally designated indigenous peoples, camp refugees have constructed for themselves a standard history of their population that represents them as the rightful natives of Burundi, deprived of their rights by Belgian incompetence and Tutsi trickery. Categorical membership gives camp refugees distinctive relations to Burundian citizens, Tanzanian citizens, and international authorities. United Nations agencies and international nongovernmental organizations do not necessarily subscribe to the refugees' own cherished histories, but these histories do reinforce Hutu claims to protection, temporary use of Tanzanian land, and political distinctness. In an unexpected location, we find a conjunction of opportunity hoarding and categorical inequality.

Within states, inclusion processes parallel the awarding of independent states to representatives of ostensible nations (and therefore the exclusion of rival claimants to representation of the same or crosscutting nations) on an international scale. We saw just such state-backed production of categorical inequality in South Africa. But it occurs, generally with less severity, in all states. States formally certify labor unions, professional organizations, firms, and political parties, thus confirming their priority within their designated spheres over rivals and enemies. Less formally, states also offer selective recognition to ethnic leaders, spokespersons for different segments of capital, representatives of organized women, and other blocs—in each case excluding others categorically from that piece of power. Included parties share in exploitation based on state-controlled resources or hoard opportunities based on resources sequestered with government support.

In principle, we might distinguish between, on the one hand, direct incorporation of unequal categories into state structure and, on the other, state intervention to enforce or alter categorically unequal practices in organizations or arenas falling under the state's jurisdiction. In either regard, state action often has strong impact on durable inequality. South African racial legislation directly inscribed racial distinctions into citizenship, and Jim Crow legislation in the United States of the late nineteenth century employed a series of devices using invisible ink to inscribe race into law often without naming the races in print, while Western states long explicitly barred all females from suffrage when large shares of adult males could vote. All these arrangements constituted direct incorporation of legal categories into state structure.

Desegregation of public accommodations; requirements of affirmative action based on race, gender, or ethnicity in private employment; and compensatory aid to minority businesses all belong to the second set of instances, where state intervention significantly affects inequality in loci outside its own structure. State-driven integration of government-run schools, elimination of inequality in recruitment to the armed forces, and legally initiated alteration of electoral districts or access to public employment straddle both cases since they involve state inter-vention in organizations and arenas the state itself operates. The line between direct incorporation and state intervention therefore becomes a continuum.

Because in all sorts of states members of dominant categories ordi-narily mobilize more effectively and enjoy more direct access to agents or instruments of state power than do members of subordinate catego-ries, states usually act to reinforce—or at least to sustain—existing cate-gorical inequalities. Through standard adaptation processes and oppor-tunity hoarding, even members of exploited categories acquire interests in the maintenance of categorical distinctions, if not in the degree or character of inequality across categorical boundaries. Democratic ar-rangements attenuate such effects by pitting the normally greater num-bers of the less privileged against the superior resources of the elite; hence, with favorable alliances, they often produce modest redistribu-tion of resources toward less favored citizens. But except under the in-fluence of state-threatening social movements, revolutionary situations, extensive military mobilizations, major defeats in war, and intense fiscal crises, we have precious few historical instances of state-led attacks on unequal categories themselves.

That the category-sustaining work of states is often inadvertent does not reduce its effect. Observers of welfare states (e.g., Haavio-Mannila 1993; Orloff 1996b; Sim 1994) have shown how national redistribution policies tend to assume and reproduce existing forms of gender inequal-ity; on the whole, for example, public welfare policies assume that men will be disproportionately involved in paid work away from home (in-cluding military service) and that women will devote themselves to un-paid care of others, especially children. Since most states attach signifi-cant rewards to military service and paid work, such an assumption channels state resources to men and affords women access to those re-sources chiefly through marriage to a wage earner or independent involvement in wage earning. Thus unmarried women who are unem-ployed or self-employed and their children almost always lose out in redistribution, protection, and access to public services.

The same inquiries, however, have also demonstrated substantial differences among welfare regimes. To take the extreme case, Scandinavian countries (where high proportions of women work for wages and labor movements have been more successful in maintaining pressure for extensive state-sponsored benefits) generally grant women more independent rights than most other capitalist regimes. Feminist analyses of differences between Scandinavia and other Western regions therefore assign major importance to national-level political processes in the generation of state-based inequality. By so doing, they implicitly raise doubts that patriarchy, male chauvinism, or other unchanging cultural characteristics drive the politics of gender inequality.

CATHOLIC EMANCIPATION IN GREAT BRITAIN

What of religion? As the history of nationalism indicates, ties between religious identity and political privilege have fluctuated enormously over the long run of European history. During the last millennium, Europe has witnessed everything from the Ottoman empire's ready (if unequal) absorption of Christians and Jews to the Nazis' programmed annihilation of those Jews they could track down. Broadly speaking, political exclusion on the basis of religious identity increased with the violently vindictive pursuit of Muslims, Jews, and Christian heretics during the fifteenth century; reached a state of war through much of Central and Western Europe during the sixteenth century; stabilized in the same regions from 1648 to 1789 with the Westphalian doctrine of *cujus regio ejus religio;* and then receded irregularly through much of the continent from the French Revolution onward.

Twentieth-century nationalism, for the most part, stresses nonreligious markers such as language and descent. To be sure, religious prejudice and unofficial discrimination survived the French Revolution, sometimes even flourishing as in nineteenth-century pogroms and the Dreyfus case. Nazi policy specifically targeted Jews for their religious difference. Nevertheless, by the twentieth century, categorical religious exclusion from political rights became rare. Even anti-Semitism took on more racist than religious content, with current beliefs and affiliations mattering much less than imputed descent (Birnbaum 1993). Until recently, at least this was true; whether the sharpening of state-identified religious divisions in the former Soviet Union, in disintegrated Yugoslavia, and potentially in France constitutes a reversal or a momentary aberration remains to be seen.

Insertion of religious, ethnic, or racial boundaries into state organization renders readily visible the parallels between manifestly political forms of action and routine smaller-scale operations of categorical inequality. South Africa under apartheid represents an extreme case of a general phenomenon. All governments survive and thrive to the extent that they successfully establish exploitation, opportunity hoarding, emulation, and adaptation. Governments differ chiefly in who benefits from these inequality-producing processes.

The politics of inclusion and exclusion on the basis of religious affiliation provides a serious challenge to organizational explanations of inequality. Here, if anywhere, we might expect deeply ingrained individual and collective attitudes to override (or explain) the installation of categorical inequality. The case of Catholic exclusion and inclusion in eighteenth- and nineteenth-century Great Britain, however, shows us exploitation, opportunity hoarding, emulation, and adaptation all recognizably at work. The story of British struggles over Catholic rights joins our earlier stories of nationalism and of South African racial divisions. We recognize them all as coming from the book of durable categorical inequality. In all of them, the construction and imposition of categories served the exploitative interests of rulers and political entrepreneurs. But in the saga of Catholic Emancipation, we see the British ruling-class interest in political control countered by increasingly salient interests in military resources and the maintenance of order.

How so? The tale of Catholic Emancipation unfolds between the Glorious Revolution of 1688–1689 and the relaxation of religious restrictions on citizenship in 1828–1829. In that tale we see Britain's ruling classes operating a system of exploitation in which state power draws effort from the Catholic (and especially Irish Catholic) masses while barring them from returns of that effort. Anglican elites hoard opportunities afforded them by the political system, and emulation builds the

distinctions Anglican-Catholic-Dissenters into a wide range of social settings, while adaptation both creates partial exemptions for elite Dissenters and organizes an uneasy but effective modus vivendi among members of diverse religious categories.

In Great Britain, the political program that eventually won the name
"Catholic Emancipation" originated in wars, both civil and international. Struggles of 1688–1689 toppled Roman Catholic James II from the
British throne, established Protestant William of Orange as king, and
restored a Protestant ruling class in colonized, largely Catholic, Ireland.
The Glorious Revolution of 1689 barred Catholics from public office,
capping their exclusion with an officeholder's oath that denied tenets of
the Catholic religion and (in the case of members of Parliament) explicitly rejected the pope's authority. Britain's and Ireland's Catholics fell
under the double suspicion of subservience to a foreign authority, the
pope, and of collaboration with Britain's historic enemy, France. The
British state, in essence, matched the interior category of officeholding
citizen to the exterior category of Anglican.

Although non-Anglican Protestants also suffered political disabilities
under the settlement of 1689, in practice subsequent regimes shut Catholics out of Parliament and public life much more effectively. Anglicans,
and to a lesser extent other Protestants, hoarded officeholding opportunities, while the British gained the benefits of Irish Catholic efforts without sharing these benefits. Once again, exploitation and opportunity
hoarding coincide. Over the longer run, however, the costs of exclusion
came to exceed its benefits to British rulers. Collective action by Catholics themselves played a significant part in that shifting balance. How
that happened is the story of Catholic Emancipation.

Oaths of abjuration individualized membership in the Catholic category and made it seem centrally a matter of belief. Certainly Catholicism
had implications for individual characteristics and behavior in the
United Kingdom, as it did elsewhere. But to be Catholic in the sense
that influenced British citizenship between 1689 and 1829 consisted of
involvement in crucial social ties: relations to priests and the church
hierarchy, relations to a publicly identified community of Catholic be-
lievers, and most of all, relations—largely negative—to an Anglican establishment.

Just as categorizing someone as a worker conveniently signals a bundle of personal characteristics but finally depends on distinction from and relation to the employer category, categorizing someone as a Catholic finally designates a boundary and a distinctive set of social ties across that boundary. Distinctions between Catholic and non-Catholic obviously existed before 1689 and after 1829; between the two dates, however, they coincided with relations between fuller and lesser citizens. As time went on, that coincidence came under increasing challenge.

Catholic exclusion had serious political consequences. When Britain won Québec from France in the Seven Years War (1756–1763), the British empire not only gained jurisdiction over an almost unanimously Catholic population but also pacified resistance to British control by large concessions to Québecois, hence to Catholic, self-rule. That settlement inserted a twin to Ireland into the British realm but granted its Catholics more favorable conditions than their Irish coreligionists enjoyed. To the extent that the British incorporated Catholic Ireland into their economy and polity, furthermore, the Irish Protestant establishment became a less effective instrument of indirect rule, and the demands of Catholic Irish on both sides of the Irish Sea for either autonomy or representation swelled. Enlargement of the armed forces during the American war, finally, rendered military recruiters increasingly eager to enroll Irish warriors, already reputed as mercenaries elsewhere in Europe but barred from British military service by the required anti-Catholic oath.

Military-inspired exemptions of Catholic soldiers from oathtaking during the later 1770s raised strident objections among defenders of Anglican supremacy. Such exemptions directly incited the formation of a nationwide Protestant Association to petition, agitate, and resist. Scottish member of Parliament Lord George Gordon, whose vociferous opposition to Catholic claims brought him to the head of the association in 1780, led an anti-Catholic campaign that at first concentrated on meetings and parliamentary petitions but during June 1780 ramified into attacks on Catholic persons and (especially) property in London. Two hundred seventy-five people died during those bloody struggles, chiefly at the hands of troops who were retaking control over London's streets. Among Britain's ruling classes, those so-called Gordon Riots gave popular anti-Catholicism an aura of violent unreason. By negation, advocacy of Catholics' political rights acquired the cachet of enlightenment.

From that time onward an important fusion occurred. Catholic Emancipation became a standard (although by no means universal) demand of reformers and radicals who campaigned for parliamentary reform. By "reform," its advocates generally meant something like elimination of parliamentary seats controlled by patrons, more uniform qualifications for voting across the country, enlargement of the electorate, and frequent parliamentary elections. (Demands for universal suffrage, for manhood suffrage, or even for equal individual-by-individual representation among the propertied rarely gained much of a following before well into the nineteenth century.) Catholic Emancipation dovetailed neatly with such proposals, since it likewise called for granting a more equal and effective voice in public affairs to currently excluded people.

Both parliamentary reform and Catholic Emancipation surged, and then collapsed, as national political issues in Great Britain several times between the 1780s and the 1820s. But Emancipation became more urgent during the Revolutionary and Napoleonic wars, when William Pitt the Younger sought to still the Irish revolutionary movement that was undermining the British state's titanic war effort against France. Pitt helped create a (dubiously) United Kingdom of Great Britain and Ireland in 1801, which meant dissolving the separate Irish Parliament and incorporating one hundred Irish Protestant members into what had been Britain's Parliament. In the process, Pitt half-promised major political concessions to Catholics.

King George III's hostility to compromising the Anglican establishment (and thereby a crown that was already suffering from the war-driven rise of parliamentary power) made that commitment impossible to keep. Pitt's consequent resignation by no means stifled Catholic demands. On the contrary, from 1801 to 1829, Catholic Emancipation remained one of the United Kingdom's thorniest political issues. The 1807 wartime resignation of the coalition "Ministry of All the Talents," for example, pivoted on the king's refusal to endorse the admission of Catholics to high military ranks.

Much more than a king's attachment to Anglican privilege, however, made the issue contentious. Anti-Catholicism continued to enjoy wide popular appeal in Great Britain, the more so as Irish immigration (responding to industrial expansion in Britain and consequent industrial contraction in Ireland) accelerated. On the other side, Irish Catholic elites resisted the even greater separation from important decisions affecting their island's fate that had resulted from the transfer of the old Dublin Parliament's powers—however Protestant it had been—to an English-dominated Parliament in distant Westminster. Repeatedly during the 1820s two movements coincided: an increasingly popular campaign for Catholic political rights led by lawyers, priests, and other elites in Ireland; and a coalition of radicals, reformers, and organized Catholics in support of Emancipation within Great Britain. Eventually a countermovement of Protestant resistance to Catholic claims mobilized as well.

The interweaving movements reached their dénouement in 1829. During the previous six years, Irish Catholic barrister Daniel O'Connell and his allies had organized successive versions of a mass-membership Catholic Association in Ireland, with some following in Great Britain. They perfected a form of organization (drawn initially and ironically from Methodist models) with which radicals and reformers had experimented during the great mobilizations of 1816 to 1819. The association collected a monthly penny—the "Catholic rent"—from thousands of peasants and workers. With the proceeds, it conducted an incessant, effective campaign of propaganda, coalition formation, lobbying, and public claim-making. Each time the British government outlawed their association, O'Connell and friends fashioned a slightly reorganized (and renamed) successor to replace it.

Efforts by Protestant supporters of Emancipation to get a bill through Parliament failed in 1812, failed repeatedly from 1816 to 1822, and failed again in 1825. But in 1828 a related campaign to expand the political rights of Protestant Dissenters (e.g., Baptists, Methodists, and Presbyterians) by repealing the seventeenth-century Test and Corporation Acts gained parliamentary and royal assent. Although it had the effect of removing important allies from the same side of the barricade, on balance such an opening made the moment auspicious for Catholic Emancipation. A regime that had defended Anglican supremacy by excluding all non-Anglicans from office in principle (despite frequent exceptions in practice for Dissenters) lost some of its rationale for excluding Catholics.

Meanwhile, Catholic Ireland moved closer to open rebellion. Despite well-organized opposition by Anglican diehards, now augmented by some of the Dissenters who had recently gained fuller political rights, Prime Minister Wellington and Home Secretary Peel finally promoted Catholic Emancipation as a lesser evil. They hoped to mute its effect by narrowing the Irish franchise dramatically, dissolving the Catholic Association definitively, and barring the association's succession to other mass organizations.

The House of Lords and the king presented larger obstacles than did the Commons, which by the early 1820s had on the whole reconciled itself to some expansion of Catholic rights. The Lords included, of course, not only peers of the realm but also bishops of the Anglican church, most of whom would not lightly sacrifice their organization's privileged political position. At their coronations, furthermore, British monarchs swore to defend Anglican primacy; in 1828 King George IV still feared that to approve Catholic Emancipation would violate his coronation oath.

When the House of Lords again forestalled Emancipation in 1828, both Irish organizers and their British allies redoubled the Emancipation campaign, not only expanding the Catholic Association but also staging massive meetings, marches, and petition drives. The technically illegal election of Catholic O'Connell to Parliament from a seat in County Clare during the fall of 1828 directly challenged national authorities, especially when O'Connell proposed to take his place in Westminster at the new Parliament's opening early in 1829.

This formidable mobilization, in turn, stimulated a large countermobilization by defenders of what they called the Protestant Constitution. In Great Britain, and to a lesser extent in Ireland itself, opponents of Emancipation organized Brunswick Clubs to manufacture meetings, marches, petitions, propaganda, and solidarity on behalf of the royal house of Brunswick. That the Commons, the Lords, and the king finally conceded major political rights—although far from perfect equality—to Catholics during the spring of 1829 resulted from an otherwise unresolvable crisis in both Ireland and Great Britain. It by no means represented a general conversion of Britons to religious toleration. Jews, for example, did not receive similar concessions until 1858. Nor did unofficial discrimination against Jews or Irish Catholics ever disappear from British life. We are speaking here of legal exclusion from political rights on the basis of religious identity.

In 1689, Great Britain built categorical inequality by religion into the very structure of citizenship, with significant consequences for Catholics' conditions of life. In 1829, the United Kingdom eliminated most traces of that inequality from citizenship rights without by any means rendering Catholics and non-Catholics equal in regard to wealth, income, prestige, or power. As in cases of legal discrimination by race, a categorization that initially implemented unequal treatment eventually became an incentive for, and a basis of, political mobilization against discrimination.

Although the vast mobilization of Catholics and their supporters in Great Britain and Ireland succeeded in displacing major barriers to Catholic participation in the United Kingdom's public life, it also laid the ground for a nearly contradictory program: the demand for Irish autonomy and, eventually, independence under Catholic hegemony. In an age of politicized ethnicity and nationalism, politicized Irish Catholics represented themselves as yet another nation denied their own rightful state.

For all its particularities, the history of legally sanctioned religious inequality in the British Isles shares its causal structure with many other varieties of categorical inequality: not only South African racial categories and Balkan ethnicities but also the divisions built into American health care, immigrant niches, local communities, and the ordinary operation of capitalist firms. Whether the organization in question is a state, a firm, or something else, we find exploitation, opportunity hoarding, emulation, and adaptation. We find people who wield power within an organization responding to organizational problems by creating or incorporating categorical differences, elaborating and using interpersonal networks within categorical boundaries, erecting social markers at the boundaries, transmitting categorical membership to new participants, giving multiple parties a stake in perpetuating the categories, and drawing even persons disadvantaged by their categorical assignment into some form of collaboration with the system. Although contempt, mistrust, and misunderstanding often characterize cross-boundary ties, negative feelings do not in themselves explain such systems of categorical inequality. Even people who do not hate generally collaborate with them.

Within the history of Catholic Emancipation, we witness the creation of social movements as major forms of political interaction, including other struggles over inequality. After 1800 most capitalist countries installed contested elections as ways of staffing their governments, of managing polity membership, and of adjudicating competing claims among polity members. Contested elections designated the members of parliaments and (directly or indirectly) high executive offices. In the same process, however, capitalist countries also generated paraelectoral and paraparliamentary politics in the form of party action, interest-group maneuvering, and social movements. Social movements in particular came to play crucial parts as ways of asserting candidacy for polity membership, of demanding redress, and of getting on the national agenda the issues that parliamentary, executive, and electoral processes were currently neglecting.

SOCIAL MOVEMENTS AND INEQUALITY

Social movements create or activate paired and unequal categories, with an important twist: they deliberately emphasize the unjust treatment of people on the weaker side of a categorical line and/or the improper behavior of people on the stronger side. The "we" referred to by social-movement activists comprises a whole category (composite or homogeneous) of unjustly treated persons or organizations. The "they" consists of others (industrialists, officials, immoral persons, sometimes competing groups) whose action or inaction allegedly causes the condition that activists are protesting in the name of their presumably aggrieved constituency. Social movements challenge the exploitation, opportunity hoarding, emulation, and adaptation that occur on the other side of the categorical line and threaten drastic collective action by members of their own constituency. Outsiders' participation in the construction of categories helps to solve four acute organizational problems: mobilizing supporters behind a set of demands, coordinating contentious and often risky action, attracting allies, and—in the case of success—establishing a structure for the distribution and hoarding of benefits gained.

A social movement is a kind of campaign, parallel in many respects to an electoral campaign. This sort of campaign, however, demands righting of a wrong, most often a wrong suffered by a well-specified population. It constructs that population as a category, often as a categorical candidate for polity membership. The population in question can range from a single individual to all humans, or even all living creatures. Whereas an electoral campaign pays off chiefly in the votes that finally result from it, a social movement pays off in effective transmission of the message that its program's supporters are WUNC (Worthy, Unified, Numerous, and Committed). These four elements compensate one another to some degree; for example, a high value on worthiness ("respectability" in the language of 1829) can make up for small numbers. Yet a visibly low value on any one of these elements (a public demonstration of unworthiness, division, dwindling numbers, and / or outright defection) discredits the whole movement.

Social-movement campaigning involves a familiar bundle of performances: creating associations and coalitions, organizing marches and demonstrations, circulating petitions, attending public meetings, shouting slogans, wearing badges, writing pamphlets, and more. Seen as means-end action, such a campaign has a peculiar diffuseness; compared with striking, voting, smashing the loom of a nonstriking weaver, or running a miscreant out of town, its actions remain essentially symbolic, cumulative, and indirect, with almost no chance that any single event will achieve its stated objective of ending an injustice or persuading authorities to enact a needed law. Social-movement mobilization gains its strength from an implicit threat to act in adjacent arenas: to withdraw support from public authorities, to provide sustenance to a regime's enemies, to ally with splinter parties, to move toward direct action or even rebellion. Skilled social-movement organizers draw tacitly on such threats to bargain with the objects of their demands.

Social movements take place as conversations—not as solo performances but as interactions among parties. The most elementary set of parties consists of an actor making a claim, the object of the actor's claim, and an audience having a stake in the fate of at least one of the first two. Whatever else they do, movements dramatize categorical differences between claimants and objects of claims. But allies, competitors, enemies, authorities, and multiple audiences also frequently play parts in movement interactions. Therein lies the complexity of social-movement organizing, not to mention the complexity of responses by authorities and objects of claims; third parties always complicate the interaction.

Examined from the viewpoint of challengers, a social movement's success depends in part on two varieties of mystification. First, as they increase, worthiness, unity, numbers, and commitment almost necessarily contradict each other; to gain numbers, for example, generally requires compromise on worthiness, unity, and/or commitment. The actual work of organizers consists recurrently of patching together provisional coalitions, suppressing risky tactics, negotiating which of the multiple agendas that participants bring with them will find public voice in their collective action, and, above all, hiding backstage struggle from public view. They almost always exaggerate their coalition's WUNC.

Second, movement activists seek to present themselves and (if different) the objects of their solicitude as a solidary group, preferably as a group with a long history and with a coherent existence outside the world of public claim-making. In that regard, they resemble state-seeking nationalists with their constructions of long, coherent, distinctive cultural histories for their nations. Thus feminists identify themselves with women's age-old struggles for rights in the streets and in everyday existence, civil rights leaders minimize class and religious differences within their racial category, and environmentalists present most of humankind as their eternal community. Organizers of the Catholic

Emancipation campaign, including Daniel O'Connell, spent much of their energy striving to create a united public front and portraying their constituents as a long-suffering solidary population who had waited far too long for justice.

The two varieties of mystification address several different audiences. They encourage activists and supporters to make high estimates of the probability that fellow adherents will take risks and incur costs for the cause, hence that their own contributions will bear fruit. They warn authorities, objects of claims, opponents, rivals, and bystanders to take the movement seriously as a force that can affect their fates.

Movements differ significantly in the relative attention they give to these various audiences, from self-absorbed tests of daring organized by small clusters of terrorists to signature of petitions by transient participants who want some authority to know their opinion. These orientations frequently vary in the course of a given social movement, for example, in transitions from internal building to ostentatious action to fighting off competitors and enemies.

Neither in the case of Catholic Emancipation nor in general does mystification mean utter falsehood. Activists and constituents of social movements vary considerably in the extent to which they actually embody worthiness, unity, numbers, and commitment and in the degree to which they spring from a single solidary group with a collective life outside the world of public politics. To the extent that the two varieties of mystification contain elements of truth, furthermore, social movements generally mobilize more effectively. A segregated ethnic community threatened by outside attack, on the average, mobilizes more readily than does the entire category consisting of all those who suffer from diverse attacks on civil liberties.

The process whereby social-movement activists achieve recognition as valid interlocutors for unjustly deprived populations does not resemble the fact-finding inquiries of novelists, social scientists, or investigative reporters. It resembles a court proceeding, in which those who make such claims, however self-evident to them, must establish themselves in the eyes of others—authorities, competitors, enemies, and relevant audiences—as voices that require attention and must commonly establish themselves in the face of vigorous opposition. They must prove that they qualify. Almost all such proofs entail suppression of some evidence and exaggeration of other evidence concerning the claimants' WUNC and their grounding in a durable, coherent, solidary, deprived population. Again, resemblances to state-seeking nationalism immediately strike the mind's eye.

Analysts of collective action, especially those who entertain sympathy for the actions they are studying, often insist on these mystified elements as intrinsic to social movements: the presence of solidarity, the construction of shared identities, the sense of grievance, the creation of sustaining organizations, and more. Without such features, analysts say, we have nothing but ordinary politics. Sometimes the myths fulfill themselves, building up the lineaments of durable connection among core participants. But most social movements remain far more contingent and volatile than their mystifications allow; these other elements do not define the social movement as a distinctive political phenomenon.

What does? Social movements involve collective claims on authorities. A social movement consists of a sustained challenge to powerholders in the name of a population living under the jurisdiction of those powerholders by means of repeated public displays of that population's numbers, commitment, unity, and worthiness. We, the aggrieved, demand that you, the perpetrators of evil or the responsible authorities, act to alleviate a condition about which we are justly indignant. Although some of our actions may express support for proposals, programs, or persons that are already advancing our aims, most of our displays dramatize not only our own WUNC but also the existence of conditions we oppose.

As they developed in Great Britain and other Western European countries during the early nineteenth century, characteristic social-movement displays (whose relative weight varied considerably from movement to movement) included creating special-purpose associations; lobbying officials; organizing public meetings, demonstrations, and marches; circulating petitions; writing pamphlets; publicizing statements in mass media; posting or wearing identifying signs; and adopting distinctive slogans. Although the advocates and opponents of

Catholic Emancipation had by no means mastered this full array of techniques in 1828 and 1829, they tried them all. They were, indeed, inventing the social movement as they went along.

Let me stress the fact of invention. For all its contentiousness, most of human history has proceeded without social movements as such. Rebellions, revolutions, avenging actions, rough justice, and many other forms of popular collective action have abounded, but not the associating, meeting, marching, petitioning, propagandizing, sloganeering, and brandishing of symbols that mark social movements.

With some eighteenth-century precedents, this complex of interactions emerges as a way of doing political business in Western Europe during the nineteenth century; however we finally sort out the priorities, Britain shares credit for the invention. In Great Britain, the actual inventors were political entrepreneurs such as John Wilkes, Lord George Gordon, William Cobbett, Daniel O'Connell, and Francis Place. They, their collaborators, and their followers bargained out space for new forms of political action—bargained it out with local and national authorities, with rivals, with enemies, with the objects of their claims. The tales of contention over Catholic Emancipation in March 1829 provide glimpses of that bargaining.

Social movements, then, center on the construction of categorical identities. Identities in general are shared experiences of distinctive social relations and the representations of those social relations. Workers become workers in relation to employers and other workers; women become women in relation to men and other women; Orthodox Jews become Orthodox Jews in relation to non-Jews, non-Orthodox Jews, and other Orthodox Jews. Like social movements, nationalism and religious qualifications for citizenship involve the construction and enforcement of unequal, paired categories.

POLITICAL IDENTITIES

Political identities are the subset of identities to which governments are parties. For all the enormous variation in the form and content of political identities, we can assert that the following propositions are true:

- Political identities are always and everywhere relational and collective.

- Most political identities are also categorical rather than specific to a tie between two particular actors.

- Political identities therefore alter as political networks, opportunities, and strategies shift.

- The validation of political identities depends on contingent performances to which other parties' acceptance or rejection of the asserted relation is crucial.

- That validation both constrains and facilitates collective action by those who share the identity.

- Deep differences separate political identities that are embedded in routine social life from those that appear chiefly in public life (embedded and disjoined collective identities).

These propositions break with three very different but common ways of understanding political identities: first, as straightforward activations of durable personal traits, whether individual or collective; second, as malleable features of individual consciousness; third, as purely discursive constructions.

The first view appears incessantly in interest-based accounts of political participation, which generally depend on some version of methodological individualism. The second view recurs in analyses of political commitment as a process of self-realization and correlates closely with an assumption of phenomenological individualism, the doctrine that personal consciousness is the primary—or, at a solipsistic extreme, the only—social reality. The third appears repeatedly in postmodern accounts of identity, many of which likewise lean toward solipsism. My own view denies neither discursive construction, personal traits, nor individual psyches but rather places relations among actors at the center of social processes.

What does "relational and collective" mean? A *political identity* is an actor's experience of a shared social relation in which at least one of the parties—including third parties—is an individual or an organization controlling concentrated means of coercion within some substantial territory. Political identities usually double with shared public *representa-*

tions of both relation and experience. Thus at various times the same people represent themselves as workers, local residents, ethnics, women, citizens, gays, partisans, and other categories that distinguish them from other parts of the population. In each case they engage in authenticating performances that establish worthiness, unity, numbers, and commitment—for example, by marching together, wearing badges, singing songs of solidarity, or shouting slogans.

Under specifiable social conditions, collective identities that people deploy in the course of contention correspond to *embedded identities*, those that inform their routine social lives: race, gender, class, ethnicity, locality, kinship, and so on. Observers tend to label as either "spontaneous" or "traditional" the forms of collective vengeance, shaming, obstruction, and mutual manipulation that spring from embedded identities. Observers also commonly imagine the central causal mechanisms to be transformations of individual consciousness, when in fact selective fortification of certain social ties and divisions at the expense of others impels the mobilization. Although they usually operate at a small scale, when they are under attack by powerholders and enemies embedded identities such as religious affiliation and ethnicity can become the basis of fierce, extensive contention. The Protestant Reformation and the breakup of the Soviet Union featured just such activation of embedded identities.

Under other conditions, people turn to *disjoined identities*, ones that as such rarely or never govern everyday social relations. Disjoined collective identities often include associational memberships, asserted nationalities, and legal categories such as "minority," "tribe," or "military veteran." In these cases, participants invoke salient social ties much more selectively than is the case with embedded identities. Political entrepreneurs, on the average, play much larger parts in their activation. Beth Roy's analysis of how Bengali villagers came to redefine local conflicts as aligning "Hindus" against "Muslims" beautifully illustrates such entrepreneurially mediated mobilization: the farther the intervening political entrepreneurs were situated from the particular village and the more heavily they were involved in national politics, the more they invoked generally recognizable categories (Roy 1994).

The distinction between embedded and disjoined collective identities marks endpoints of a continuum. The collective identity "citizen," for example, falls somewhere in between, typically shaping relations between employers and workers and strongly affecting political involvements but making little difference to a wide range of other social routines. The embedded-disjoined distinction denies, however, two common (and contradictory) ways of understanding the identities that prevail in contentious politics: either as simple activations of preexisting, even primordial, individual attributes or as pure discursive constructions having little or no grounding in social organization. From embedded to disjoined, collective identities resemble linguistic genres in entailing coherent interpersonal collaboration but varying contingently in content, form, and applicability from setting to setting.

The embedded-disjoined contrast also parallels my earlier distinction between interior and exterior categorical pairs. An identity based on location in a categorical pair counts as embedded in a given setting to the extent that people organize a wide range of routine social interactions around it, disjoined to the extent that it becomes salient only on special occasions. Thus, from the perspective of most firms, membership or nonmembership in a sports team remains invisible most of the time; but on the day before a big match, it becomes a basis of differentiation. Within schools, however, sports team membership often makes a difference for a wide range of social relations; it operates in the interior as an embedded category.

Reinforced by contention, internal organization, or acquisition of privileges, disjoined identities sometimes become salient in everyday social relations as well, but they begin elsewhere. Through its various policies from 1903 to 1981, as we have seen, the South African state reified and ratified racial categories that eventually came to loom large in social routines. Eventually, the state and its diverse agents mapped such categories as Zulu, Xhosa, Afrikaner, and Coloured onto the entire population with such force that the categories governed significant shares of everyday social relations. Thus initially disjoined collective identities embedded themselves.

Through sharpening categorical boundaries and promoting shared activities, participation in social movements has likewise partially embedded disjoined identities in routine social life among women, ethnic minorities, or military veterans. The process also runs in the other direction, generalizing and disjoining embedded identities, as when carpenters in one shop, machinists in another, and pipefitters in a third band together not in those identities but as generalized workers. Nevertheless, the distinction matters: the degree to which political identities are embedded or disjoined strongly affects the quantity of widely available knowledge they draw on, the density of underpinning social ties, the strength of conflicting commitments, the ease of emulation from one setting to another, and therefore the effectiveness of different organizing strategies.

The distinction between embedded and disjoined collective identities corresponds approximately to the difference between local contention and national social-movement politics in early nineteenth-century Europe, when a major shift toward the national arena was transforming popular politics (Tarrow 1994; Traugott 1995). As they made claims through such forms of interaction as shaming ceremonies, grain seizures, and the burning of effigies, people generally deployed collective identities corresponding closely to those that prevailed in routine social life: householder, carpenter, neighbor, and so on. We can designate these forms of interaction as *parochial* and *particularistic*, since they ordinarily occurred within localized webs of social relations, incorporating practices and understandings peculiar to those localized webs. They also often took a *patronized* form, relying on appeals to privileged intermediaries for intercession with more distant authorities.

In demonstrations, electoral campaigns, and public meetings, on the other hand, participants often presented themselves as party supporters, association members, citizens, and similar disjoined collective identities. These types of claim-making can be described as *national, modular,* and *autonomous,* calling attention to their frequent fixation on national issues and objects, their standardization from one setting or issue to another, and the frequency with which participants directly addressed powerholders they did not see in everyday social contacts. The difference signified large contrasts in social relations among participants, mobilization patterns, and the organization of action itself. The shift from parochial, particularistic, often patronized forms of claim-making to autonomous, national, and modular forms articulated with profound alterations in social structure.

These shifts in Europe's predominant forms of claim-making of course took place in different versions at different times and paces from one region to another. Altogether, they constituted a dramatic alteration of contentious *repertoires*. Repertoires of contention resemble conversational conventions linking particular sets of interlocutors to each other: far narrower than the technical capacities of the parties would allow or their interests alone prescribe, repertoires form and change through mutual claim-making itself. Like economic institutions that evolve through interaction among organizations but significantly constrain the forms of economic relations at any particular point in time, they limit possibilities for collective action and interaction (Nelson 1995).

Evolution of the demonstration as a means of claim-making, to take an obvious example, tilts activists, police, spectators, rivals, and political officials toward well-defined ways of organizing, anticipating, and responding to the claims made in this medium and to sharp distinctions from claims laid by bombing or bribing (Favre 1990). Strikes, sit-ins, mass meetings, and other forms of claim-making link well-defined identities to each other, involve incessant innovation, and change configuration over the long run but accumulate their own histories, memories, lore, laws, and standard practices. Repertoires, in short, are historically evolving, strongly constraining, cultural products. They combine emulation and adaptation almost seamlessly.

What difference, then, does the presence or absence of a government make to the operation of exploitation and opportunity hoarding? Politicization of categorical inequality increases the salience of government-enforced law, of coercive means, and of polity positions on either side of categorical boundaries. Mobilization of support through elections, social movements, and influence networks becomes a means by which those contesting control of particular resources—whether government-dominated or otherwise—increase their leverage. Since, however, current control of crucial resources augments the capacity of any actor to mobilize political support through elections, influence networks, and even social movements, in ordinary circumstances the operations of states sustain existing patterns of categorical inequality rather than subverting them.

INEQUALITY AND BASIC POLITICAL PROCESSES

The previous discussion implies a general answer to our second question, the issue of how the character and extent of categorical inequality in an organization or population affect its basic political processes. Clearly, they affect those processes profoundly. Categorical inequality forms one of the major grounds and constraints of political life. Let me take up just one implication, the relation between inequality and democracy. Let us call a polity democratic to the extent that it features these elements:

Broad citizenship

Equal citizenship

Binding consultation of citizens with respect to state personnel and performance

Protection of citizens, especially members of minorities, against arbitrary action by state agents

In one obvious way and two less obvious ways, the definition itself incorporates questions of inequality. By definition, obviously, unequal citizenship (e.g., votes for men only or two-tiered systems of state-guaranteed benefits) diminishes democracy. Since 1792, when the French Revolution abolished distinctions between "active" citizens (that is, essentially, propertied adult males) and "passive" citizens (that is, essentially unpropertied adult males who were nevertheless subject to military service), Western struggles for democracy have frequently centered, precisely, on the equalization of rights among previously distinguished categories of citizens.

Less obviously, narrow citizenship entails substantial inequality with respect to rights within a state's territory; some subjects of the state enjoy citizenship while others do not. Before 1865 American slaves did not possess citizenship in any meaningful sense of the word. Apartheid South Africa's virtual exclusion of black Africans from citizenship at a national scale constituted one of its most undemocratic features. Kuwait today excludes the great majority of its work force, recruited immigrants, from citizenship.

Where armed forces enjoy autonomous political power, finally, their autonomy constitutes a violation of equal citizenship, binding consultation, and protection. (If you had to judge whether a state was democratic or not on the basis of a single organizational feature, whether the police reported to the military or to civilian authorities would serve as an excellent guide.) Western countries struggled to their halfway democracies only by containing autonomous military power, and those that failed to do so (for example, Spain and Portugal) saw nominally democratic regimes fail repeatedly.

That inequalities within citizenship, inequalities between citizens and noncitizens, or unequal political autonomy between armed forces and civilians violate democracy by definition does not reduce their substantive threat to democratic politics. Outside the zone of definition, deep categorical inequality also threatens democracy. The main dynamic is simple: to the extent that people on the advantaged sides of categorical divides are small in number and rich in resources, they combine the incentive and the capacity to buy their way out of democratic processes. They can and will effectively narrow citizenship, render it unequal, subvert binding consultation, and undermine protection. In popular elections, for example, the co-presence of a few very rich people and many very poor people encourages the buying of candidates, votes, and election judges, as well as extraelectoral patronage. Where elections are relatively honest, exploiters and opportunity hoarders can still afford to protect their interests by buying or subverting state authorities.

Answers to our first two questions—how states relate to the operation of categorical inequality and how the character of categorical inequality affects basic political processes—therefore imply answers to the other two: ascertaining when inequality itself becomes an object of political struggle and when political struggle and/or governmental action actually changes prevailing patterns of inequality. Let us return to each question briefly.

Because exploitation and opportunity hoarding often involve an effective means of control over members of excluded and subordinated categories, because emulation naturalizes distinctions by making them ubiquitous, and because adaptation ties even exploited groups to the structure of exploitation, most categorical inequality stays in place without sustained, overt struggle. James Scott (1985, 1990) has argued the contrary, indicating that subordinate groups commonly use "weapons of the weak" based on "hidden transcripts" of opposition to subvert powerholders. The histories of landlord-tenant relations, religious inequalities, and social movements indicate, however, that organizers generally have a difficult time stimulating shared awareness of oppression and determination to resist, that even with intense organizing efforts they fail except in special structural circumstances.

What are these circumstances? In the broadest terms, they occur when the benefits from exploitation and opportunity hoarding decline and/or the costs of exploitation, opportunity hoarding, emulation, and adaptation increase. In those circumstances, the beneficiaries of categorical inequality tend to split, with some of them becoming available as the underdogs' allies against other exploiters and hoarders. Contradictions between beliefs sustaining categorical boundaries and day-to-day social life then become more visible, which undermines inequality-sustaining beliefs and practices both by making justification more difficult and by promoting mobilization in the name of justice. When the altered structural position of a subordinated population increases its leverage or internal connectedness—as when Irish soldiers became more essential to British armies and Irish workers more essential to British industry— eventually the costs of controlling that population expand, along with capacity to resist control. Finally, exploiters themselves sometimes inadvertently create opportunities for claim-making, as when British rulers' concessions to organized Protestant Dissenters in 1828 weakened their grounds for excluding organized Catholics in 1829, or when the U.S. government's modest concessions to black civil rights demands in the 1960s established a powerful model for claim-making on behalf of other subordinated populations such as women, gays, older people, Hispanics, Native Americans.

The principles and cases we have been exploring recommend rough distinctions among top-down, competitive, and bottom-up situations. From the *top down*, inequality typically becomes an object of political struggle when would-be exploiters or opportunity hoarders seek to subordinate or exclude from relevant resources members of categories that have previously held collective rights to more favorable circumstances. State-led nationalism's generation of resistance by minorities provides a case in point, but so do plant shutdowns that incite worker takeovers.

Among *competitive* situations, the invasion of an established ethnic occupational niche by members of a new immigrant population frequently causes bitter conflict. So, as we have seen, does the confrontation of rival claimants to statehood within the same territory. Both internal changes (e.g., shifts in the demographic balance between two previously accommodated populations) and external changes (e.g., collapse of a previously restraining national authority) generate such struggles (Margadant 1992; Olzak 1992). For recent American history, Orlando Patterson describes the "paradox of desegregation":

> When blacks and whites were segregated from each other there was little opportunity for conflict. The two groups lived in largely separate worlds, and when they did come in contact their interactions were highly structured by the perverse etiquette of racial relations. The system may have worked well in minimizing conflict, as long as both groups played by the rules, but it was clearly a pernicious arrangement for blacks since it condemned them to inferior status and excluded them from participation in the political life of their society and from nearly all the more desirable opportunities for economic advancement.
>
> Desegregation meant partial access to the far superior facilities and opportunities open previously only to whites. Hence, it entailed a great improvement in the condition and dignity of blacks. All this should be terribly obvious, but it must be spelled out because it is precisely this obvious improvement that is so often implicitly denied when we acknowledge one of the inevitable consequences of desegregation: namely that, as individuals in both groups meet more and more, the possibility for conflict is bound to increase. (Patterson 1995, 26)

Patterson is identifying a crucial aspect not only of recent African American experience but of inequality's competitive politics in general.

From the *bottom up*, South African experience gives us insight into situations where members of subordinate categories acquire increased collective capacity to withhold valuable resources, resist control, exploit elite divisions, and enlist outside allies. Parallels with British Catholics' demands for political participation, American blacks' mobilization for civil rights, and Western women's campaigns for equal pay should become obvious. In short, classic conditions for collective action obtain (Calhoun 1991; Marwell and Oliver 1993; Oliver 1993; Tarrow 1994; Traugott 1995).

When do struggle and/or governmental action change—even reduce—prevailing patterns of inequality? When members of subordinate categories not only mobilize broadly but actually gain power, substantial alterations of inequality often occur rapidly. In the extreme case of revolutions, alliances of underdogs with fragments of the ruling coalition, acquisition of armed force by members of a revolutionary coalition, neutralization or defection of the regime's armed force, and revolutionary control over some significant part of the state apparatus all promote the overturning of the old regime.

Short of revolution, similar conditions foster extensive change in inequality. In South Africa, for example, fragmentation of the white elite not only provided opportunities for black mobilization but also opened up alliances that facilitated black sharing of power. The increasing reliance of white-controlled urban enterprises on black labor; the consequent mismatch between the apartheid system of control and the actual daily movements of the black population; black mobilization within the townships, enclaves, and migration networks that had been created or reinforced by apartheid arrangements; and international sanctions against the regime and its major corporations—all these conditions not only increased the costs to political elites of operating the system of categorical inequality but also diminished returns to holders of capitalist property. These circumstances inclined some members of the ruling coalition to form alliances across categorical boundaries and made their still-resisting fellow rulers more vulnerable to attack. Although income and wealth inequality still divide South Africans more deeply than in almost any other country of the world, at least in the public sector substantial equalization occurred within a few years. Over the medium run, that shift in political power will most likely cause some equalization in wealth, income, education, health, housing, and living conditions across what had been one of the world's starkest divisions of categorical inequality.

South Africa's partial revolution does not bespeak a worldwide trend toward equality. Material inequality is increasing in the major capitalist countries, while in many parts of the world political mobilization on behalf of religious, ethnic, and national categories is promoting new, destructive forms of inequality. These two trends toward inequality make democracy more difficult to sustain or achieve. To the extent that categorical differences in life chances by race, gender, ethnicity, citizenship, and other well-marked boundaries already divide social life, those visible differences, their sustaining practices, and their rationalizing beliefs are readily available for incorporation into new forms of exploitation and opportunity hoarding. In addition to inequality's immediate effects on welfare, threats to democracy give us one more reason for worrying about the general trend toward inequality in the capitalist and postsocialist worlds.

𝟪 Future Inequalities

Jane Austen's *Northanger Abbey* tells the story of Catherine Morland, a seventeen-year-old who lived to unlearn lessons acquired from too much reading of Gothic novels. In Bath, Catherine discussed history with her new friends Henry Tilney (who would eventually, after suitable tribulations, marry Catherine) and Henry's sister Eleanor. "I can read poetry and plays, and things of that sort, and do not dislike travels," declares Catherine,

> "but history, real solemn history, I cannot be interested in. Can you?"
> [Eleanor:] "Yes, I am fond of history."
> [Catherine:] "I wish I were too. I read it a little as a duty, but it tells me nothing that does not either vex or weary me. The quarrels of popes and kings, with wars or pestilences, in every page; the men all so good for nothing, and hardly any women at all—it is very tiresome: yet I often think it odd that it should be so dull, for a great deal of it must be invention. The speeches that are put into the heroes' mouths, their

thoughts and designs—the chief of all this must be invention, and invention is what delights me in other books."

"Historians, you think," said Miss Tilney, "are not happy in their flights of fancy. They display imagination without raising interest. I am fond of history—and am very well contented to take the false with the true. In the principal facts they have sources of intelligence in former histories and records, which may be as much depended on, I conclude, as any thing that does not actually pass under one's own observation; and as for the little embellishments you speak of, they are embellishments, and I like them as such. If a speech be well drawn up, I read it with pleasure, by whomsoever it may be made—and probably with much greater, if the production of Mr. Hume or Mr. Robertson, than if the genuine words of Caractatus, Agricola, or Alfred the Great."

[Catherine:] "You are fond of history!—and so are Mr. Allen and my father; and I have two brothers who do not dislike it. So many instances within my small circle of friends is remarkable! At this rate, I shall not pity the writers of history any longer. If people like to read their books, it is all very well, but to be at so much trouble in filling great volumes, which, as I used to think, nobody would willingly ever look into, to be labouring only for the torment of little boys and girls, always struck me as a hard fate; and though I know it is all very right and necessary, I have often wondered at the person's courage that could sit down on purpose to do it." (Austen 1995 [1818], 97–98)

Inequality's history includes "the quarrels of popes and kings, with wars or pestilences, in every page," but it also includes the daily lives of ordinary people. In that history I have tried to read not only moral tales but also causal principles. More sanguine than Catherine Morland about the possibility of compelling, systematic, and valid historical analysis, I have claimed to identify recurrent causal mechanisms behind the multifarious forms of durable inequality.

Exploitation, opportunity hoarding, emulation, and adaptation that incorporate asymmetrically paired categories have for millennia promoted most of the inequality that historians commonly attribute to individual differences in capacity or enterprise. These causal principles combine with a vast historical record to provide the means of constructing counterfactual accounts of durable inequality: forms of inequality or equality that have existed in some times and places, that could have existed, that could exist now, that could take shape in the future.

A clearer analysis of inequality's structural origins becomes more urgent as inequality in general sharpens. One simple indication of recent changes in American inequality comes from tracking the share of all family income received by the highest 5 percent of families. As Figure 7 shows, that share declined from about 17 percent to 15 percent of the total during the postwar years, hovered at just above 15 percent between 1960 and 1980, and then shot upward. In 1994, census reports showed the wealthiest twentieth of American families receiving more than a fifth of all family income. More refined analyses reveal that overall income inequality generally declined between 1947 and 1966 but then rose almost incessantly from 1968 to the 1990s. During the latter period, real income coming to the country's bottom 60 percent of families has remained essentially constant, whereas the top 5 percent have seen their real income increase by about half (Weinberg 1996; see also Fischer et al. 1996; Danziger and Gottschalk 1995; Massey 1996).

At least four trends have contributed to this massive change: (1) large shifts from relatively well-paid employment in manufacturing to lower-paid employment in services as the U.S. manufacturing base has shrunk; (2) deteriorating employment conditions for poorer American households, especially black and Hispanic, as minimum-wage jobs, sweatshops operating below the minimum wage, part-time employment, temporary employment, and just plain unemployment have all become more prevalent; (3) increases in nonwage income for rich people: stock options, bonuses, commissions, returns from investments; (4) widening disparities in compensation within large firms. On the fourth point, Paul Krugman sums up:

> In 1970 the CEO of a typical Fortune 500 corporation earned about 35 times as much as the average manufacturing employee. It would have been unthinkable to pay him 150 times the average, as is now common, and downright outrageous to do so while announcing mass layoffs and cutting the real earnings of many of the company's workers, especially those who were paid the least to start with. (Krugman 1996, 47)

Between 1970 and the 1990s, unions lost much of their political power, large firms built up their administrative hierarchies while cutting back lower-level jobs, and venture capitalists gained power in corporate

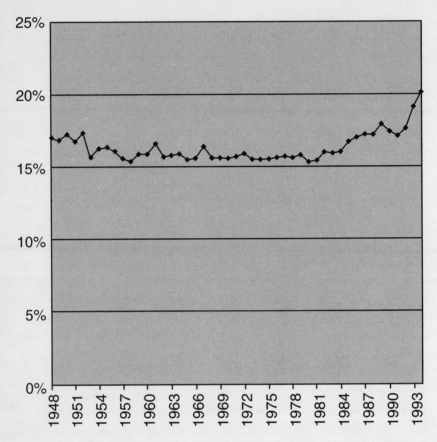

Figure 7.   Share of U.S. Family Income Received by the Top 5 Percent of Families, 1948–1994

SOURCE: Statistics from U.S. Census Bureau, August 1996, *Report on Income Inequality: A Brief Look at Postwar U.S. Income Inequality,* Table 1, electronic version, World Wide Web (*http:// www.census.gov/ hhes/income/incineq/p60 + b1.html*).

governance and used it both to press for larger short-term profits and to reward lavishly those top executives who delivered such profits, while governments (no doubt moved in part by the increasing dependence of elected officials on corporate campaign contributors) became much more charitable to large-firm CEOs and holders of capital. In the name of investment, growth, competitiveness, and efficiency, American government facilitated these changes by means of powerful fiscal incentives. All these shifts weakened the position of labor and strengthened the position of capital. A huge transfer of income from bottom to top intensified American inequality.

Widening American inequality appears not only in income but also in employment and quality of work. Richard Freeman has recently summarized U.S. trends over the past two decades in these terms:

> An economic disaster has befallen low-skilled Americans, especially young men. Researchers using several data sources—including household survey data from the Current Population Survey, other households surveys, and establishment surveys—have documented that wage inequality and skill differentials in earnings and employment increased sharply in the United States from the mid-1970s through the 1980s and into the 1990s. The drop in the relative position of the less skilled shows up in a number of ways: greater earnings differentials between older and younger workers; greater differentials between high-skilled and low-skilled occupations; in a wider earnings distribution overall and within demographic and skill groups; and in less time worked by low-skill and low-paid workers. (Freeman 1995, 17–18)

By now such findings have become drearily familiar. While we certainly should continue to grill the usual suspects—low-wage immigration, competition from offshore production, weakening of organized labor's political position, technological displacement of middle-level workers, short-term corporate profit-taking, and so on—my analysis suggests that alteration of categorical inequalities will turn out to be a key mechanism by which aggregate inequality has been increasing. The channeling of undocumented Asian immigrants into segregated garment sweatshops constitutes one such mechanism, the concentration of black youths in high-turnover, minimum-wage service jobs another. Under conditions of growing freedom for capital, exploitation is increasing.

Articulate radical economist David Gordon, my colleague for years at the New School for Social Research, died while I was writing this book. Gordon took just such a relational line in a book of his own, published within days of his death. "I argue," he declared, that a critically important source of falling wages has been U.S. corporations' increasingly aggressive stance with their employees, their mounting power to gain the upper hand in those struggles, and the shifts in the institutional environment that this mounting power has helped foster. The management offensive since the 1970s has driven three important institutional changes in labor relations and the political environment affecting them—the decline in the real value of the minimum wage, the erosion of union reach and power, and the emergence of "disposable" employment. These three changes appear to underlie much if not most of the wage squeeze. (Gordon 1996, 9)

Gordon's book documents large increases in the share of the American labor force consisting of managers and supervisors, coupled with even larger increases in executive compensation. For all their talk of "lean and mean," American capitalists have opted for a new version of the drive incentive system, with categorically segregated African American males either excluded entirely from workplaces or relegated to the least remunerative jobs (Gordon 1996, 129–135; see also Wilson 1996a). As categorical inequality intensifies, so does aggregate inequality of rewards in the American economy.

Deep down, nevertheless, do all these categorical differences ultimately depend on genetic variation from individual to individual and group to group? The Herrnstein-Murray *Bell Curve* analysis has brought the question, long whispered but not much broadcast, back into public discussion in the United States. Its answer matters analytically, morally, and politically. As Steven Fraser says of *The Bell Curve*:

If group differences in intelligence are to some large degree hereditary and therefore intractable, and if we have become a hierarchical society, polarized into an empowered "cognitive elite" at the top and a sociopathic "cognitive underclass" at the bottom—a hierarchy that merely replicates an ascending slope of IQ scores—then, the authors feel obligated to tell us, public policy stands helpless to do anything about it; thus "success and failure in the American economy, and all that goes with it, are increasingly a matter of the genes that people inherit," and "programs to expand opportunities for the disadvantaged are not going to make much difference." Grim pronouncements indeed. Inequality, inequality of the most fundamental sort, is our inexorable fate however much the nation's democratic and egalitarian credo might groan in protest. (Fraser 1995, 2–3)

Neither the argument nor the evidence in this book has addressed genetic differences directly. Five features of the cases we have reviewed, however, argue for a large organizational component in the variability that reductionists trace to inherited capacity:

- The organizational logics of exploitation, opportunity hoarding, emulation, and adaptation predict to the changing fault lines along which categorical differences array. Instead of the continuous distributions—bell-curved or otherwise—predicted by individual-level variation in capacity, we find organized social discontinuity. In attenuated forms, South African modes of boundary drawing appear everywhere.

- Rapid changes in such alignments as a consequence of new immigration streams, government intervention, shifts in political opportunity, or alterations in corporate policy reveal much greater plasticity than slow-moving genetic differences could account for. Catholic Emancipation, Korean penetration of the New York grocery trade, and affirmative action in American bureaucracies realign categories with a rapidity that depends on organizationally induced changes in social relations.

- Similarity and interchangeability of paired categories in different organizations suggest that very general and compelling organizational processes are occurring. That race, gender, and citizenship should mark similar boundaries in different organizations tells against any simple reductionism to genes.

- At times—as in the formation of immigrant niches and the reorganization of ethnicity in Bosnia—we can observe the processes of category formation directly.

- The indirect effects of categorical inequality on capacity and style loom so large that categorically differentiated experience could plausibly account for most or all of the average intergroup differences in test performances on which Herrnstein, Murray, and other genetic determinists base their arguments. As the evidence on nutrition with which this book opened indicates, genetic variation is much more likely to explain differences *within* than *between* categories.

If we reject genetic explanations, however, a question persists: do non-categorical inequalities respond to the same sorts of organizational processes as categorical inequalities? My reading of the evidence produces no certainties but runs toward strong working hypotheses. We should find that once categories are fixed in place they greatly attenuate the effects of individual variation in knowledge, skill, attitude, and performance on either side of categorical divides. Even aside from such extreme genetic reductionism as *The Bell Curve*, differential rewards do not correspond closely to variation in individual attributes. We should also find that categorical organization helps produce individual differences as a consequence of structured differentials in contacts, experiences, opportunities, and assistance or resistance from others. Bonds, not essences, provide the bases of durable inequality.

CATEGORICAL INEQUALITY GENERALIZED

Categorical inequality therefore has strong links to inequality in general. Following a research tradition dating back to John Stuart Mill in the 1850s but given great impetus by Simon Kuznets a century later, economists and economically minded social scientists have generally explained income differentials as the rewards of variable productivity. At the level of firms, industries, and whole economies, according to this line of reasoning, the factors of production whose increments cause larger increases of output also receive larger returns.

Similar reasoning operates at the individual level. At that level, economists typically see individually carried human capital as a major contributor to productivity and as employers' most frequent proxy for the contribution; employers, clients, and other consumers of labor power set its rewards in accordance with the laborer's human capital, which includes not only education but also productivity-enhancing knowledge acquired on the job. Hence an unequal distribution of human capital predicts to unequal income.

The actual value of human capital in such a model, however, depends on its correspondence to available work; technological obsolescence or oversupply of certain skills, for example, depresses the value of those skills. Ability to operate a typewriter commanded much higher rewards in 1920 than in 1990. Assuming a relatively efficient labor market that tends toward equilibrium, the argument predicts a long-term movement of employment toward the cheapest workers that can make a given contribution to productivity as well as a movement of workers toward the best income available for their human capital.

Even neoclassical economists recognize the rigidities, stickiness, lumpiness, and segregation among markets that hinder efficient moves toward general equilibrium—for example, laid-off older workers do not easily move to where their diminishing talents would gain their maximum reward, or any reward at all. Following John Stuart Mill, economists often recognize the presence (however temporary) of noncompeting labor markets, such as agricultural and industrial specialties between which little or no equilibrating movement ever occurs. By extension, then, the standard competitive view of income inequality allows for substantial leads and lags among jobs, trades, industries, and even factors of production (land, labor, capital, technology) in the relation between income and value added.

Simon Kuznets saw intersectoral lags as typically broadening income inequality during early industrialization (with an undersupply of skilled labor and excess workers tied up in relatively unproductive industries) but eventually diminishing with mature industrialization; this is the famous inverted-U path of change in income inequality. Jeffrey Williamson has offered a sophisticated, modified version of Kuznets's doctrine as a general account of changes in income inequality during industrialization (e.g., Williamson 1985; Williamson and Lindert 1980). Williamson and like-minded analysts argue, furthermore, that current income differences drive longer-run differences in wealth, hence differences in a wide range of material advantages.

Williamson's collaborator Peter Lindert sums up the five main "forces" that interact to produce changing income inequality:

1. *labour force growth*, as governed by the demographic transition and international migration;

2. *skills deepening,* or the rate of improvement in the average skill endowment of the labour force;

3. *technological imbalance,* or sectoral differences in exogenous total-factor productivity change that imply shifts in relative factor demands;

4. *Engel effects* translating exogenous contributions to growth in income per capita into biases in factor demand ["Engel's Law" describes the tendency of expenditures to shift proportionately away from subsistence necessities as income rises]; and

5. *the prior distribution of wealth,* both human and non-human as influenced by revolutions, land reform and other historic forces. (Lindert 1991, 223)

Over the long run, in such a view, efficient markets produce equalizing effects as all factors of production move toward their most efficient uses. At equilibrium, factors and the individuals that embody or deploy them get returns proportionate to the contributions they make to total productivity.

Lindert himself presents all five forces in quite individualistic terms, as if the skills commanded by more and more individual workers altered wage bargains one by one, with the cumulative effect of equalizing wages. Even his sectors serve his explanations primarily as accounting rubrics within which individual efforts wreak their consequences rather than as organized social structures. Nevertheless, by now it should be clear that most of these effects have categorical elements: categorical construction of skill, categorical distribution of wealth, and so on. Our challenge is to see how many of these effects depend on categorical organization.

Institutional and Marxist economists, not to mention many economic sociologists, commonly consider most labor markets to be segmented, crossed by strong barriers separating relatively favored industries, firms, and their workers from less favored sectors (Tilly and Tilly 1994, 294). In general, analyses of labor market segmentation argue that employers in capital-intensive and/or monopoly-exploiting firms share some of the rents accruing from their favored positions with selected workers who reciprocate with loyalty, effort, and accumulation of productive, firm-specific knowledge.

In more competitive sectors, goes the usual argument, the wage bill looms so large within total production that employers cannot afford the luxury of buying off their workers; they turn to the cheapest available labor consistent with their productive requirements and drive that labor hard. As I see it, however, segmentation cuts across firms and industries, for example, dividing pools characterized by drive, loyalty, and task incentive systems and their corresponding command-mobility arrangements within the very same establishments. Yet segmentation does occur very widely, does correspond to the segregation of recruitment and employment networks, and does fit with contrasting systems of rewards for work.

Where, then, do categories come in? Categorical inequality actually accounts for a major share of interindividual and interhousehold inequality in material welfare. Production of qualifications for, and connections to, different kinds of work—human capital, broadly defined—operates categorically, with systematic differences by race, gender, ethnicity, and citizenship. Actual matching of workers with jobs likewise follows categorical lines, with the fitting of exterior to interior categories installing systematic differences in income.

As we have seen, close analyses of job segregation by gender (the best-documented form of categorical inequality in this regard) typically indicate that more than half of male/female income differences, *net of human capital,* result not from wage variability within the same jobs but from the assignment of males and females to differentially rewarded jobs. Since human-capital differences themselves result to an important degree from categorical processes, categorical inequality actually lies behind much of what economists now measure as interindividual or interhousehold inequality. Once we consider both indirect and direct effects of categorically organized inequality, we discover that a large share of the variation in rewards and resources commonly attributed to individual differences in capacity and effort actually results from the categorical organization of production and reproduction.

If so, we should reverse the conventional procedure for analyzing discrimination: instead of treating it as the residual difference between categories once all possible sources of individual variation are taken into account, treat it as the portion of inequality that corresponds to locally relevant categories, and then see how much of the residual can be explained by variation in human capital, effort, and similar individual-level factors. The recurrent finding that job segregation according to race, ethnicity, and, especially, gender rather than wage discrimination within jobs accounts for a large share of all wage differentials encourages such a reversal of reasoning.

To be sure, differences begin right there: differences between states and other organizations; between the asymmetrical, coercive imposition of categories and their slow emergence from unequal social interaction; between creation of new categories and insertion of existing categories into new settings; between life-shaping categorical inequalities and narrow ones. Common features result from the general properties of categorical work, which brings with it a visible boundary, defined ties across that boundary, mechanisms for placing new persons and social relations with respect to the boundary, and segregated social structures attaching life on one side of the boundary or the other to larger webs of social ties. Systematic variation in categorical work results chiefly from differences in the kinds of resources involved, the scope of the boundaries in question, the implication of categories in social ties outside the organization, and the configurations of interested parties.

Because of these local, historical, and organizational contingencies, different sorts of categorical pairs occupy distinct positions in social life. Gender and race, to take an extreme contrast, work differently because gender distinctions cut through households, communities, and social classes, while race often coincides with household, community, and class boundaries. Indeed, where race operates as a major basis of inequality it ordinarily does so through just such exclusions. People build ostensibly racial systems by means of inheritance, restrictions on cohabitation, network segmentation, and spatial segregation to a degree that they accomplish with gender only in very special circumstances: religious communities, military units, not much more.

A momentous contrast results: on one side, reduction of racial inequality usually depends on extensive creation of social ties where few exist and on deep alteration of existing relations but relatively little change in organizational structure. On the other side, emulation and adaptation embed unequal gender relations in so many different sorts of structures that reduction of gender inequality depends on massive alteration of existing organizations but little creation of new social ties. For all the common properties we have discovered in various systems of categorical inequality, deliberate intervention to change them therefore requires deep knowledge of their peculiarities and historical settings.

Like any serious inquiry into important social processes, my analysis of inequality-generating mechanisms clarifies some questions but makes others seem more urgent and difficult than before. Two problems stand out: First, how much, and how, does historically accumulated culture differentiate the operation of various sorts of categorical inequality: gender, race, citizenship, and so on? Second, to what degree, and how, do indirect effects of categorically differentiated experience and connections modify, limit, or determine the direct effects on which the analysis has concentrated? In the first regard, we have seen abundant evidence that such categorical sets as ethnicity, race, citizenship, gender, and religion accumulate significantly different beliefs, symbols, and practices wherever they coexist and that these historically accumulated cultural features inform the day-to-day operation of inequality. Students of inequality must still examine whether such historical accumulations have such regularity and power that exploitation, opportunity hoarding, emulation, and adaptation work differently depending on which categorical distinctions they employ.

In the second regard, we could still discover that categorically differentiated experiences in household, kin group, neighborhood, school, and previous workplaces override, modify, or even explain categorical differences in positions occupied by people of diverse origins in resource-controlling organizations. Instead of concentrating on sorting by race or religion into superior and inferior categories at the point of unequal rewards, we might then shift our explanatory focus to characteristically different life histories that produce people who differ so greatly in knowledge, skill, style, motivation, and personal connections as to affect reward-generating performances deeply. Such an outcome would not contradict this book's major arguments, but it would reduce the scope of the point-of-reward organizational mechanisms it has emphasized. The relational analysis of inequality has just begun.

FUTURES

Setting aside doubts and calls for further research, suppose that organizationally based exploitation, opportunity hoarding, emulation, and adaptation have roughly the effects I have claimed. What futures might we then envisage for inequality over the world at large, and within rich capitalist countries in particular? This book's analyses lead to no firm unitary predictions, precisely because they treat inequality as a historical product, deeply subject to human agency. To discipline our thinking, nevertheless, we might sketch the following possibilities:

- **More of the Same:** Present trends in inequality are perpetuated, with categorical differences in access to capital increasingly salient in a capital-divided world; educational institutions exercise greater and greater influence on the sorting of people into categories and hence into the receipt of differential rewards; race and ethnicity acquire or lose significance chiefly as they intertwine with class and political power; gender becomes less critical as a basis of material inequality; and governmental intervention (whether promoted by popular political mobilization or otherwise) continues to make a strong difference in the institutionalization or attenuation of categorical differences. In this scenario, exploitation, opportunity hoarding, emulation, and adaptation simply follow their current courses throughout the world.

- **Balkanization:** Technological and organizational changes reduce the feasibility and attractiveness of exploitation—especially the subordination of excluded persons' efforts—while expanding the scope of opportunity hoarding. As a result, the world segments increasingly into partly insulated clusters of producers-consumers whose exchanges equalize them to some degree but which become vulnerable to invasion and attack from members of other clusters that combine extensive solidarity-generating internal networks, poor resource bases, and little current opportunity to hoard. Small, segregated camps of hoarders emerge.

- **Material Equalization:** Authoritative intervention (democratically sanctioned or otherwise) inhibits the matching of interior with exterior categories within reward-distributing organizations, redistributes enough of the surplus generated by such organizations to guarantee all individuals a socially acceptable package of income and services, ensures that sorting institutions such as schools resist the installation of exterior categories and attenuate the performance effects of previous categorically differentiated experiences, reduces the transmission of categorically organized advantages from generation to generation, and generally weakens the links among exploitation, opportunity hoarding, and widely prevalent categorical pairs.

- **New Categories:** As has frequently happened in history, new categorical pairs form, or existing categorical pairs gain salience, through incremental action and/or political mobilization. Ethnicities become recognized nations and acquire their own states, social movements establish new polity members, the line between citizens and noncitizens becomes the basis of increasing discrimination, revolutionary coalitions seize control over existing states, prophets gather followings that turn into powerful religious organizations, and so on, through a wide range of possible transformations. Much depends on whether these sorts of mobilizations disrupt, capture, or coincide with previously existing control of surplus-generating resources—whether, that is, they have serious impacts on existing patterns of exploitation, opportunity hoarding, emulation, and adaptation.

Although I admit a strong personal preference for the third scenario (material equalization) over the first, second, and fourth, the point of this little exercise is neither to weigh the desirability of one future or another nor to estimate their relative probabilities. It is instead to assert that in the future, as in the past, the same sorts of causal mechanisms will continue to generate forms and degrees of inequality. People will continue to invent, borrow, or connect chains, hierachies, triads, organizations, and categorical pairs as they solve workaday problems. Scripting and the accumulation of local knowledge will continue to characterize social interaction, equal or unequal. Changes in the categorical organization of exploitation, opportunity hoarding, emulation, and adaptation will continue to produce major differences in welfare, power, and opportunity. Immutable economic laws will not lay down inevitable material inequalities, both because economic processes result from accumulated, discretionary agency and because inequality-generating economic processes operate within stringent limits set by political institutions and public policies.

Suppose we decide to push our world gently toward (or away from) one of the four scenarios. Suppose we adopt this book's view of durable inequality as an outcome of categorically organized exploitation, opportunity hoarding, emulation, and adaptation. That view, if correct, has three strong implications for intervention:

- First, changes in attitudes will have weak and indirect effects on existing patterns of inequality. Education for tolerance and understanding may ease the way, but it will not attack the root causes of discrimination.

- Second, alteration of categorical differences in human capital through education, on-the-job training, or transformation of social environments will affect categorical inequality but will do so chiefly through their impact on the organization of opportunity rather than their improvement of individual capacities.

- Finally, reorganization of workplaces and other sites of differential rewards with respect to the location and character of categorical boundaries can produce rapid, far-reaching changes in categorical inequality. Breaking connections between interior categories and widely adopted exterior categories, diminishing cross-boundary reward differentials, or facilitating mobility across boundaries should produce significant reductions in overall inequality.

Just as they usually concentrate on individual admissions to colleges and universities, American advocates of affirmative action in employment (e.g., Bergmann 1997) ordinarily focus attention on hiring agents' individual decisions at the point of initial hiring. Surely the elimination of exclusion at hiring and/or the establishment of categorically preferential hiring can affect the extent and character of categorical inequality within firms. To the extent that initial jobs connect with internal labor markets, the effect of affirmative action at initial hiring multiplies. Concentrating on individual decisions at the point of hire is neither surprising nor stupid. After all, antidiscrimination law also concentrates there; for advocates, that law establishes a claim for governmental intervention on behalf of equality.

The law concentrates on initial admission to a school or a firm, however, largely because analysts, advocates, and legislators have accepted a narrow, individualistic view of inequality. Analysts, advocates, and legislators who believe this book's arguments should shift their thinking to organizational processes. They should examine every organization and labor market as a collection of sites for exploitation, opportunity hoarding, emulation, and adaptation. They should plot how either to foil those sites' inequality-producing effects or to turn them toward the promotion of equality. If existing employees of a firm continue to play predominant parts in the recruitment of applicants for new jobs, for example, altering the networks through which information about new openings flows is likely to have a larger effect at lower cost than enforcing strictly egalitarian standards in hiring decisions. An improved understanding of the organizational processes that generate inequality will multiply the possible points and means of intervention.

The implications of this analysis run far beyond sites of work. As my tales of Catholic Emancipation and South African racism have indicated most directly, the extent of large-scale categorical inequality matters not only because of deprivation among members of subordinate categories but also because it affects the viability of democratic institutions (Muller 1995; Rueschemeyer, Stephens, and Stephens 1992). A polity is democratic, as I understand it, to the extent that it institutionalizes broad, relatively equal citizenship, protects citizens from arbitrary action by state agents, and gives citizens significant collective control over state personnel and policy. Widespread categorical inequality threatens democratic institutions twice: by giving members of powerful categories incentives and means to exclude others from full benefits, and by providing visible markers for inclusion and exclusion. Current American efforts to shrink state-mediated entitlements and tie benefits to employment strike me, despite their obfuscatory language of market rationalization, as embodying just such threats to democracy.

Caution: I do not consider it possible—or even desirable—to delete all categorical inequalities from social life; I appreciate the advantages, for example, of licensing professionals who make risky interventions in our bodies and of attaching special obligations-cum-rights to citizenship. The two situations require categorical distinctions of professionals from nonprofessionals and citizens from noncitizens. Nor do I think we can easily check the propensity of people who run large organizations to create segregated patron-client chains within them and then to defend those patronage systems by means of category work. I am not certain either that we should block immigrant niche making, so long as it imposes no net harm on persons outside the niche.

We can, nevertheless, envisage three crucial steps toward equality of opportunity: first, analyzing present-day organizational structures to detect the operation of unnecessary categorical inequalities within them; second, constructing verified counterfactuals, alternative paths by which inequality-sustaining organizations could do similar work without pernicious inequality; third, thwarting routines by which exterior categories come to match differentially rewarded interior categories and thereby exclude members of subordinate categories from their share of organizationally distributed rewards. Guided by adequate understanding of categorical inequality and its consequences, familiar forms of organizational analysis and intervention could foster substantial, beneficial social change.

Here is a field of analysis and action worthy of social-scientific intelligence. Here is a chance to work seriously toward reducing durable inequality. We must move away from, not toward, the gross inequalities of James Gillray's era. In the midst of twenty-first-century abundance, we should leave no place for bitter confrontations of the tall and the short, the fat and the thin, the overfed and the hungry.

References

Abrahamson, Mark. 1996. *Urban Enclaves: Identity and Place in America.* New York: St. Martin's.

Adams, Julia. 1994. "Trading States, Trading Places: The Role of Patrimonialism in Early Modern Dutch Development." *Comparative Studies in Society and History* 36: 319–355.

Ahrne, Göran. 1994. *Social Organizations: Interaction Inside, Outside, and Between Organizations.* London: Sage.

———. 1996. "Civil Society and Civil Organizations." *Organization* 3: 109–120.

Akerlof, George A. 1984. "Gift Exchange and Efficiency Wage Theory: Four Views." *American Economic Review: Papers and Proceedings* 74: 79–83.

Aldrich, Howard, Trevor P. Jones, and David McEvoy. 1984. "Ethnic Advantage and Minority Business Development." In *Ethnic Communities in Business: Strategies for Economic Survival,* edited by Robin Ward and Richard Jenkins. Cambridge: Cambridge University Press.

Allan, Jim. 1993. "Male Elementary Teachers: Experiences and Perspectives." In *Doing "Women's Work": Men in Nontraditional Occupations,* edited by Christine L. Williams. Newbury Park, Calif.: Sage.

248   REFERENCES

Allen, Mike. 1996. "What to Wear, What to Touch, What to Say, What to Tuck." *New York Times*, August 11, E7.

Almquist, Elizabeth M. 1987. "Labor Market Gender Inequality in Minority Groups." *Gender and Society* 1: 400–414.

Amott, Teresa L., and Julie A. Matthaei. 1991. *Race, Gender, and Work: A Multicultural Economic History of Women in the United States*. Boston: South End Press.

Anderson, Benedict. 1991. *Imagined Communities: Reflections on the Origin and Spread of Nationalism*. Rev. ed. London: Verso.

Anderson, Grace M. 1974. *Networks of Contact: The Portuguese and Toronto*. Waterloo, Ontario: Wilfrid Laurier University Publications.

Andrews, George Reid, and Herrick Chapman, eds. 1995. *The Social Construction of Democracy, 1870–1990*. New York: New York University Press.

Armstrong, John A. 1982. *Nations Before Nationalism*. Chapel Hill: University of North Carolina Press.

Ashenfelter, Orley, and Albert Rees, eds. 1973. *Discrimination in Labor Markets*. Princeton: Princeton University Press.

Ashforth, Adam. 1990. *The Politics of Official Discourse in Twentieth-Century South Africa*. Oxford: Clarendon Press.

Austen, Jane. 1995. *Northanger Abbey*. London: Penguin. First published in 1818.

Avalos, Manuel. 1996. "Gender Inequality: Sorting Out the Effects of Race/Ethnicity and Gender in the Anglo Male–Latino Female Earnings Gap." *Sociological Perspectives* 39: 497–516.

Ayres, Ian, and Peter Siegelman. 1995. "Race and Gender Discrimination in Bargaining for a New Car." *American Economic Review* 85: 304–321.

Baer, Ellen D. 1990. "Nurses." In *Women, Health, and Medicine in America: A Historical Handbook*, edited by Rima D. Apple. New York: Garland.

Bahl, Vinay. 1989. "Women in the Third World: Problems in Proletarianization and Class Consciousness." *Sage Race Relations Abstracts* 14: 3–27.

Bailey, Thomas R. 1987. *Immigrant and Native Workers: Contrasts and Competition*. Boulder: Westview.

Baily, Samuel L. 1983. "The Adjustment of Italian Immigrants in Buenos Aires and New York, 1870–1914." *American Historical Review* 88: 281–305.

Barbalet, J. M. 1988. *Citizenship*. Minneapolis: University of Minnesota Press.

Barnett, Rosalind C., and Grace K. Baruch. 1987. "Social Roles, Gender, and Psychological Distress." In *Gender and Stress*, edited by Rosalind C. Barnett, Lois Biener, and Grace K. Baruch. New York: Free Press.

Baron, Ava. 1982. "Women and the Making of the American Working Class: A Study of the Proletarianization of Printers." *Review of Radical Political Economics* 14: 23–42.

———. 1991a. "Gender and Labor History: Learning from the Past, Looking to the Future." In *Work Engendered: Toward a New History of American Labor,* edited by Ava Baron. Ithaca: Cornell University Press.

———. 1991b. "An 'Other' Side of Gender Antagonism at Work: Men, Boys, and the Remasculinization of Printers' Work, 1830–1920." In *Work Engendered: Toward a New History of American Labor,* edited by Ava Baron. Ithaca: Cornell University Press.

Baron, James N. 1984. "Organizational Perspectives on Stratification." *Annual Review of Sociology* 10: 37–69.

———. 1994. "Reflections on Recent Generations of Mobility Research." In *Social Stratification: Class, Race, and Gender,* edited by David B. Grusky. Boulder: Westview.

Baron, James N., and William T. Bielby. 1980. "Bringing the Firm Back In: Stratification, Segmentation, and the Organization of Work." *American Sociological Review* 45: 737–755.

———. 1984. "The Organization of Work in a Segmented Economy." *American Sociological Review* 49: 454–473.

Barth, Fredrik. 1981. *Process and Form in Social Life: Selected Essays of Fredrik Barth.* Vol. 1. London: Routledge and Kegan Paul.

Barton, Josef J. 1975. *Peasants and Strangers: Italians, Rumanians, and Slovaks in an American City, 1890–1950.* Cambridge: Harvard University Press.

Bax, Mart. 1976. *Harpstrings and Confessions: Machine-Style Politics in the Irish Republic.* Amsterdam: Van Gorcum.

Bearman, Peter S. 1993. *Relations into Rhetorics: Local Elite Social Structure in Norfolk, England, 1540–1640.* New Brunswick, N. J.: Rutgers University Press.

Beckert, Jens. 1996. "What Is Sociological About Economic Sociology? Uncertainty and the Embeddedness of Economic Action." *Theory and Society* 25: 803–840.

Beinart, William. 1987. "Worker Consciousness, Ethnic Particularism, and Nationalism: The Experiences of a South African Migrant, 1930–1960." In *The Politics of Race, Class, and Nationalism in Twentieth-Century South Africa,* edited by Shula Marks and Stanley Trapido. London: Longman.

Benford, Robert D., and Scott A. Hunt. 1992. "Dramaturgy and Social Movements: The Social Construction and Communication of Power." *Sociological Inquiry* 62: 35–55.

Beramendi, Justo G., Ramón Máiz, and Xosé M. Núñez, eds. 1994. *Nationalism in Europe, Past and Present.* 2 vols. Santiago: Universidad de Santiago de Compostela.

Bergmann, Barbara R. 1986. *The Economic Emergence of Women.* New York: Basic Books.

———. 1997. "A Business Showcases Its Segregated Staff." *Dollars and Sense* 209 (January–February): 10–11.

Bernhardt, Annette, Martina Morris, and Mark S. Handcock. 1995. "Women's Gains or Men's Losses? A Closer Look at the Shrinking Gender Gap in Earnings." *American Journal of Sociology* 101: 302–328.

Berry, Albert, François Bourguignon, and Christian Morrisson. 1991. "Global Economic Inequality and Its Trends Since 1950." In *Economic Inequality and Poverty: International Perspectives,* edited by Lars Osberg. Armonk, N.Y.: M. E. Sharpe.

Besley, Timothy. 1995. "Nonmarket Institutions for Credit and Risk Sharing in Low-Income Countries." *Journal of Economic Perspectives* 9: 169–188.

Best, G. F. A. 1958. "The Protestant Constitution and Its Supporters, 1800–1829." *Transactions of the Royal Historical Society,* 5th ser., 8: 105–127.

———. 1967. "Popular Protestantism in Victorian Britain," In *Ideas and Institutions of Victorian Britain,* edited by Robert Robson. London: G. Bell and Sons.

Best, Michael H. 1990. *The New Competition: Institutions of Industrial Restructuring.* Cambridge: Harvard University Press.

Bielby, Denise D., and William T. Bielby. 1988. "She Works Hard for the Money: Household Responsibilities and the Allocation of Work Effort." *American Journal of Sociology* 93: 1031–1059.

———. 1995. "Cumulative Versus Continuous Disadvantage in an Unstructured Labor Market: Gender Differences in the Careers of Television Writers." In *Gender Inequality at Work,* edited by Jerry A. Jacobs. Thousand Oaks, Calif.: Sage.

Bielby, William T., and James N. Baron. 1986. "Men and Women at Work: Sex Segregation and Statistical Discrimination," *American Journal of Sociology* 91: 759–799.

Birkelund, Gunn Elisabeth, Leo A. Goodman, and David Rose. 1996. "The Latent Structure of Job Characteristics of Men and Women." *American Journal of Sociology* 102: 80–113.

Birnbaum, Pierre. 1993. *"La France aux Français": Histoire des haines nationalistes.* Paris: Seuil.

Bjørn, Claus, Alexander Grant, and Keith J. Stringer, eds. 1994a. *Nations, Nationalism, and Patriotism in the European Past.* Copenhagen: Academic Press.

———. 1994b. *Social and Political Identities in Western History.* Copenhagen: Academic Press.

Blanc, Maurice, ed. 1992. *Pour une sociologie de la transaction sociale.* Paris: L'Harmattan.

Blau, Francine D., and Marianne A. Ferber. 1985. "Women in the Labor Market: The Last Twenty Years." *Women and Work: An Annual Review* 1: 19–49.

———. 1986. *The Economics of Women, Men, and Work.* Englewood Cliffs, N.J.: Prentice-Hall.

Blau, Francine D., and Lawrence M. Kahn. 1992. "The Gender Earnings Gap:

Some International Evidence." Working Paper 4224, National Bureau of Economic Research, Cambridge, Mass.

———. 1994. "Rising Wage Inequality and the U.S. Gender Gap." *American Economic Review: Papers and Proceedings* 84: 23–28.

Blau, Peter M. 1977. *Inequality and Heterogeneity: A Primitive Theory of Social Structure.* New York: Free Press.

Bodnar, John. 1982. *Workers' World: Kinship, Community, and Protest in an Industrial Society, 1900–1940.* Baltimore: Johns Hopkins University Press.

———. 1985. *The Transplanted: A History of Immigrants in Urban America.* Bloomington: Indiana University Press.

Bodnar, John, Roger Simon, and Michael P. Weber. 1982. *Lives of Their Own: Blacks, Italians, and Poles in Pittsburgh, 1900–1960.* Urbana: University of Illinois Press.

Bögenhold, Dieter. 1996. *Das Dienstleistungsjahrhundert: Kontinuitäten und Diskontinuitäten in Wirtschaft und Gesellschaft.* Stuttgart: Enke.

Borjas, George J. 1995a. "The Economic Benefits from Immigration." *Journal of Economic Perspectives* 9: 3–22.

———. 1995b. "Ethnicity, Neighborhoods, and Human Capital Externalities." *American Economic Review* 85: 365–390.

Bottomore, Thomas, ed. 1983. *A Dictionary of Marxist Thought.* Cambridge: Harvard University Press.

Botwinick, Howard. 1993. *Persistent Inequalities: Wage Disparity Under Capitalist Competition.* Princeton: Princeton University Press.

Bound, John, and Richard B. Freeman. 1992. "What Went Wrong? The Erosion of the Relative Earnings and Employment of Young Black Men in the 1980s." *Quarterly Journal of Economics* 107: 201–232.

Bourdieu, Pierre. 1979. *La Distinction: Critique Sociale du Jugement.* Paris: Editions de Minuit.

Bourdieu, Pierre, and Loïc J. D. Wacquant. 1992. *Invitation to Reflexive Sociology.* Chicago: University of Chicago Press.

Bouton, Cynthia A. 1993. *The Flour War: Gender, Class, and Community in Late Ancien Régime French Society.* University Park: Pennsylvania State University Press.

Bower, Gordon H., and Daniel G. Morrow. 1990. "Mental Models in Narrative Comprehension." *Science* 247: 44–48.

Bowles, Samuel, and Herbert Gintis. 1976. *Schooling in Capitalist America: Educational Reform and the Contradictions of Economic Life.* New York: Basic Books.

———. 1993. "The Revenge of Homo Economicus: Contested Exchange and the Revival of Political Economy." *Journal of Economic Perspectives* 7: 83–114 (with comments by Oliver Williamson and Joseph Stiglitz).

Boyd, Monica, Mary Ann Mulvihill, and John Myles. 1995. "Gender, Power, and Postindustrialism." In *Gender Inequality at Work,* edited by Jerry A. Jacobs. Thousand Oaks, Calif.: Sage.

Brachet-Marquez, Viviane. 1994. *The Dynamics of Domination: State, Class, and Social Reform in Mexico, 1910–1990.* Pittsburgh: University of Pittsburgh Press.

Brass, Tom. 1991. "Moral Economists, Subalterns, New Social Movements, and the (Re-)Emergence of a (Post-)Modernized (Middle) Peasant." *Journal of Peasant Studies* 18: 173–205.

Breiger, Ronald L. 1995. "Social Structure and the Phenomenology of Attainment." *Annual Review of Sociology* 21: 115–136.

Breton, Raymond, Wsevolod W. Isajiw, Warren E. Kalbach, and Jeffrey G. Reitz. 1990. *Ethnic Identity and Equality: Varieties of Experience in a Canadian City.* Toronto: University of Toronto Press.

Breuilly, John. 1994. *Nationalism and the State.* 2d ed. Chicago: University of Chicago Press.

Bridges, William P. 1982. "The Sexual Segregation of Occupations: Theories of Labor Stratification in Industry." *American Journal of Sociology* 88: 270–295.

Brines, Julie. 1994. "Economic Dependency, Gender, and the Division of Labor at Home." *American Journal of Sociology* 100: 652–688.

Brockett, Charles D. 1992. "Measuring Political Violence and Land Inequality in Central America." *American Political Science Review* 86: 169–176.

Brown, Charles. 1980. "Equalizing Differences in the Labor Market." *Quarterly Journal of Economics* 94: 114–134.

Brubaker, Rogers. 1992. *Citizenship and Nationhood in France and Germany.* Cambridge: Harvard University Press.

———. 1996. *Nationalism Reframed: Nationhood and the National Question in the New Europe.* Cambridge: Cambridge University Press.

Buchmann, Marlis. 1989. *The Script of Life in Modern Society: Entry into Adulthood in a Changing World.* Chicago: University of Chicago Press.

Bulow, Jeremy I., and Lawrence H. Summers. 1986. "A Theory of Dual Labor Markets with Application to Industrial Policy, Discrimination, and Keynesian Unemployment." *Journal of Labor Economics* 4: 376–414.

Bunge, Mario. 1996. *Finding Philosophy in Social Science.* New Haven: Yale University Press.

Buoye, Thomas. 1993. "From Patrimony to Commodity: Changing Concepts of Land and Social Conflict in Guangdong Province During the Qianlong Reign (1736–1795)." *Late Imperial China* 14: 33–59.

Burawoy, Michael. 1979. *Manufacturing Consent: Changes in the Labor Process Under Monopoly Capitalism.* Chicago: University of Chicago Press.

Burbridge, Lynn C. 1994. "The Reliance of African-American Women on Government and Third-Sector Employment." *American Economic Review: Papers and Proceedings* 84: 103–107.

Burt, Ronald S., and Marc Knez. 1995. "Kinds of Third-Party Effects on Trust." *Rationality and Society* 7: 255–292.

Butler, Richard J., and James B. McDonald. 1986. "Income Inequality in the United States, 1948–1980." *Research in Labor Economics* 8: 85–140.

Butterfield, Fox. 1997. "Many Black Men Barred from Voting." *New York Times,* January 30, A12.

Cain, Glen G. 1991. "The Uses and Limits of Statistical Analysis in Measuring Economic Discrimination." In *Essays on the Economics of Discrimination,* edited by Emily P. Hoffman. Kalamazoo, Mich.: W. E. Upjohn Institute for Employment Research.

Calhoun, Craig. 1991. "The Problem of Identity in Collective Action." In *Macro-Micro Linkages in Sociology,* edited by Joan Huber. Newbury Park, Calif.: Sage.

———. 1993a. "Nationalism and Ethnicity." *Annual Review of Sociology* 19: 211–239.

———. 1993b. " 'New Social Movements' of the Early Nineteenth Century." *Social Science History* 17: 385–428.

Campbell, Karen E., Peter V. Marsden, and Jeanne S. Hurlbert. 1986. "Social Resources and Socioeconomic Status." *Social Networks* 8: 97–117.

Campbell, Karen, and Rachel Rosenfeld. 1986. "Job Search and Job Mobility: Sex and Race Differences." *Research in the Sociology of Work* 3, entire issue.

Carlos, Ann M. 1992. "Principal-Agent Problems in Early Trading Companies: A Tale of Two Firms." *American Economic Review: Papers and Proceedings* 82: 140–145.

Castells, Manuel. 1996. *The Rise of the Network Society.* Oxford: Blackwell.

Cates, Jerry R. 1983. *Insuring Inequality: Administrative Leadership in Social Security, 1935–53.* Ann Arbor: University of Michigan Press.

Cattacin, Sandro, and Florence Passy. 1993. "Der Niedergang von Bewegungsorganisationen: Zur Analyse von organisatorischen Laufbahnen." *Kölner Zeitschrift für Soziologie und Sozialpsychologie* 45: 419–438.

Cavalli-Sforza, Luca, Paolo Menozzi, and Alberto Piazza. 1994. *The History and Geography of Human Genes.* Abridged ed. Princeton: Princeton University Press.

Cerutti, Simona, Robert Descimon, and Maarten Prak, eds. 1995. "Cittadinanze." *Quaderni Storici* 30, no. 89: 281–514.

Chambliss, William J. 1994. "Policing the Ghetto Underclass: The Politics of Law and Law Enforcement." *Social Problems* 41: 177–194.

Charles, Maria. 1992. "Cross-National Variation in Occupational Sex Segregation." *American Sociological Review* 57: 483–502.

Cheng, Lucie, and Edna Bonacich, eds. 1984. *Labor Immigration Under Capitalism: Asian Workers in the United States Before World War II.* Berkeley: University of California Press.

Chirot, Daniel, and Karen Barkey. 1983. "States in Search of Legitimacy: Was There Nationalism in the Balkans of the Early Nineteenth Century?" *International Journal of Comparative Sociology* 24: 30–45.

Chiswick, Barry R., Carmel U. Chiswick, and Paul W. Miller. 1985. "Are Immigrants and Natives Perfect Substitutes in Production?" *International Migration Review* 19: 674–685.

Christensen, Søren, Peter Karnøe, Jesper Strangaard Pedersen, and Frank Dobbin, eds. 1997. "Action in Institutions." *American Behavioral Scientist* 40, no. 4, entire issue.

Christenson, Eva. 1995. "Belastningsskador och Könssegregeringsprocesser på en Elekronikindustri." Arbetsrapport 1, Projekt Arbetsskador. Genus och Arbetsorganisation, Sociologiska Institutionen, Stockholm University.

Clark, Anna. 1995. *The Struggle for the Breeches: Gender and the Making of the British Working Class.* Berkeley: University of California Press.

Clark, Samuel. 1995. *State and Status: The Rise of the State and Aristocratic Power in Western Europe.* Montreal: McGill-Queen's University Press.

Clemens, Elisabeth S. 1993. "Organizational Repertoires and Institutional Change: Women's Groups and the Transformation of U.S. Politics, 1890–1920." *American Journal of Sociology* 98: 755–798.

Coase, Ronald. 1992. "The Institutional Structure of Production." *American Economic Review* 82: 713–719.

Cobble, Dorothy Sue. 1991. " 'Drawing the Line': The Construction of a Gendered Work Force in the Food Service Industry," In *Work Engendered: Toward a New History of American Labor,* edited by Ava Baron. Ithaca: Cornell University Press.

Cockburn, Cynthia. 1983. *Brothers: Male Dominance and Technological Change.* London: Pluto Press.

———. 1991. *In the Way of Women: Men's Resistance to Sex Equality in Organizations.* Ithaca: ILR Press.

Cohn, Samuel. 1985. *The Process of Occupational Sex-Typing: The Feminization of Clerical Labor in Great Britain.* Philadelphia: Temple University Press.

———. 1993. *When Strikes Make Sense—and Why.* New York: Plenum.

Cole, Jonathan R., and Harriet Zuckerman. 1984. "The Productivity Puzzle: Persistence and Change in Patterns of Publication of Men and Women Scientists." *Advances in Motivation and Achievement* 2: 217–258.

Coleman, James S. 1990. *Foundations of Social Theory.* Cambridge: Harvard University Press.

Colley, Linda. 1992. *Britons: Forging the Nation, 1707–1837.* New Haven: Yale University Press.

Comaroff, John. 1991. "Humanity, Ethnicity, Nationality: Conceptual and Comparative Perspectives on the U.S.S.R." *Theory and Society* 20: 661–688.

Comaroff, John, and Jean Comaroff. 1992. *Ethnography and the Historical Imagination.* Boulder: Westview.

Comaroff, John L., and Paul C. Stern, eds. 1995. *Perspectives on Nationalism and War.* Luxembourg: Gordon and Breach.

Commons, John R. 1934. *Institutional Economics: Its Place in Political Economy.* New York: Macmillan.

Conell, Carol, and Samuel Cohn. 1995. "Learning from Other People's Actions: Environmental Variation and Diffusion in French Coal Mining Strikes, 1890–1935." *American Journal of Sociology* 101: 366–403.

Conell, Carol, and Kim Voss. 1990. "Formal Organization and the Fate of Social Movements: Craft Association and Class Alliance in the Knights of Labor." *American Sociological Review* 55: 255–269.

Conlisk, John. 1996. "Why Bounded Rationality?" *Journal of Economic Literature* 34: 669–700.

Connor, Walker. 1987. "Ethnonationalism." In *Understanding Political Development,* edited by Myron Weiner and Samuel P. Huntington. Boston: Little, Brown.

Cooper, Carole. 1989. "The Militarisation of the Bantustans: Control and Contradictions." In *War and Society: The Militarisation of South Africa,* edited by Jacklyn Cok and Laurie Nathan. Cape Town and Johannesburg: David Philip.

Cooper, Frederick. 1987. *On the African Waterfront: Urban Disorder and the Transformation of Work in Colonial Mombasa.* New Haven: Yale University Press.

———. 1994. "Conflict and Connection: Rethinking Colonial African History." *American Historical Review* 99: 1516–1545.

Cooper, Patricia. 1991. "The Faces of Gender: Sex Segregation and Work Relations at Philco, 1928–1938." In *Work Engendered: Toward a New History of American Labor,* edited by Ava Baron. Ithaca: Cornell University Press.

Corcoran, Mary, Linda Datcher, and Greg J. Duncan. 1980. "Most Workers Find Jobs Through Word of Mouth." *Monthly Labor Review,* August, 33–35.

Cotter, David A., et al. 1995. "Occupational Gender Segregation and the Earnings Gap: Changes in the 1980s." *Social Science Research* 24: 439–454.

Coverman, Shelley. 1983. "Gender, Domestic Labor Time, and Wage Inequality." *American Sociological Review* 48: 623–636.

Cowan, Ruth Schwartz. 1983. *More Work for Mother: The Ironies of Household Technology from the Open Hearth to the Microwave.* New York: Basic Books.

Crafts, N. F. R. 1985. *British Economic Growth During the Industrial Revolution.* Oxford: Clarendon Press.

———. 1989. "Real Wages, Inequality, and Economic Growth in Britain, 1750–1850: A Review of Recent Research," In *Real Wages in 19th and 20th Century*

Europe: Historical and Comparative Perspectives, edited by Peter Scholliers. New York: Berg.

Crosby, Alfred W. 1986. *Ecological Imperialism: The Biological Expansion of Europe, 900–1900.* Cambridge: Cambridge University Press.

Cruz, Rafael. 1992–1993. "La Lógica de la Guerra: Ejército, Estado y Revolución en la España Contemporánea." *Studia Historica-Historia Contemporánea* 10–11: 207–222.

Curtin, Philip D. 1984. *Cross-Cultural Trade in World History.* Cambridge: Cambridge University Press.

Dagens Nyheter. 1996. "Största studien visar: Lågutbildade får mindre barn." February 13, A1, A5.

Danziger, Sheldon, and Peter Gottschalk. 1995. *American Unequal.* New York: Russell Sage Foundation; Cambridge: Harvard University Press.

———, eds. 1992. *Uneven Tides: Rising Inequality in the 1980's.* New York: Russell Sage Foundation.

Darity, William, Jr. 1992. "Dressing for Success? Economic History and the Economic Performance of Racial and Ethnic Minorities in the USA." [forthcoming in *Cambridge Economic History of the United States.*]

———, ed. 1984. *Labor Economics: Modern Views.* Boston: Kluwer-Nijhoff.

Dasgupta, Partha. 1995. "The Population Problem: Theory and Evidence." *Journal of Economic Literature* 33: 1879–1902.

Davies, Margery W. 1975. "Woman's Place Is at the Typewriter: The Feminization of the Clerical Labor Force." In *Labor Market Segmentation,* edited by Richard Edwards, Michael Reich, and David Gordon. Lexington, Mass.: D. C. Heath.

———. 1982. *Woman's Place Is at the Typewriter: Office Work and Office Workers, 1870–1930.* Philadelphia: Temple University Press.

Davis, Gerald F., and Tracy A. Thompson. 1994. "A Social Movement Perspective on Corporate Control." *Administrative Science Quarterly* 39: 141–173.

Defnet, Mary A., Jean Ducat, Thierry Eggerickx, and Michel Poulain. 1986. *From Grez-Doiceau to Wisconsin.* Brussels: De Boeck-Wesmael.

della Porta, Donatella. 1995. *Social Movements, Political Violence, and the State: A Comparative Analysis of Italy and Germany.* Cambridge: Cambridge University. Press.

Dembe, Allard E. 1996. *Occupation and Disease: How Social Factors Affect the Conception of Work-Related Disorders.* New Haven: Yale University Press.

Deneckere, Gita. 1990. "Norm en deviantie: Een bijdrage over diagnoses van collectieve populaire actie in de Nieuwste Geschiedenis." *Tijdschrift voor Sociale Geschiedenis* 16: 105–127.

De Schweinitz, Dorothea. 1932. *How Workers Find Jobs: A Study of Four Thousand Hosiery Workers in Philadelphia.* Philadelphia: University of Pennsylvania Press.

DeVault, Marjorie. 1991. *Feeding the Family: The Social Organization of Caring as Gendered Work.* Chicago: University of Chicago Press.

Dex, Shirley. 1985. *The Sexual Division of Work: Conceptual Revolutions in the Social Sciences.* Brighton: Wheatsheaf Books.

Diani, Mario. 1988. *Isole nell'arcipelago: Il movimento ecologista in Italia.* Bologna: Il Mulino.

———. 1992. "The Concept of Social Movement." *Sociological Review* 40: 1–25.

———. 1995. *Green Networks: A Structural Analysis of the Italian Environmental Movement.* Edinburgh: Edinburgh University Press.

Dickens, William T., and Kevin Lang. 1985. "A Test of Dual Labor Market Theory." *American Economic Review* 75: 792–805.

DiPrete, Thomas A., and Patricia A. McManus. 1996. "Institutions, Technical Change, and Diverging Life Chances: Earnings Mobility in the United States and Germany." *American Journal of Sociology* 102: 34–79.

Domínguez, Virginia R. 1986. *White by Definition: Social Classification in Creole Louisiana.* New Brunswick, N.J.: Rutgers University Press.

Downs, Laura Lee. 1995. *Manufacturing Inequality: Gender Division in the French and British Metalworking Industries, 1914–1939.* Ithaca: Cornell University Press.

Drew, Christopher, and David Cay Johnston. 1996. "For Wealthy Americans, Death Is More Certain Than Taxes." *New York Times,* December 22, 1, 30–31.

Druckman, Daniel. 1994. "Nationalism, Patriotism, and Group Loyalty: A Social Psychological Perspective." *Mershon International Studies Review* 38: 43–68.

Duin, Pieter van. 1992. "White Building Workers and Coloured Competition in the South African Labour Market, c. 1890–1940." *International Review of Social History* 37: 59–90.

Duncan, Otis Dudley. 1966. "Methodological Issues in the Study of Social Mobility." In *Social Structure and Mobility in Economic Development,* edited by Neil J. Smelser and Seymour Martin Lipset. Chicago: Aldine.

Earle, Carville. 1993. "Divisions of Labor: The Splintered Geography of Labor Markets and Movements in Industrializing America, 1790–1930." *International Review of Social History* 38, supplement no. 1: 5–38.

Eisenberg, Susan. 1990. "Shaping a New Decade: Women in the Building Trades." *Radical America* 23, nos. 2–3: 29–38.

———. 1992a. "Tradeswomen: Pioneers—or What?" *Sojourner: The Women's Forum* 17: 17–18.

———. 1992b. "Welcoming Sisters into the Brotherhood." *Sojourner: The Women's Forum* 18: 20–21.

Elias, Norbert. 1982. *Power and Civility.* Vol. 2, *The Civilizing Process.* New York: Pantheon.

Elias, Norbert, and John L. Scotson. 1994. *The Established and the Outsiders: A Sociological Enquiry into Community Problems.* 2d ed. London: Sage.

Elster, Jon. 1983. *Explaining Technical Change: A Case Study in the Philosophy of Science.* Cambridge: Cambridge University Press.

———. 1985. *Making Sense of Marx.* Cambridge: Cambridge University Press; Paris: Editions de la Maison des Sciences de l'Homme.

England, Paula. 1992. *Comparable Worth: Theories and Evidence.* New York: Aldine de Gruyter.

England, Paula, and George Farkas. 1986. *Households, Employment, and Gender: A Social, Economic, and Demographic View.* Chicago: Aldine.

England, Paula, George Farkas, Barbara Stanek Kilbourne, and Thomas Dou. 1988. "Explaining Occupational Sex Segregation and Wages: Findings from a Model with Fixed Effects." *American Sociological Review* 53: 544–558.

England, Paula, and Barbara Stanek Kilbourne. 1990. "Feminist Critiques of the Separative Model of Self: Implications for Rational Choice Theory." *Rationality and Society* 2: 156–171.

England, Paula, and Lori McCreary. 1987. "Gender Inequality in Paid Employment." In *Analyzing Gender: A Handbook of Social Science Research,* edited by Beth B. Hess and Myra Marx Ferree. Newbury Park, Calif.: Sage.

England, Paula, Lori L. Reid, and Barbara Stanek Kilbourne. 1996. "The Effect of Sex Composition of Jobs on Starting Wages in an Organization: Findings from the NLSY." *Demography* 33: 511–522.

Ennis, James G. 1987. "Fields of Action: Structure in Movements' Tactical Repertoires." *Sociological Forum* 2: 520–533.

Epstein, Cynthia Fuchs. 1981. *Women in Law.* New York: Basic Books.

———. 1992. "Tinkerbells and Pinups: The Construction and Reconstruction of Gender Boundaries at Work." In *Cultivating Differences: Symbolic Boundaries and the Making of Inequality,* edited by Michèle Lamont and Marcel Fournier. Chicago: University of Chicago Press.

Erickson, Bonnie H. 1996. "The Structure of Ignorance." Keynote address to the International Sunbelt Social Network Conference, Charleston, S.C.

Erikson, Robert, and Jan O. Jonsson. 1996a. "Income Attainment Among Young Employees in Sweden: The Importance of Credentials, School Performance, Job Matching, and Industrial Branch." Swedish Institute for Social Research, Stockholm University. Typescript.

———. 1996b. "Introduction: Explaining Class Inequality in Education: The Swedish Test Case." In *Can Education Be Equalized? The Swedish Case in Comparative Perspective,* edited by Robert Erikson and Jan O. Jonsson. Boulder: Westview.

Esping-Anderson, Gøsta, ed. 1993. *Changing Classes: Stratification and Mobility in Post-Industrial Societies.* Newbury Park, Calif.: Sage.

Evans, Ivan. 1990. "The Native Affairs Department and the Reserves in the 1940s and 1950s." In *Repression and Resistance: Insider Accounts of Apartheid*, edited by Robin Cohen, Yvonne G. Muthien, and Abebe Zegeye. London: Hans Zell.

Favre, Pierre, ed. 1990. *La Manifestation.* Paris: Presses de la Fondation Nationale des Sciences Politiques.

Ferber, Marianne A., and Carole A. Green. 1991. "Occupational Segregation and the Earnings Gap: Further Evidence." In *Essays on the Economics of Discrimination*, edited by Emily P. Hoffman. Kalamazoo, Mich.: W. E. Upjohn Institute for Employment Research.

Fernandez, Roberto, and Doug McAdam. 1988. "Social Networks and Social Movements: Multiorganizational Fields and Recruitment to Mississippi Freedom Summer." *Sociological Forum* 3: 357–382.

Fernández-Kelly, M. Patricia. 1983. *For We Are Sold, I and My People: Women and Industry in Mexico's Frontier.* Albany: State University of New York Press.

———. 1994. "Broadening the Scope: Gender and the Study of International Development." In *Comparative National Development: Society and Economy in the New Global Order*, edited by A. Douglas Kincaid and Alejandro Portes. Chapel Hill: University of North Carolina Press.

Ferree, Myra Marx. 1987. "She Works Hard for a Living: Gender and Class on the Job." In *Analyzing Gender: A Handbook of Social Science Research*, edited by Beth B. Hess and Myra Marx Ferree. Newbury Park, Calif.: Sage.

Fillieule, Olivier, ed., 1993. *Sociologie de la protestation: Les formes de l'action collective dans la France contemporaine.* Paris: L'Harmattan.

Fine, Janice, and Richard Locke. 1996. "Unions Get Smart: New Tactics for a New Labor Movement." *Dollars and Sense* 207: 16–19, 42.

Fischer, Claude S., Martín Sánchez Jankowski, Samuel R. Lucas, Ann Swidler, and Kim Voss. 1996. *Inequality by Design: Cracking the Bell Curve Myth.* Princeton: Princeton University Press.

Fligstein, Neil. 1981. *Going North: Migration of Blacks and Whites from the South, 1900–1950.* New York: Academic Press.

Floud, Roderick, Kenneth Wachter, and Annabel Gregory. 1990. *Height, Health, and History: Nutritional Status in the United Kingdom, 1750–1980.* Cambridge: Cambridge University Press.

Fogel, Robert W. 1993. "New Sources and New Techniques for the Study of Secular Trends in Nutritional Status, Health, Mortality, and the Process of Aging." *Historical Methods* 26: 5–43.

———. 1994. "Economic Growth, Population Theory, and Physiology: The Bearing of Long-Term Processes on the Making of Economic Policy." *American Economic Review* 84: 369–395.

Fogel, Robert W., and Dora L. Costa. 1997. "A Theory of Technophysio Evolution, with Some Implications for Forecasting Population, Health Care Costs, and Pension Costs." *Demography* 34: 49–66.

Frader, Laura L., and Sonya O. Rose, eds. 1996. *Gender and Class in Modern Europe.* Ithaca: Cornell University Press.

Franzosi, Roberto. 1995. *The Puzzle of Strikes: Class and State Strategies in Postwar Italy.* Cambridge: Cambridge University Press.

Fraser, Steven, ed. 1995. *The Bell Curve Wars: Race, Intelligence, and the Future of America.* New York: Basic Books.

Fredrickson, George M. 1981. *White Supremacy: A Comparative Study in American and South African History.* Oxford: Oxford University Press.

———. 1995. *Black Liberation: A Comparative History of Black Ideologies in the United States and South Africa.* New York: Oxford University Press.

Freeman, Richard B. 1995. "Are Your Wages Set in Beijing?" *Journal of Economic Perspectives* 9: 15–32.

———. 1996. "Why Do So Many Young American Men Commit Crimes and What Might We Do About It?" *Journal of Economic Perspectives* 10: 25–42.

Friedberg, Rachel M., and Jennifer Hunt. 1995. "The Impact of Immigrants on Host Country Wages, Employment, and Growth." *Journal of Economic Perspectives* 9: 23–44.

Friedman, Jeffrey, ed. 1996. *The Rational Choice Controversy: Economic Models of Politics Reconsidered.* New Haven: Yale University Press.

Fullbrook, Mary. 1993. *National Histories and European History.* Boulder: Westview.

Gailus, Manfred, and Heinrich Volkmann, eds. 1994. *Der Kampf um das tägliche Brot: Nahrungsmangel, Versorgungspolitik und Protest 1770–1990.* Opladen: Westdeutscher Verlag.

Gal, Susan. 1987. "Codeswitching and Consciousness in the European Periphery." *American Ethnologist* 14: 637–653.

———. 1989. "Language and Political Economy." *Annual Review of Anthropology* 18: 345–369.

Gamson, William A., Bruce Fireman, and Steven Rytina. 1982. *Encounters with Unjust Authority.* Homewood, Ill.: Dorsey.

Gans, Herbert J. 1995. *The War Against the Poor: The Underclass and Antipoverty Policy.* New York: Basic Books.

George, M. Dorothy. 1967. *Hogarth to Cruikshank: Social Change in Graphic Satire.* New York: Viking.

Gerber, Theodore P., and Michael Hout. 1995. "Educational Stratification in Russia During the Soviet Period." *American Journal of Sociology* 101: 611–660.

Geremek, Bronislaw. 1994. *Poverty: A History.* Oxford: Blackwell.

Giele, Janet Z. 1988. "Gender and Sex Roles." In *Handbook of Sociology*, edited by Neil J. Smelser. Newbury Park, Calif.: Sage.

Giliomee, Hermann. 1995. "Democratization in South Africa." *Political Science Quarterly* 110: 83–104.

Giugni, Marco. 1995. *Entre stratégie et opportunité: Les nouveaux mouvements sociaux en Suisse.* Zürich: Seismo.

Giugni, Marco G., and Florence Passy. 1993. "Etat et nouveaux mouvements sociaux, comparaison de deux cas contrastés: la France et la Suisse." *Revue Suisse de Sociologie* 19: 545–570.

Glazer, Nona Y. 1991. " 'Between a Rock and a Hard Place': Women's Professional Organizations in Nursing and Class, Racial, and Ethnic Inequalities." *Gender and Society* 5: 351–372.

———. 1993. *Women's Paid and Unpaid Labor: The Work Transfer in Health Care and Retailing.* Philadelphia: Temple University Press.

Goffman, Erving. 1963. *Stigma: Notes on the Management of Spoiled Identity.* New York: Simon and Schuster.

———. 1981. *Forms of Talk.* Oxford: Blackwell.

Goldberger, Arthur S., and Charles F. Manski. 1995. "Review Article: *The Bell Curve* by Herrnstein and Murray." *Journal of Economic Literature* 33: 762–776.

Goldin, Claudia. 1987. "Women's Employment and Technological Change: A Historical Perspective." In *Computer Chips and Paper Clips: Technology and Women's Employment,* edited by Heidi Hartmann. Vol. 2. Washington, D.C.: National Academy Press.

———. 1990. *Understanding the Gender Gap: An Economic History of American Women.* New York: Oxford University Press.

———. 1994. "Labor Markets in the Twentieth Century." Working Paper Series on Historical Factors in Long Run Growth, Historical Paper no. 58, National Bureau of Economic Research, Cambridge, Mass.

Goldin, Ian. 1987. "The Reconstitution of Coloured Identity in the Western Cape." In *The Politics of Race, Class, and Nationalism in Twentieth-Century South Africa,* edited by Shula Marks and Stanley Trapido. London: Longman.

Goodnow, Jacqueline J., and Jennifer M. Bowes. 1994. *Men, Women, and Household Work.* Oxford: Oxford University Press.

Gordon, David M. 1996. *Fat and Mean: The Corporate Squeeze of Working Americans and the Myth of Managerial "Downsizing."* New York: Free Press.

Gordon, David M., Richard Edwards, and Michael Reich. 1982. *Segmented Work, Divided Workers: The Historical Transformations of Labor in the United States.* New York: Cambridge University Press.

Gossiaux, Jean-François. 1996. "Yougoslavie: Quand la démocratie n'est plus un jeu." *Annales: Histoire, Sciences Sociales* 51: 837–848.

Goudsblom, Johan, E. L. Jones, and Stephen Mennell. 1989. *Human History and*

Social Process. Exeter Studies in History, no. 26. Exeter: University of Exeter Press.

Gould, Roger V. 1995. *Insurgent Identities: Class, Community, and Protest in Paris from 1848 to the Commune.* Chicago: University of Chicago Press.

Gould, Stephen Jay. 1981. *The Mismeasure of Man.* New York: Norton.

Granovetter, Mark. 1981. "Toward a Sociological Theory of Income Differences." In *Sociological Perspectives on Labor Markets,* edited by Ivar Berg. New York: Academic Press.

———. 1985. "Economic Action and Social Structure: The Problem of Embeddedness." *American Journal of Sociology* 91: 481–510.

———. 1986. "Labor Mobility, Internal Markets, and Job-Matching: A Comparison of the Sociological and the Economic Approaches," *Research in Social Stratification and Mobility* 5: 3–39.

———. 1988. "The Sociological and Economic Approaches to Labor Markets," In *Industries, Firms, and Jobs: Sociological and Economic Approaches,* edited by George Farkas and Paula England. New York: Plenum.

———. 1995. *Getting a Job: A Study of Contacts and Careers.* 2d ed. Chicago: University of Chicago Press.

Granovetter, Mark, and Charles Tilly. 1988. "Inequality and Labor Processes." *Handbook of Sociology,* edited by Neil J. Smelser. Newbury Park, Calif.: Sage.

Grant, David, Melvin Oliver, and Angela James. 1996. "African Americans: Social and Economic Bifurcation." In *Ethnic Los Angeles,* edited by Roger Waldinger and Mehdi Bozorgmehr. New York: Russell Sage Foundation.

Graubard, Stephen R., ed. 1993. "Reconstructing Nations and States." *Daedalus* 122, entire issue.

———. 1995. "American Education: Still Separate, Still Unequal." *Daedalus* 124, entire issue.

Gray, Robert. 1993. "Factory Legislation and the Gendering of Jobs in Britain, 1830–1860." *Gender and History* 5: 56–80.

Green, Donald P., and Ian Shapiro. 1994. *Pathologies of Rational Choice Theory: A Critique of Applications in Political Science.* New Haven: Yale University Press.

Green, Nancy L. 1996. "Women and Immigrants in the Sweatshop: Categories of Labor Segmentation Revisited." *Comparative Studies in Society and History* 38: 411–433.

Greenfeld, Liah. 1992. *Nationalism: Five Roads to Modernity.* Cambridge: Harvard University Press.

———. 1996. "The Modern Religion?" *Critical Review* 10: 169–192.

Greif, Avner. 1989. "Reputation and Coalitions in Medieval Trade: Evidence on the Maghribi Traders." *Journal of Economic History* 49: 857–882.

Greif, Avner, Paul Milgrom, and Barry R. Weingast. 1994. "Coordination, Commitment, and Enforcement: The Case of the Merchant Guild." *Journal of Political Economy* 102: 745–775.

Grieco, Margaret. 1987. *Keeping It in the Family: Social Networks and Employment Chance.* London: Tavistock.

Guardino, Peter. 1994. "Identity and Nationalism in Mexico: Guerrero, 1780–1840." *Journal of Historical Sociology* 7: 314–342.

Gurr, Ted Robert. 1993. *Minorities at Risk: A Global View of Ethnopolitical Conflicts.* Washington, D.C.: U.S. Institute of Peace Press.

———. 1994. "Peoples Against States: Ethnopolitical Conflict and the Changing World System." *International Studies Quarterly* 38: 347–378.

Gurr, Ted Robert, and Barbara Harff. 1994. *Ethnic Conflict in World Politics.* Boulder: Westview.

Gustafsson, Harald. 1994a. *Political Interaction in the Old Regime: Central Power and Local Society in the Eighteenth-Century Nordic States.* Lund: Studentlitteratur.

———. 1994b. "Vad var staten? Den tidigmoderna svenska staten: sex synpunkter och en modell." *Historisk Tidskrift,* no. 2, 203–227.

Haas, Ernst. 1986. "What Is Nationalism and Why Should We Study It?" *International Organization* 40: 707–744.

Haavio-Mannila, Elina. 1993. *Women in the Workplace in Three Types of Societies.* Ann Arbor: Center for the Education of Women, University of Michigan.

Hall, Elaine J. 1993. "Waitering/Waitressing: Engendering the Work of Table Servers." *Gender and Society* 7: 329–346.

Hall, Jacqueline Dowd. 1991. "Private Eyes, Public Women: Images of Class and Sex in the Urban South, Atlanta, Georgia, 1913–1915." In *Work Engendered: Toward a New History of American Labor,* edited by Ava Baron. Ithaca: Cornell University Press.

Halpern, Rick. 1992. "Race, Ethnicity, and Union in the Chicago Stockyards, 1917–1922." *International Review of Social History* 37: 25–58.

Hanagan, Michael P. 1980. *The Logic of Solidarity: Artisans and Industrial Workers in Three French Towns, 1871–1914.* Urbana: University of Illinois Press.

———. 1994. "New Perspectives on Class Formation: Culture, Reproduction, and Agency." *Social Science History* 18: 77–94.

Hanagan, Michael, and Charles Tilly, eds. 1988. "Solidary Logics." *Theory and Society* 17, no. 3, special issue.

Harff, Barbara, and Ted Robert Gurr. 1990. "Victims of the State: Genocides, Politicides, and Group Repression Since 1945." *International Review of Victimology* 1: 23–41.

Harney, Robert. 1984. *Dalla frontiera alle Little Italies.* Rome: Bonacci.

————, ed. 1985. *Gathering Place: Peoples and Neighborhoods of Toronto, 1834–1945.* Toronto: Multicultural History Society of Ontario.

Harvey, David. 1989. *The Condition of Postmodernity.* Oxford: Blackwell.

Haveman, Robert, and Barbara Wolfe. 1995. "The Determinants of Children's Attainments: A Review of Methods and Findings." *Journal of Economic Literature* 33: 1829–1878.

Hawthorn, Geoffrey. 1991. *Plausible Worlds: Possibility and Understanding in History and the Social Sciences.* Cambridge: Cambridge University Press.

Head, Simon. 1996. "The New, Ruthless Economy." *New York Review of Books* 29 (February) 47–52.

Hedström, Peter. 1991. "Organizational Differentiation and Earnings Dispersion." *American Journal of Sociology* 97: 96–113.

Heimer, Carol A. 1984. "Career Development and Social Mobility in Engineering Project Work." Report no. 38, Institute of Industrial Economics, Bergen, Norway.

Heimer, Carol A., and Lisa R. Staffen. 1995. "Interdependence and Reintegrative Social Control." *American Sociological Review* 60: 635–654.

Henshall, Nicholas. 1992. *The Myth of Absolutism: Change and Continuity in Early Modern European Monarchy.* London: Longman.

Herrnstein, Richard J., and Charles Murray. 1994. *The Bell Curve: Intelligence and Class Structure in American Life.* New York: Free Press.

Hibbert, Christopher. 1958. *King Mob: The Story of Lord George Gordon and the London Riots of 1780.* Cleveland: World.

Hill, Draper, ed. 1976. *The Satirical Etchings of James Gillray.* New York: Dover.

Hinde, Wendy. 1992. *Catholic Emancipation: A Shake to Men's Minds.* Oxford: Blackwell.

Hirsch, Eric L. 1990a. "Sacrifice for the Cause: Group Processes, Recruitment, and Commitment in a Student Social Movement." *American Sociological Review* 55: 243–254.

————. 1990b. *Urban Revolt: Ethnic Politics in the Nineteenth-Century Chicago Labor Movement.* Berkeley: University of California Press.

Hirsch, Susan. 1986. "Rethinking the Sexual Division of Labor: Pullman Repair Shops, 1900–1969." *Radical History* 35: 26–48.

Hirschman, Albert O. 1995. *A Propensity to Self-Subversion.* Cambridge: Harvard University Press.

Hirschman, Charles. 1982. "Immigrants and Minorities: Old Questions for New Directions in Research." *International Migration Review* 16: 474–490.

Hobsbawm, E. J. 1990. *Nations and Nationalism Since 1789: Programme, Myth, Reality.* Cambridge: Cambridge University Press.

————. 1994. "What Is Ethnic Conflict and How Does It Differ from Other Conflicts?" In *Ethnic Conflict and International Security,* edited by Anthony McDermott. Oslo: Norwegian Institute of International Affairs.

Hochschild, Jennifer L. 1995. *Facing Up to the American Dream: Race, Class, and the Soul of the Nation.* Princeton: Princeton University Press.

Hoerder, Dirk. 1988. "German Immigrant Workers' Views of 'America' in the 1880s." In *A l'ombre de la statue de la Liberté: Immigrants et ouvriers dans la République américaine, 1880–1920,* edited by Marianne Debouzy. Saint-Denis: Presses Universitaires de Vincennes.

———, ed. 1983. *American Labor and Immigration History, 1877–1920s: Recent European Research.* Urbana: University of Illinois Press.

Hofmeyr, Isabel. 1987. "Building a Nation from Words: Afrikaans Language, Literature, and Ethnic Identity, 1902–1924." In *The Politics of Race, Class, and Nationalism in Twentieth-Century South Africa,* edited by Shula Marks and Stanley Trapido. London: Longman.

Holton, Robert J. 1995. "Rational Choice Theory in Sociology." *Critical Review* 9: 519–537.

Holzer, Harry J. 1987. "Informal Job Search and Black Youth Unemployment." *American Economic Review* 77: 446–452.

Horowitz, Donald. 1985. *Ethnic Groups in Conflict.* Berkeley: University of California Press.

Horowitz, Irving Louis. 1966. *Three Worlds of Development: The Theory and Practice of International Stratification.* New York: Oxford University Press.

Hout, Michael, Richard Arum, and Kim Voss. 1996. "The Political Economy of Inequality in the 'Age of Extremes.' " *Demography* 33: 421–425.

Hout, Michael, and Daniel P. Dohan. 1996. "Two Paths to Educational Opportunity: Class and Educational Selection in Sweden and the United States." In *Can Education Be Equalized? The Swedish Case in Comparative Perspective,* edited by Robert Erikson and Jan O. Jonsson. Boulder: Westview.

Hoy, Pat C. 1996. "Soldiers and Scholars." *Harvard Magazine* 98 (May–June): 64–70.

Huber, Joan. 1986. "Trends in Gender Stratification, 1970–1985," *Sociological Forum* 1: 476–495.

Hubscher, Ronald. 1996. "L'invention d'une profession: les vétérinaires au XIXe siècle." *Revue d'Histoire Moderne et Contemporaine* 43: 686–708.

Huffman, Matt L. 1995. "Organizations, Internal Labor Market Policies, and Gender Inequality in Workplace Supervisory Authority." *Sociological Perspectives* 38: 381–398.

Ikegami, Eiko. 1995. *The Taming of the Samurai: Honorific Individualism and the Making of Modern Japan.* Cambridge: Harvard University Press.

Ikegami, Eiko, and Charles Tilly. 1994. "State Formation and Contention in Japan and France." In *Edo and Paris: Urban Life and the State in the Early Modern Era,* edited by James L. McClain, John M. Merriman, and Ugawa Kaoru. Ithaca: Cornell University Press.

International Herald Tribune. 1996. "Sex Harassment: Tales of the Assembly Line." May 3, 2.

Jackman, Mary R. 1994. *The Velvet Glove: Paternalism and Conflict in Gender, Class, and Race Relations.* Berkeley: University of California Press.

Jackson, Robert Max. 1984. *The Formation of Craft Labor Markets.* Orlando: Academic Press.

Jacobs, Jerry A. 1989. *Revolving Doors: Sex Segregation and Women's Careers.* Stanford: Stanford University Press.

———. 1992. "Women's Entry into Management: Trends in Earnings, Authority, and Values Among Salaried Managers." *Administrative Science Quarterly* 37: 282–301.

———, ed. 1995. *Gender Inequality at Work.* Thousand Oaks, Calif.: Sage.

Jacobs, Jerry A., and Suet T. Lim. 1995. "Trends in Occupational and Industrial Sex Segregation in 56 Countries, 1960–1980." In *Gender Inequality at Work,* edited by Jerry A. Jacobs. Thousand Oaks, Calif.: Sage.

Jacobs, Jerry A. and Ronnie J. Steinberg. 1990. "Compensating Differentials and the Male-Female Wage Gap: Evidence from the New York State Comparable Worth Study." *Social Forces* 69: 439–468.

Jacoby, Sanford M. 1990. "The New Institutionalism: What Can It Learn from the Old?" *Industrial Relations* 29: 316–340.

———, ed. 1991. *Masters to Managers: Historical and Comparative Perspectives on American Employers.* New York: Columbia University Press.

James, Wilmot G. 1990. "Class Conflict, Mine Hostels, and the Reproduction of a Labour Force in the 1980s." In *Repression and Resistance: Insider Accounts of Apartheid,* edited by Robin Cohen, Yvonne G. Muthien, and Abebe Zegeye. London: Hans Zell.

Jaynes, Gerald David, and Robin M. Williams Jr., eds., 1989. *A Common Destiny: Blacks and American Society.* Washington, D.C.: National Academy Press.

Jencks, Christopher, et al. 1972. *Inequality: A Reassessment of the Effect of Family and Schooling in America.* New York: Basic Books.

Jenson, Jane. 1993. "Naming Nations: Making Nationalist Claims in Canadian Public Discourse." *Canadian Review of Sociology and Anthropology* 30: 337–358.

Johansson, Sten, and Ola Nygren. 1991. "The Missing Girls of China: A New Demographic Account." *Population and Development Review* 17: 35–52.

Jung, Courtney, and Ian Shapiro. 1995. "South Africa's Negotiated Transition: Democracy, Opposition, and the New Constitutional Order." *Politics and Society* 23: 269–308.

Jütte, Robert. 1994. *Poverty and Deviance in Early Modern Europe.* Cambridge: Cambridge University Press.

Kadalie, Rhoda. 1995. "Constitutional Equality: The Implications for Women in South Africa." *Social Politics: International Studies in Gender, State, and Society* 2: 208–224.

Kaelble, Hartmut. 1983. *Industrialisierung und soziale Ungleichheit*. Göttingen: Vandenhoeck & Ruprecht.

Kalb, Don. 1993. "Frameworks of Culture and Class in Historical Research." *Theory and Society* 22: 513–537.

Kangas, Olli. 1991. *The Politics of Social Rights: Studies on the Dimensions of Sickness Insurance in OECD Countries*. Dissertation Series, no. 19. Stockholm: Swedish Institute for Social Research.

Kanter, Rosabeth Moss. 1993. *Men and Women of the Corporation*. Rev. ed. New York: Basic Books.

Katz, Michael B., ed. 1993. *The "Underclass" Debate: Views from History*. Princeton: Princeton University Press.

Kazal, Russell A. 1995. "Revisiting Assimilation: The Rise, Fall, and Reappraisal of a Concept in American Ethnic History." *American Historical Review* 100: 437–471.

Kessler-Harris, Alice. 1982. *Out to Work: A History of Wage-Earning Women in the United States*. Oxford: Oxford University Press.

———. 1985. "The Debate Over Equality for Women in the Work Place: Recognizing Differences." *Women and Work: An Annual Review* 1: 141–161.

———. 1989. "Gender Ideology in Historical Reconstruction: A Case Study from the 1930s." *Gender and History* 1: 31–49.

———. 1990. *A Woman's Wage: Historical Meanings and Social Consequences*. Lexington: University Press of Kentucky.

Kettering, Sharon. 1993. "Brokerage at the Court of Louis XIV." *Historical Journal* 36: 69–87.

Kevles, Daniel J. 1995. "Genetics, Race, and IQ: Historical Reflections from Binet to *The Bell Curve*." *Contention* 5: 3–18.

Khawaja, Marwan. 1993. "Repression and Popular Collective Action: Evidence from the West Bank." *Sociological Forum* 8: 47–71.

Kilbourne, Barbara Stanek, et al. 1994. "Returns to Skill, Compensating Differentials, and Gender Bias: Effects of Occupational Characteristics on the Wages of White Women and Men." *American Journal of Sociology* 100: 689–719.

Kirschenman, Joleen, Philip Moss, and Chris Tilly. 1995. "Employer Screening Methods and Racial Exclusion: Evidence from New In-Depth Interviews with Employers." Working Paper 77, Russell Sage Foundation, New York.

Klein, Herbert S. 1983. "The Integration of Italian Immigrants into the United States and Argentina: A Comparative Analysis." *American Historical Review* 88: 306–329.

Knoke, David. 1990a. *Organizing for Collective Action: The Political Economies of Associations.* New York: Aldine de Gruyter.

—. 1990b. *Political Networks: The Structural Perspective.* Cambridge: Cambridge University Press.

Komlos, John. 1987. "The Height and Weight of West Point Cadets: Dietary Change in Antebellum America." *Journal of Economic History* 47: 897–927.

—. 1990. "Height and Social Status in Eighteenth-Century Germany." *Journal of Interdisciplinary History* 20: 607–622.

—, ed. 1994. *Stature, Living Standards, and Economic Development: Essays in Anthropometric History.* Chicago: University of Chicago Press.

Kriesi, Hanspeter. 1981. *AKW-Gegner in der Schweiz: Eine Fallstudie zum Aufbau des Widerstands gegen das geplante AKW in Graben.* Diessenhofen: Verlag Ruegger.

—. 1993. *Political Mobilization and Social Change: The Dutch Case in Comparative Perspective.* Aldershot: Avebury.

Krugman, Paul. 1996. "The Spiral of Inequality." *Mother Jones*, November–December, 44–49.

Kuper, Leo. 1975. *Race, Class, and Power: Ideology and Revolutionary Change in Plural Societies.* Chicago: Aldine.

Kuznets, Simon. 1966. *Modern Economic Growth: Rate, Structure, and Spread.* New Haven: Yale University Press.

Laitin, David D. 1985. "Hegemony and Religious Conflict: British Imperial Control and Political Cleavages in Yorubaland." In *Bringing the State Back In*, edited by Peter Evans, Dietrich Rueschemeyer, and Theda Skocpol. Cambridge: Cambridge University Press.

—. 1991. "The National Uprisings in the Soviet Union." *World Politics* 44: 139–177.

Langford, Christopher, and Pamela Storey. 1993. "Sex Differentials in Mortality Early in the Twentieth Century: Sri Lanka and India Compared." *Population and Development Review* 19: 263–282.

Lapidus, Gail W. 1992. "The Interaction of Women's Work and Family Roles in the Former USSR." In *Women's Work and Women's Lives: The Continuing Struggle Worldwide*, edited by Hilda Kahne and Janet Z. Giele. Boulder: Westview.

Laumann, Edward O. 1973. *Bonds of Pluralism: The Form and Substance of Urban Social Networks.* New York: Wiley Interscience.

Laumann, Edward O., and Franz U. Pappi. 1976. *Networks of Collective Action: A Perspective on Community Influence Systems.* New York: Academic Press.

Lazear, Edward P. 1989. "Symposium on Women in the Labor Market." *Journal of Economic Perspectives* 3: 3–8.

—. 1991. "Discrimination in Labor Markets." In *Essays on the Economics of*

Discrimination, edited by Emily P. Hoffman. Kalamazoo, Mich.: W. E. Upjohn Institute for Employment Research.

Lazonick, William. 1991. *Business Organization and the Myth of the Market Economy.* Cambridge: Cambridge University Press.

Lee, Ching Kwan. 1995. "Engendering the Worlds of Labor: Women Workers, Labor Markets, and Production Politics in the South China Economic Miracle." *American Sociological Review* 60: 378–397.

Lee, James, Cameron Campbell, and Guofu Tan. 1992. "Infanticide and Family Planning in Late Imperial China: The Price and Population History of Rural Liaoning, 1774–1873." In *Chinese History in Economic Perspective,* edited by Thomas G. Rawski and Lillian M. Li. Berkeley: University of California Press.

Lee, James, Wang Feng, and Cameron Campbell. 1994. "Infant and Child Mortality Among the Qing Nobility: Implications for Two Types of Positive Check." *Population Studies* 48: 395–411.

Lee, Ok-Jie. 1993. "Gender-Differentiated Employment Practices in the South Korean Textile Industry." *Gender and Society* 7: 507–528.

Leeuwen, Marco H. D. Van, and Ineke Maas. 1996. "Long-Term Social Mobility: Research Agenda and a Case Study (Berlin, 1825–1957)." *Continuity and Change* 11: 399–433.

le Grand, Carl. 1991. "Explaining the Male-Female Wage Gap: Job Segregation and Solidarity Wage Bargaining in Sweden." *Acta Sociologica* 34: 261–278.

le Grand, Carl, Ryszard Szulkin, and Michael Tåhlin. 1994. "Organizational Structures and Job Rewards in Sweden." *Acta Sociologica* 37: 231–251.

———. 1996. "Why Do Some Employers Pay More Than Others? Earnings Variation Across Establishments in Sweden." *Research in Social Stratification and Mobility* 14: 265–296.

Leigh, J. Paul. 1991. "No Evidence of Compensating Differentials for Occupational Fatalities." *Industrial Relations* 30: 382–395.

Leiman, Melvin N. 1993. *Political Economy of Racism.* London: Pluto Press.

Lenski, Gerhard. 1966. *Power and Privilege.* New York: McGraw-Hill.

Lerner, Adam J., ed. 1991. "Reimagining the Nation." *Millennium* 20, entire issue.

Levine, David, ed. 1984. *Proletarianization and Family History.* Orlando: Academic Press.

Lewin, Shira. 1996. "Economics and Psychology: Lessons for Our Own Day from the Early Twentieth Century." *Journal of Economic Literature* 34: 1293–1323.

Lewin-Epstein, Noah, and Moshe Semyonov. 1994. "Sheltered Labor Markets, Public Sector Employment, and Socioeconomic Returns to Education of Arabs in Israel." *American Journal of Sociology* 100: 622–651.

Lichbach, Mark Irving. 1995. *The Rebel's Dilemma*. Ann Arbor: University of Michigan Press.

Lieberson, Stanley. 1980. *A Piece of the Pie: Blacks and White Immigrants Since 1880*. Berkeley: University of California Press.

Lieberson, Stanley, and Mary C. Waters. 1988. *From Many Strands: Ethnic and Racial Groups in Contemporary America*. New York: Russell Sage Foundation.

Light, Ivan. 1984. "Immigrant and Ethnic Enterprise in North America." *Ethnic and Racial Studies* 7: 195–216.

Light, Ivan, and Edna Bonacich. 1988. *Immigrant Entrepreneurs: Koreans in Los Angeles, 1965–1982*. Berkeley: University of California Press.

Lin, Nan. 1982. "Social Resources and Instrumental Action." In *Social Structure and Network Analysis*, edited by Peter V. Marsden and Nan Lin. Beverly Hills: Sage.

Lin, Nan, and Mary Dumin. 1986. "Access to Occupations Through Social Ties." *Social Networks* 8: 365–385.

Linard, André. 1996. "La pêche, enjeu de toutes les convoîtises." In *Conflits fin de siècle*, edited by Ignacio Ramonet, Christian de Brie, and Alain Gresh. Manière de Voir, no. 29. Paris: Le Monde Diplomatique.

Lindert, Peter H. 1991. "Toward a Comparative History of Income and Wealth Inequality." In *Income Distribution in Historical Perspective*, edited by Y. S. Brenner, Hartmut Kaelble, and Mark Thomas. Cambridge: Cambridge University Press.

Lipartito, Kenneth. 1994. "When Women Were Switches: Technology, Work, and Gender in the Telephone Industry, 1890–1920." *American Historical Review* 99: 1074–1111.

Lis, Catharina. 1986. *Social Change and the Labouring Poor: Antwerp, 1770–1860*. New Haven: Yale University Press.

Lis, Catharina, Jan Lucassen, and Hugo Soly, eds. 1994. "Before the Unions: Wage Earners and Collective Action in Europe, 1300–1850." *International Review of Social History* 39, supplement no. 2, entire issue.

———. 1996. *Disordered Lives: Eighteenth-Century Families and Their Unruly Relatives*. Oxford: Polity Press.

Litoff, Judy Barrett. 1978. *American Midwives 1860 to the Present*. Westport, Conn.: Greenwood.

Lodge, Tom. c. 1984. "The Poqo Insurrection." In *Resistance and Ideology in Settler Societies*, edited by Tom Lodge. Southern African Studies, vol. 4. Johannesburg: Ravan Press.

———. 1987. "Political Mobilisation During the 1950s: An East London Case Study." In *The Politics of Race, Class, and Nationalism in Twentieth-Century South Africa*, edited by Shula Marks and Stanley Trapido. London: Longman.

———. 1996. "South Africa: Democracy and Development in a Post-Apartheid Society." In *Democracy and Development: Theory and Practice,* edited by Adrian Leftwich. London: Polity Press.

MacDonald, John S., and Leatrice D. MacDonald. 1964. "Chain Migration, Ethnic Neighborhood Formation, and Social Networks." *Milbank Memorial Fund Quarterly* 42: 82–97.

Machin, G. I. T. 1963. "The No-Popery Movement in Britain in 1828–9." *Historical Journal* 6: 193–211.

———. 1964. *The Catholic Question in English Politics, 1820 to 1830.* Oxford: Clarendon Press.

———. 1979. "Resistance to Repeal of the Test and Corporation Acts, 1828." *Historical Journal* 22: 115–139.

MacLeod, Jay. 1987. *Ain't No Makin' It: Leveled Aspirations in a Low-Income Neighborhood.* Boulder: Westview.

Madden, Janice Fanning. 1985. "The Persistence of Pay Differentials: The Economics of Sex Discrimination." *Women and Work: An Annual Review* 1: 76–114.

Malkki, Liisa H. 1996. "Speechless Emissaries: Refugees, Humanitarianism, and Dehistoricization." *Cultural Anthropology* 11: 377–404.

Maloney, Thomas N. 1995. "Degrees of Inequality: The Advance of Black Male Workers in the Northern Meat Packing and Steel Industries Before World War II." *Social Science History* 19: 31–62.

Margadant, Ted. 1979. *French Peasants in Revolt: The Insurrection of 1851.* Princeton: Princeton University Press.

———. 1992. *Urban Rivalries in the French Revolution.* Princeton: Princeton University Press.

Markoff, John. 1995. "Violence, Emancipation, and Democracy: The Countryside and the French Revolution." *American Historical Review* 100: 360–386.

———. 1996. *Waves of Democracy: Social Movements and Political Change.* Thousand Oaks, Calif.: Pine Grove Press.

Marks, Carole. 1981. "Split Labor Markets and Black-White Relations, 1865–1920." *Phylon* 42: 293–308.

———. 1983. "Lines of Communication, Recruitment Mechanisms, and the Great Migration of 1916–1918." *Social Problems* 31: 73–83.

Marks, Shula, and Stanley Trapido. 1987. "The Politics of Race, Class, and Nationalism." In *The Politics of Race, Class, and Nationalism in Twentieth-Century South Africa,* edited by Shula Marks and Stanley Trapido. London: Longman.

Marsden, Peter V., and Jeanne S. Hurlbert. 1988. "Social Resources and Mobility Outcomes: A Replication and Extension." *Social Forces* 66: 1038–1059.

Marwell, Gerald, and Pamela Oliver. 1993. *The Critical Mass in Collective Action: A Micro-Social Theory.* Cambridge: Cambridge University Press.

Marx, Anthony W. 1992. *Lessons of Struggle: South African International Opposition, 1960–1990.* New York: Oxford University Press.

——. 1995. "Contested Citizenship: The Dynamics of Racial Identity and Social Movements." *International Review of Social History* 40: 159–183.

Massey, Douglas S. 1995. "The New Immigration and Ethnicity in the United States." *Population and Development Review* 21: 631–652.

——. 1996. "The Age of Extremes: Concentrated Affluence and Poverty in the Twenty-First Century." *Demography* 33: 395–412.

Massey, Douglas S., and Nancy A. Denton. 1993. *American Apartheid: Segregation and the Making of the Underclass.* Cambridge: Harvard University Press.

Massey, Douglas S., Andrew B. Gross, and Kumiko Shibuya. 1994. "Migration, Segregation, and the Geographic Concentration of Poverty." *American Sociological Review* 59: 425–446.

Mayer, Philip. 1971. *Townsmen or Tribesmen: Conservatism and the Process of Urbanization in a South African City.* Cape Town: Oxford University Press.

McAdam, Doug. 1982. *Political Process and the Development of Black Insurgency, 1930–1970.* Chicago: University of Chicago Press.

——. 1988. *Freedom Summer.* New York: Oxford University Press.

McAdam, Doug, John D. McCarthy, and Mayer N. Zald. 1988. "Social Movements." In *Handbook of Sociology,* edited by Neil J. Smelser. Newbury Park, Calif.: Sage.

——, eds. 1996. *Comparative Perspectives on Social Movements: Political Opportunities, Mobilizing Structures, and Cultural Framings.* Cambridge: Cambridge University Press.

McCarthy, John D., David W. Britt, and Mark Wolfson. 1991. "The Institutional Channeling of Social Movements by the State in the United States." *Research in Social Movements, Conflicts, and Change* 13: 45–76.

McGuire, Gail M., and Barbara F. Reskin. 1993. "Authority Hierarchies at Work: The Impacts of Race and Sex." *Gender and Society* 7: 487–506.

McPhail, Clark. 1991. *The Myth of the Madding Crowd.* New York: Aldine De Gruyter.

Mehmedinovic, Semezdin. 1996. "A Small Map of the World." *Voice Literary Supplement,* June, 29–30.

Merton, Robert K. 1936. "The Unanticipated Consequences of Purposive Social Action." *American Sociological Review* 1: 894–904.

——. 1989. "Unanticipated Consequences and Kindred Sociological Ideas: A Personal Gloss." In *L'Opera di R. K. Merton e la Sociologia Contemporanea,* edited by Carlo Mongardini and Simonetta Tabboni. Genoa: Edizioni Culturali Internazionali.

Meyer, David S. 1993. "Institutionalizing Dissent: The United States Structure of Political Opportunity and the End of the Nuclear Freeze Movement." *Sociological Forum* 8: 157–179.

Midlarsky, Manus, ed. 1986. *Inequality and Contemporary Revolutions.* Monograph Series in World Affairs, vol. 22, book 2. Denver: Graduate School of International Studies, University of Denver.

Mies, Maria. 1986. *Patriarchy and Accumulation on a World Scale: Women in the International Division of Labour.* London: Zed Books.

Mikkelsen, Flemming, ed. 1986. *Protest og Opror.* Aarhus: Modtryk.

———. 1992. *Arbeidskonflikter i Skandinavien 1848–1980.* Odense: Odense Universitetsforlag.

Milgram, Stanley. 1967. "The Small-World Problem." *Psychology Today* 1: 62–67.

Milkman, Ruth. 1987. *Gender at Work: The Dynamics of Job Segregation by Sex During World War II.* Urbana: University of Illinois Press.

Milkman, Ruth, and Eleanor Townsley. 1994. "Gender and the Economy." In *Handbook of Economic Sociology,* edited by Neil J. Smelser and Richard Swedberg. Princeton: Princeton University Press; New York: Russell Sage Foundation.

Miller, Ann R. 1994. "The Industrial Affiliation of Workers: Differences by Nativity and Country of Origin." In *After Ellis Island: Newcomers and Natives in the 1910 Census,* edited by Susan Cotts Watkins. New York: Russell Sage Foundation.

Miller, Joanne. 1988. "Jobs and Work." In *Handbook of Sociology,* edited by Neil J. Smelser. Newbury Park, Calif.: Sage.

Miller, Jon. 1986. *Pathways in the Workplace: The Effects of Gender and Race on Access to Organizational Resources.* Cambridge: Cambridge University Press.

Miller, Paul, Charles Muley, and Nick Martin. 1995. "What Do Twins Studies Reveal About the Economic Returns to Education? A Comparison of Australian and U.S. Findings." *American Economic Review* 85: 586–599.

Moch, Leslie Page. 1992. *Moving Europeans: Migration in Western Europe Since 1650.* Bloomington: Indiana University Press.

———. 1996. "The European Perspective: Changing Conditions and Multiple Migrations, 1750–1914." In *European Migrants: Global and Local Perspectives,* edited by Dirk Hoerder and Leslie Page Moch. Boston: Northeastern University Press.

Model, Suzanne. 1985. "A Comparative Perspective on the Ethnic Enclave: Blacks, Italians, and Jews in New York City." *International Migration Review* 19: 64–81.

———. 1988a. "The Economic Progress of European and East Asian Americans." *Annual Review of Sociology* 14: 363–380.

———. 1988b. "Italian and Jewish Intergenerational Mobility: New York, 1910." *Social Science History* 12: 31–48.

———. 1989. "The Effects of Ethnicity in the Workplace on Blacks, Italians, and Jews in 1910 New York." *Journal of Urban History* 16: 29–51.

———. 1990. "Work and Family: Blacks and Immigrants from South and East Europe." In *Immigration Reconsidered: History, Sociology, and Politics,* edited by Virginia Yans-McLaughlin. New York: Oxford University Press.

———. 1991. "Caribbean Immigrants: A Black Success Story?" *International Migration Review* 25: 248–276.

———. 1992. "The Ethnic Economy: Cubans and Chinese Reconsidered." *Sociological Quarterly* 33: 63–82.

———. 1996. "An Occupational Tale of Two Cities: Minorities in London and New York." Paper presented to the Conference on Social Stratification in Modern Welfare States, Stockholm University.

Montgomery, David. 1987. *The Fall of the House of Labor: The Workplace, the State, and American Labor Activism, 1865–1925.* Cambridge: Cambridge University Press.

———. 1993. *Citizen Worker: The Experience of Workers in the United States with Democracy and the Free Market During the Nineteenth Century.* Cambridge: Cambridge University Press.

Montgomery, James D. 1991. "Social Networks and Labor Market Outcomes: Toward an Economic Analysis." *American Economic Review* 81: 1408–1418.

———. 1992. "Job Search and Network Composition: Implications of the Strength-of-Weak-Ties Hypothesis." *American Sociological Review* 57: 586–596.

———. 1994. "Weak Ties, Employment, and Inequality: An Equilibrium Analysis." *American Journal of Sociology* 99: 1212–1236.

Moodie, T. Dunbar. 1975. *The Rise of Afrikanderdom: Power, Apartheid, and the Afrikaner Civil Religion.* Berkeley: University of California Press.

———. 1994. *Going for Gold: Men, Mines, and Migration.* Berkeley: University of California Press.

Moore, Kelly. 1996. "Organizing Integrity: American Science and the Creation of Public Interest Organizations, 1955–1975." *American Journal of Sociology* 101: 1592–1627.

Morawska, Ewa. 1985. *For Bread with Butter: Life-Worlds of East Central Europeans in Johnstown, Pennsylvania, 1890–1940.* Cambridge: Cambridge University Press.

———. 1990. "The Sociology and Historiography of Immigration." In *Immigration Reconsidered: History, Sociology, and Politics,* edited by Virginia Yans-McLaughlin. New York: Oxford University Press.

———. 1994. "Afterword: America's Immigrants in the 1910 Census Monograph: Where Can We Who Do It Differently Go from Here?" In *After Ellis Island: Newcomers and Natives in the 1910 Census,* edited by Susan Cotts Watkins. New York: Russell Sage Foundation.

———. 1996. *Insecure Prosperity: Small-Town Jews in Industrial America, 1890–1940.* Princeton: Princeton University Press.

Morokvasic, Mirjana. 1987. "Immigrants in the Parisian Garment Industry." *Work, Employment, and Society* 1: 441–462.

Morris, Aldon D. 1984. *The Origins of the Civil Rights Movement: Black Communities Organizing for Change.* New York: Free Press.

———. 1993. "Birmingham Confrontation Reconsidered: An Analysis of the Dynamics and Tactics of Mobilization." *American Sociological Review* 58: 621–636.

Morris, Martina, Annette D. Bernhardt, and Mark S. Handcock. 1994. "Economic Inequality: New Methods for New Trends." *American Sociological Review* 59: 205–219.

Moss, Philip, and Chris Tilly. 1991. "Why Black Men Are Doing Worse in the Labor Market: A Review of Supply-Side and Demand-Side Explanations." New York: Committee for Research on the Urban Underclass, Social Science Research Council.

———. 1995a. "Raised Hurdles for Black Men: Evidence from Interviews with Employers." Working Paper 81, Russell Sage Foundation, New York.

———. 1995b. "Skills and Race in Hiring: Quantitative Findings from Face-to-Face Interviews." *Eastern Economic Journal* 21: 357–374.

———. 1996. " 'Soft' Skills and Race: An Investigation of Black Men's Employment Problems." Working Paper 80, Russell Sage Foundation, New York.

Motyl, Alexander J. 1992a. "From Imperial Decay to Imperial Collapse: The Fall of the Soviet Empire in Comparative Perspective." In *Nationalism and Empire: The Habsburg Empire and the Soviet Union,* edited by Richard J. Rudolph and David F. Good. New York: St. Martin's.

———, ed. 1992b. *Thinking Theoretically About Soviet Nationalities: History and Comparison in the Study of the USSR.* New York: Columbia University Press.

Mueser, Peter. 1989. "Discrimination." In *Social Economics,* edited by John Eatwell, Murray Milner, and Peter Newman. New York: Norton.

Muhuri, Pradip K., and Samuel H. Preston. 1991. "Effects of Family Composition on Mortality Differentials by Sex Among Children in Matlab, Bangladesh." *Population and Development Review* 17: 415–434.

Muller, Edward N. 1985. "Income Inequality, Regime Repressiveness, and Political Violence." *American Sociological Review* 50: 47–61.

———. 1995. "Economic Determinants of Democracy." *American Sociological Review* 60: 966–982.

Murray, Stephen O., Joseph H. Rankin, and Dennis W. Magill. 1981. "Strong Ties and Job Information." *Sociology of Work and Occupations* 8: 119–136.

Muthein, Yvonne G. 1990. "Protest and Resistance in Cape Town, 1939–1965."

In *Repression and Resistance: Insider Accounts of Apartheid*, edited by Robin Cohen, Yvonne G. Muthien, and Abebe Zegeye. London: Hans Zell.

Nagi, Saad Z. 1992. "Ethnic Identification and Nationalist Movements." *Human Organization* 51: 307–317.

Nee, Victor. 1991. "Social Inequalities in Reforming State Socialism: Between Redistribution and Markets in China." *American Sociological Review* 56: 267–282.

———. 1996. "The Emergence of a Market Society: Changing Mechanisms of Stratification in China." *American Journal of Sociology* 101: 908–949.

Nee, Victor G., and Brett de Bary Nee. 1986. *Longtime Californ': A Documentary Study of an American Chinatown*. Stanford: Stanford University Press.

Nee, Victor, Jimy M. Sanders, and Scott Sernau. 1994. "Job Transitions in an Immigrant Metropolis: Ethnic Boundaries and the Mixed Economy." *American Sociological Review* 59: 849–872.

Nelson K. D., et al. 1996. "Partially Molten Middle Crust Beneath Southern Tibet: Synthesis of Project INDEPTH Results." *Science* 274: 1684–1688.

Nelson, Richard R. 1995. "Recent Evolutionary Theorizing About Economic Change." *Journal of Economic Literature* 33: 48–90.

Newby, Robert G., ed. 1995. "The Bell Curve: Laying Bare the Resurgence of Scientific Racism." *American Behavioral Scientist* 39, no. 1, entire issue.

Newman, Katherine, and Chauncy Lennon. 1995. "The Job Ghetto." *American Prospect* 22: 66–67.

New York Times. 1996a. "Citadel Suspends Second Cadet in the Inquiry on Hazing Women." December 18, A23.

———. 1996b. "The Downsizing of America." March 5–14, electronic version, World Wide Web *(http://www.nytimes.com/specials/downsize)*.

———. 1997. "Citing Abuse, 2 Women Leave Citadel." January 13, A10.

Nielsen, François and Arthur S. Alderson. 1995. "Income Inequality, Development, and Dualism: Results from an Unbalanced Cross-National Panel." *American Sociological Review* 60: 674–701.

Nightingale, Carl Husemoller. 1993. *On the Edge: A History of Poor Black Children and Their American Dreams*. New York: Basic Books.

Noiriel, Gérard. 1991. *La tyrannie du National: Le droit d'asile en Europe, 1793–1993.* Paris: Calmann-Lévy.

———. 1993. "L'identification des citoyens: Naissance de l'état civil républicain." *Genèses* 13: 3–28.

North, Douglas C. 1985. "Transaction Costs in History." *Journal of European Economic History* 14: 557–576.

———. 1991. "Institutions." *Journal of Economic Perspectives* 5: 97–112.

Numbers, Ronald L. 1985. "The Fall and Rise of the American Medical Profession." In *Sickness and Health in America: Readings in the History of Medicine and Public Health*, edited by Judith Walzer Leavitt and Ronald L. Numbers. Madison: University of Wisconsin Press.

O'Ferrall, Fergus. 1985. *Catholic Emancipation: Daniel O'Connell and the Birth of Irish Democracy, 1820–30.* Dublin: Gill and Macmillan.

Ohlemacher, Thomas. 1993. *Brücken der Mobilisierung: Soziale Relais und persönliche Netzwerke in Bürgerinitiativen gegen militärischen Tiefflug.* Wiesbaden: Deutscher Universitäts Verlag.

Öhngren, Bo. 1974. *Folk i rörelse: Samhällsutveckling, flyttningsmonster och folkrörelser i Eskilstuna 1870–1900.* Studia Historica Upsaliensia, 55. Uppsala: Almqvist and Wicksell.

Oliver, Melvin L., and Thomas M. Shapiro. 1997. *Black Wealth/White Wealth: A New Perspective on Racial Inequality.* New York: Routledge.

Oliver, Pamela E. 1993. "Formal Models of Collective Action." *Annual Review of Sociology* 271–300.

Olivier, Johan. 1991. "State Repression and Collective Action in South Africa, 1970–84." *South African Journal of Sociology* 22: 109–117.

Olson, Mancur. 1982. *The Rise and Decline of Nations: Economic Growth, Stagflation, and Social Rigidities.* New Haven: Yale University Press.

Olzak, Susan. 1992. *The Dynamics of Ethnic Competition and Conflict.* Stanford: Stanford University Press.

Olzak, Susan, and Joane Nagel, eds. 1986. *Competitive Ethnic Relations.* Orlando: Academic Press.

Orloff, Ann Shola. 1993. "Gender and the Social Rights of Citizenship: The Comparative Analysis of Gender Relations and Welfare States." *American Sociological Review* 58: 303–328.

———. 1996a. "Gender in the Liberal Welfare States: Australia, Canada, the United Kingdom, and the United States." Working Paper 1996/80, Instituto Juan March de Estudios e Investigaciones, Madrid.

———. 1996b. "Gender and the Welfare State." Working Paper 1996/79, Instituto Juan March de Estudios e Investigaciones, Madrid.

Ortoll, Servando, and Avital H. Bloch. 1985. "Xenofobia y nacionalismo revolucionario, los tumultos de Guadalajara, México, en 1910," *Cristianismo y Sociedad* 86: 63–78.

Osofsky, Gilbert. 1963. *Harlem: The Making of a Ghetto, 1890–1930.* New York: Harper and Row.

Östberg, Viveca. 1996. *Social Structure and Children's Life Chances: An Analysis of Child Mortality in Sweden.* Dissertation Series, no. 26. Stockholm: Swedish Institute for Social Research.

Østergard, Uffe. 1991. " 'Denationalizing' National History: The Comparative Study of Nation-States." *Culture and History* 9/10: 9–41.

———. 1992. "Peasants and Danes: The Danish National Identity and Political Culture." *Comparative Studies in Society and History* 34: 3–27.

Osterman, Paul. 1975. "An Empirical Study of Labor Market Segmentation." *Industrial and Labor Relations Review* 28: 508–523.

———. 1980. *Getting Started.* Cambridge: MIT Press.

———. 1982. "Employment Structures Within Firms." *British Journal of Industrial Relations* 20: 349–361.

———. 1985. "Technology and White-Collar Employment: A Research Strategy." *Proceedings of the 38th Annual Meeting of the Industrial Relations Research Association,* 52–59.

———. 1987. "Choice of Employment Systems in Internal Labor Markets." *Industrial Relations* 26: 46–67.

———. 1988. *Employment Futures: Reorganization, Dislocation, and Public Policy.* New York: Oxford University Press.

———. 1993. "Why Don't 'They' Work? Employment Patterns in a High Pressure Economy." *Social Science Research* 22: 115–130.

———, ed. 1984. *Internal Labor Markets.* Cambridge: MIT Press.

Padgett, John F., and Christopher K. Ansell. 1993. "Robust Action and the Rise of the Medici, 1400–1434." *American Journal of Sociology* 98: 1259–1319.

Paige, Karen, and Jeffrey Paige. 1981. *The Politics of Reproductive Ritual.* Berkeley: University of California Press.

Palmer, Phyllis. 1989. *Domesticity and Dirt: Housewives and Domestic Servants in the United States, 1920–1945.* Philadelphia: Temple University Press.

Parcel, Toby L., and Charles W. Mueller. 1983. *Ascription and Labor Markets: Race and Sex Differences in Earnings.* New York: Academic Press.

Parkin, Frank. 1979. *Marxism and Class Theory: A Bourgeois Critique.* London: Tavistock.

Patterson, Orlando. 1995. "The Paradox of Integration." *New Republic,* November 6, 24–27.

Paulsen, Ronnelle. 1994. "Status and Action: How Stratification Affects the Protest Participation of Young Adults." *Sociological Perspectives* 37: 635–650.

Peattie, Lisa, and Martin Rein. 1983. *Women's Claims: A Study in Political Economy.* Oxford: Oxford University Press.

Peled, Yoav. 1992. "Ethnic Democracy and the Legal Construction of Citizenship: Arab Citizens of the Jewish State." *American Political Science Review* 86: 432–443.

Perman, Lauri, and Beth Stevens. 1989. "Industrial Segregation and the Gender Distribution of Fringe Benefits." *Gender and Society* 3:388–404.

Petersen, Trond. 1992. "Payment Systems and the Structure of Inequality: Conceptual Issues and an Analysis of Salespersons in Department Stores." *American Journal of Sociology* 98: 67–104.

Petersen, Trond, and Laurie A. Morgan. 1995. "Separate and Unequal: Occupation-Establishment Sex Segregation and the Gender Wage Gap." *American Journal of Sociology* 101: 329–365.

Peterson, Paul E., ed. 1995. *Classifying by Race.* Princeton: Princeton University Press.

Picchio, Antonella. 1992. *Social Reproduction: The Political Economy of the Labour Market*. Cambridge: Cambridge University Press.

Pierce, Jennifer. 1995. *Gender Trials: Emotional Lives in Contemporary Law Firms*. Berkeley: University of California Press.

Piore, Michael. 1975. "Notes for a Theory of Labor Market Stratification." In *Labor Market Segmentation*, edited by Richard Edwards, Michael Reich, and David Gordon. Lexington, Mass.: D. C. Heath.

———. 1979a. *Birds of Passage*. Cambridge: Cambridge University Press.

———. 1979b. "Qualitative Research in Economics." *Administrative Science Quarterly* 24: 560–569.

———. 1987. "Historical Perspectives and the Interpretation of Unemployment." *Journal of Economic Literature* 25: 1834–1850.

———. 1996. "Review of *The Handbook of Economic Sociology*." *Journal of Economic Literature* 34: 741–754.

Portes, Alejandro, ed. 1995. *The Economic Sociology of Immigration: Essays on Networks, Ethnicity, and Entrepreneurship*. New York: Russell Sage Foundation.

———. 1996. *The New Second Generation*. New York: Russell Sage Foundation.

Portes, Alejandro, Manuel Castells, and Lauren A. Benton, eds. 1989. *The Informal Economy: Studies in Advanced and Less Developed Countries*. Baltimore: Johns Hopkins University Press.

Portes, Alejandro, and Robert D. Manning. 1986. "The Immigrant Enclave: Theory and Empirical Examples." In *Competitive Ethnic Relations*, edited by Susan Olzak and Joane Nagel. Orlando: Academic Press.

Portes, Alejandro, and Rubén Rumbaut. 1990. *Immigrant America: A Portrait*. Berkeley: University of California Press.

Portes, Alejandro, and Julia Sensenbrenner. 1993. "Embeddedness and Immigration: Notes on the Social Determinants of Economic Action." *American Journal of Sociology* 98: 1320–1350.

Portes, Alejandro, and John Walton. 1981. *Labor, Class, and the International System*. New York: Academic Press.

Portes, Alejandro, and Min Zhou. 1992. "Gaining the Upper Hand: Economic Mobility Among Immigrant and Domestic Minorities." *Ethnic and Racial Studies* 15: 491–522.

Posel, Deborah. 1995. "State, Power, and Gender: Conflict over the Registration of African Customary Marriage in South Africa, 1910–1970." *Journal of Historical Sociology* 8: 223–257.

Powell, Walter W., and Paul J. DiMaggio, eds. 1991. *The New Institutionalism in Organizational Analysis*. Chicago: University of Chicago Press.

Powers, James F. 1988. *A Society Organized for War: The Iberian Municipal Militias in the Central Middle Ages, 1000–1284*. Berkeley: University of California Press.

Rebitzer, James B. 1993. "Radical Political Economy and the Economics of Labor Markets." *Journal of Economic Literature* 31: 1394–1434.

Reitz, Jeffrey G. 1980. *The Survival of Ethnic Groups.* Toronto: McGraw-Hill Ryerson.

———. 1988. "The Institutional Structure of Immigration as a Determinant of Inter-Racial Competition: A Comparison of Britain and Canada." *International Migration Review* 22:117–146.

———. 1990. "Ethnic Concentrations in Labour Markets and Their Implications for Ethnic Inequality." In *Ethnic Identity and Equality: Varieties of Experience in a Canadian City,* edited by Raymond Breton, Wsevolod W. Isajiw, Warren E. Kalbach, and Jeffrey G. Reitz. Toronto: University of Toronto Press.

Reskin, Barbara F. 1988. "Bringing the Men Back In: Sex Differentiation and the Devaluation of Women's Work." *Gender and Society* 2: 58–81.

———. 1993. "Sex Segregation in the Workplace." *Annual Review of Sociology* 19: 241–270.

———, ed. 1984. *Sex Segregation in the Workplace: Trends, Explanations, Remedies.* Washington, D.C.: National Academy Press.

Reskin, Barbara F., and Heidi Hartmann, eds. 1986. *Women's Work, Men's Work: Sex Segregation on the Job.* Washington, D.C.: National Academy Press.

Reskin, Barbara, and Irene Padavic. 1994. *Women and Men at Work.* Thousand Oaks, Calif.: Pine Forge Press.

Reskin, Barbara F., and Patricia A. Roos. 1990. *Job Queues, Gender Queues: Explaining Women's Inroads into Male Occupations.* Philadelphia: Temple University Press.

Reskin, Barbara F., and Catherine E. Ross. 1995. "Jobs, Authority, and Earnings Among Managers: The Continuing Significance of Sex." In *Gender Inequality at Work,* edited by Jerry A. Jacobs. Thousand Oaks, Calif.: Sage.

Rhomberg, Chris. 1995. "Collective Actors and Urban Regimes: Class Formation and the 1946 Oakland General Strike." *Theory and Society* 24: 567–594.

Rich, Brian L. 1995. "Explaining Feminization in the U.S. Banking Industry, 1940–1980: Human Capital, Dual Labor Markets, or Gender Queuing?" *Sociological Perspectives* 38: 357–380.

Rieder, Jonathan. 1985. *Canarsie: The Jews and Italians of Brooklyn Against Liberalism.* Cambridge: Harvard University Press.

Riley, Matilda White. 1996. "Age Stratification." In *Encyclopedia of Gerontology,* vol. 1, edited by James E. Birren. San Diego: Academic Press.

Roach, Sharyn L. 1990. "Men and Women Lawyers in In-House Legal Departments: Recruitment and Career Patterns." *Gender and Society* 4: 207–219.

Roemer, John. 1982. *A General Theory of Exploitation and Class.* Cambridge: Harvard University Press.

Rollins, Judith. 1985. *Between Women: Domestics and Their Employers*. Philadelphia: Temple University Press.

Romero, Mary. 1996. "Maid in the U.S.A.: Women Domestic Workers, the Service Economy, and Labor." Comparative Labor History Series, Working Paper no. 7, Center for Labor Studies, University of Washington, Seattle.

Roos, Patricia. 1985. *Gender and Work: A Comparative Analysis of Industrial Societies*. Albany: State University of New York Press.

Rose, Sonya O. 1986. " 'Gender at Work': Sex, Class, and Industrial Capitalism." *History Workshop* 21: 113–131.

———. 1992. *Limited Livelihoods: Gender and Class in Nineteenth-Century England*. Berkeley: University of California Press.

Rosenberg, Janet, Harry Perlstadt, and William R. F. Phillips. 1993. "Now That We Are Here: Discrimination, Disparagement, and Harassment at Work and the Experience of Women Lawyers." *Gender and Society* 7: 415–433.

Rosenfeld, Rachel A. 1992. "Job Mobility and Career Processes." *Annual Review of Sociology* 18:39–61.

Rosenfeld, Rachel A., and Arne L. Kalleberg. 1991. "Gender Inequality in the Labor Market: A Cross-National Perspective." *Acta Sociologica* 34:207–226.

Rosenfeld, Rachel A., and Kenneth I. Spenner. 1995. "Occupational Sex Segregation and Women's Early Career Job Shifts." In *Gender Inequality at Work*, edited by Jerry A. Jacobs. Thousand Oaks, Calif.: Sage.

Rothman, David J. 1980. *Conscience and Convenience: The Asylum and Its Alternatives in Progressive America*. Boston: Little, Brown.

———. 1991. *Strangers at the Bedside: A History of How Law and Bioethics Transformed Medical Decision Making*. New York: Basic Books.

Roy, Beth. 1994. *Some Trouble with Cows: Making Sense of Social Conflict*. Berkeley: University of California Press.

Rueschemeyer, Dietrich, Evelyne Huber Stephens, and John D. Stephens. 1992. *Capitalist Development and Democracy*. Chicago: University of Chicago Press.

Rumberger, Russell, and Martin Carnoy. 1980. "Segmentation in the U.S. Labour Market—Its Effect on the Mobility and Earnings of Blacks and Whites." *Cambridge Journal of Economics* 4: 117–132.

Rutten, Rosanne. 1994. "Courting the Workers' Vote in a Hacienda Region: Rhetoric and Response in the 1992 Philippine Elections." *Pilipinas* 22: 1–34.

Sahlins, Peter. 1989. *Boundaries: The Making of France and Spain in the Pyrenees*. Berkeley: University of California Press.

Sapelli, Giulio. 1994. "L'emigrazione per l'eterogeneità: L'esperienza dell'Europea del sud dopo la seconda guerra mondiale." *Società e Storia* 17, no. 64: 361–390.

Saul, John S. 1994. "Globalism, Socialism, and Democracy in the South African Transition." *Socialist Register*, 171–202.

Schneider, Cathy Lisa. 1995. *Shantytown Protest in Pinochet's Chile*. Philadelphia: Temple University Press.

Schram, Stuart, ed. 1985. *The Scope of State Power in China*. Publication of the European Science Foundation. London: School of Oriental and African Studies, University of London; Hong Kong: Chinese University Press of Hong Kong.

———. 1987. *Foundations and Limits of State Power in China*. Publication of the European Science Foundation. London: School of Oriental and African Studies, University of London; Hong Kong: Chinese University Press of Hong Kong.

Schroedel, Jean Reith. 1985. *Alone in a Crowd: Women in the Trades Tell Their Stories*. Philadelphia: Temple University Press.

Scott, James. 1985. *Weapons of the Weak: Everyday Forms of Peasant Resistance*. New Haven: Yale University Press.

———. 1990. *Domination and the Arts of Resistance: Hidden Transcripts*. New Haven: Yale University Press.

Scott, James C., and Benedict Kerkvliet, eds. 1986. *Everyday Forms of Peasant Resistance in South-East Asia*. London: Frank Cass.

Scott, Joan W. 1974. *The Glassworkers of Carmaux: French Craftsmen and Political Action in a Nineteenth-Century City*. Cambridge: Harvard University Press.

Seidman, Gay W. 1993. " 'No Freedom Without the Women': Mobilization and Gender in South Africa, 1970–1992." *Signs* 18: 291–320.

Semyonov, Moshe. 1996. "Gender-Occupational Segregation and Gender-Occupational Inequality in a Comparative Perspective." Paper presented to the Conference on Social Stratification in Modern Welfare States, Stockholm University.

Sen, Amartya. 1981. *Poverty and Famines: An Essay on Entitlement and Deprivation*. Oxford: Clarendon Press.

———. 1982. *Choice, Welfare, and Measurement*. Cambridge: MIT Press.

———. 1983. "Women, Technology, and Sexual Divisions." *Trade and Development* 6: 195–223.

———. 1992. *Inequality Reexamined*. Cambridge: Harvard University Press.

Sethi, Rajiv, and E. Somanathan. 1996. "The Evolution of Social Norms in Common Property Resource Use." *American Economic Review* 86: 766–788.

Sexton, Patricia Cayo. 1991. *The War on Labor and the Left: Understanding America's Unique Conservatism*. Boulder: Westview.

Shanahan, Suzanne Elise, and Nancy Brandon Tuma. 1994. "The Sociology of Distribution and Redistribution." In *Handbook of Economic Sociology*, edited by Neil J. Smelser and Richard Swedberg. Princeton: Princeton University Press; New York: Russell Sage Foundation.

Shapiro, Bruce. 1996. "A House Divided: Racism at the State Department." *The Nation*, February 12, 11–16.

Shell, Marc. 1993. *Children of the Earth: Literature, Politics, and Nationhood.* New York: Oxford University Press.

Shue, Vivienne. 1988. *The Reach of the State: Sketches of the Chinese Body Politic.* Stanford: Stanford University Press.

Sidanius, Jim, Felicia Pratto, Stacey Sinclair, and Colette van Laar. 1996. "Mother Teresa Meets Genghis Khan: The Dialectics of Hierarchy-Attenuating Career Choices." *Social Justice Research* 9: 145–170.

Sim, Biirte. 1994. "Engendering Democracy: Social Citizenship and Political Participation for Women in Scandinavia." *Social Politics: International Studies in Gender, State, and Society* 1: 286–305.

Simon, Curtis J. and John T. Warner. 1992. "Matchmaker, Matchmaker: The Effect of Old Boy Networks on Job Match Quality, Earnings, and Tenure." *Journal of Labor Economics* 10: 306–331.

Simon, Herbert. 1976. *Administrative Behavior: A Study of Decision-Making Processes in Administrative Organization.* 3d ed. New York: Free Press.

———. 1991. "Organizations and Markets." *Journal of Economic Perspectives* 5: 25–44.

Skinner, G. William. 1964. "Marketing and Social Structure in Rural China." *Journal of Asian Studies* 24: 3–43.

———. 1985. "The Structure of Chinese History." *Journal of Asian Studies* 44: 271–292.

Skocpol, Theda. 1995. "African Americans in U.S. Social Policy." In *Classifying by Race,* edited by Paul E. Peterson. Princeton: Princeton University Press.

Smeeding, Timothy M. 1991. "Cross-National Comparisons of Inequality and Poverty." In *Economic Inequality and Poverty: International Perspectives,* edited by Lars Osberg. Armonk, N.Y.: M. E. Sharpe.

Smith, Adam. 1910. *The Wealth of Nations.* 2 vols. London: J. M. Dent. First published in 1776.

Smith, Anthony D. 1981. *The Ethnic Revival.* Cambridge: Cambridge University Press.

———. 1990. "The Supersession of Nationalism?" *International Journal of Comparative Sociology* 31: 1–31.

Smith, Carol A. 1995. "Race-Class-Gender Ideology in Guatemala: Modern and Anti-Modern Forms." *Comparative Studies in Society and History* 37: 723–749.

Somers, Margaret R. 1992. "Narrativity, Narrative Identity, and Social Action: Rethinking English Working-Class Formation." *Social Science History* 16: 591–630.

———. 1993. "Citizenship and the Place of the Public Sphere: Law, Community, and Political Culture in the Transition to Democracy." *American Sociological Review* 58: 587–620.

Sørensen, Aage B. 1994a. "The Basic Concepts of Stratification Research: Class,

Status, and Power." In *Social Stratification: Class, Race, and Gender in Sociological Perspective*, edited by David B. Grusky. Boulder: Westview.

———. 1994b. "Firms, Wages, and Incentives." In *Handbook of Economic Sociology*, edited by Neil J. Smelser and Richard Swedberg. Princeton: Princeton University Press; New York: Russell Sage Foundation.

———. 1996. "The Structural Basis of Social Inequality." *American Journal of Sociology*. 101: 1333–1365.

Sørensen, Annemette, and Heike Trappe. 1995. "The Persistence of Gender Inequality in Earnings in the German Democratic Republic." *American Sociological Review* 60: 398–406.

Sorokin, Pitirim A. 1959. *Social and Cultural Mobility*. Glencoe: Free Press. Includes Sorokin's *Social Mobility*, first published in 1927.

Stansell, Christine. 1987. *City of Women: Sex and Class in New York, 1789–1860*. Urbana: University of Illinois Press.

Starr, Paul. 1982. *The Social Transformation of American Medicine*. New York: Basic Books.

Steckel, Richard H. 1995. "Stature and the Standard of Living." *Journal of Economic Literature* 33: 1903–1940.

Steinberg, Marc W. 1994. "The Dialogue of Struggle: The Contest over Ideological Boundaries in the Case of London Silk Weavers in the Early Nineteenth Century." *Social Science History* 18: 505–542.

Steinberg, Ronnie J. 1995. "Gendered Instructions: Cultural Lag and Gender Bias in the Hay System of Job Evaluation." In *Gender Inequality at Work*, edited by Jerry A. Jacobs. Thousand Oaks, Calif.: Sage.

Steinfeld, Robert J. 1991. *The Invention of Free Labor: The Employment Relation in English and American Law and Culture, 1350–1870*. Chapel Hill: University of North Carolina Press.

Steinmetz, George. 1993. "Reflections on the Role of Social Narratives in Working-Class Formation: Narrative Theory in the Social Sciences." *Social Science History* 16: 489–516.

Stepan-Norris, Judith, ed. 1995. "On Inequality." *Sociological Perspectives* 38, no. 3, entire issue.

Stevens, Thomas S., and Gregory T. Stevens. 1996. "Emergence, Self-Organization, and Social Interaction: Arousal-Dependent Structure in Social Systems." *Sociological Theory* 14: 131–153.

Stinchcombe, Arthur L. 1959. "Bureaucratic and Craft Administration of Production." *Administrative Science Quarterly* 4: 168–187.

———. 1972. "The Social Determinants of Success." *Science* 178: 603–604.

———. 1975. "Merton's Theory of Social Structure." In *The Idea of Social Structure*, edited by Lewis Coser. New York: Harcourt Brace Jovanovich.

———. 1978a. "Generations and Cohorts in Social Mobility: Economic Development and Social Mobility in Norway." Memorandum no. 18, Institute of Applied Social Research, Oslo.

———. 1978b. *Theoretical Methods in Social History.* New York: Academic Press.

———. 1979. "Social Mobility in Industrial Labor Markets." *Acta Sociologica* 22: 217–245.

———. 1990a. *Information and Organizations.* Berkeley: University of California Press.

———. 1990b. "Work Institutions and the Sociology of Everyday Life." In *The Nature of Work: Sociological Perspectives,* edited by Kai Erikson and Steven Peter Vallas, New Haven: Yale University Press.

———. 1995. *Sugar Island Slavery in the Age of Enlightenment: The Political Economy of the Caribbean World.* Princeton: Princeton University Press.

———. 1996. "Monopolistic Competition as a Mechanism: Corporations, Universities, and Nation States in Competitive Fields." Paper presented to the Conference on Social Mechanisms, Stockholm University.

Strom, Sharon Hartman. 1992. *Beyond the Typewriter: Gender, Class, and the Origins of Modern American Office Work, 1900–1930.* Urbana: University of Illinois Press.

Sturino, Franc. 1978. "Family and Kin Cohesion Among South Italian Immigrants in Toronto." In *The Italian Immigrant Woman in North America,* edited by Betty Boyd Caroli, Robert F. Harney, and Lydio F. Tomasi. Toronto: Multicultural History Society of Ontario.

Sugden, Robert. 1993. "Welfare, Resources, and Capabilities: A Review of *Inequality Reexamined* by Amartya Sen." *Journal of Economic Literature* 31: 1947–1962.

Sugimoto, Yoshio. 1981. *Popular Disturbance in Postwar Japan.* Hong Kong: Asian Research Service.

Sugrue, Thomas J. 1996. *The Origins of the Urban Crisis: Race and Inequality in Postwar Detroit.* Princeton: Princeton University Press.

Swerdlow, Marian. 1989. "Men's Accommodations to Women Entering a Nontraditional Occupation: A Case of Rapid Transit Operatives." *Gender and Society* 3: 373–387.

Szreter, Simon. 1996. *Fertility, Class, and Gender in Britain, 1860–1940.* Cambridge: Cambridge University Press.

Tabili, Laura. 1996. "Women 'of a Very Low Type': Crossing Racial Boundaries in Imperial Britain." In *Gender and Class in Modern Europe,* edited by Laura L. Frader and Sonya O. Rose. Ithaca: Cornell University Press.

Tam, Tony. 1997. "Sex Segregation and Occupational Gender Inequality in the United States: Devaluation or Specialized Training?" *American Journal of Sociology* 102: 1652–1692.

Tanner, James M. 1994. "Introduction: Growth in Height as a Mirror of the

Standard of Living." In *Stature, Living Standards, and Economic Development: Essays in Anthropometric History,* edited by John Komlos. Chicago: University of Chicago Press.

Tarrow, Sidney. 1988. "National Politics and Collective Action: Recent Theory and Research in Western Europe and the United States." *Annual Review of Sociology:* 421–440.

———. 1989. *Democracy and Disorder: Social Conflict, Political Protest, and Democracy in Italy, 1965–1975.* New York: Oxford University Press.

———. 1993. "La mondialisation des conflits: encore un siècle de rébellion?" *Etudes Internationales* 24: 513–532.

———. 1994. *Power in Movement.* Cambridge: Cambridge University Press.

Taubman, Paul J. 1991. "Discrimination Within the Family: The Treatment of Daughters and Sons." In *Essays on the Economics of Discrimination,* edited by Emily P. Hoffman. Kalamazoo, Mich.: W. E. Upjohn Institute for Employment Research.

Taylor, J. Edward. 1986. "Differential Migration, Networks, Information, and Risk." *Research in Human Capital and Development* 4: 147–171.

Taylor, Rupert. 1990. "South Africa: Consociation or Democracy?" *Telos* 85: 17–32.

Thomas, Robert J. 1985. *Citizenship, Gender, and Work: Social Organization of Industrial Agriculture.* Berkeley: University of California Press.

Thompson, Leonard. 1990. *A History of South Africa.* New Haven: Yale University Press.

Thompson, Richard H. 1989. *Theories of Ethnicity: A Critical Appraisal.* New York: Greenwood.

Tilly, Chris. 1992. "Dualism in Part-Time Employment." *Industrial Relations* 31: 330–347.

———. 1996. *Half a Job: Bad and Good Part-Time Jobs in a Changing Labor Market.* Philadelphia: Temple University Press.

Tilly, Chris, and Charles Tilly. 1994. "Capitalist Work and Labor Markets." In *Handbook of Economic Sociology,* edited by Neil J. Smelser and Richard Swedberg. New York: Russell Sage Foundation; Princeton: Princeton University Press.

Tilly, Louise A. 1992a. "Industrialization and Gender Inequality." Working Paper 148, Center for Studies of Social Change, New School for Social Research.

———. 1992b. *Politics and Class in Milan, 1881–1901.* New York: Oxford University Press.

Tilly, Louise A., and Joan W. Scott. 1987. *Women, Work, and Family.* 2d ed. New York: Methuen.

Tomaskovic-Devey, Donald. 1993. *Gender and Racial Inequality at Work: The Sources and Consequences of Job Segregation.* Ithaca: ILR Press.

————. 1995. "Sex Composition and Gendered Earnings Inequality: A Comparison of Job and Occupational Models." In *Gender Inequality at Work*, edited by Jerry A. Jacobs. Thousand Oaks, Calif.: Sage.

Tomaskovic-Devey, Donald, and Jacqueline Johnson. 1996. "The Job Matching Process and the Organizational Production of Gender Segregation." Paper presented to the Conference on Social Stratification in Modern Welfare States, Stockholm University.

Tomlins, Christopher L. 1993. *Law, Labor, and Ideology in the Early American Republic.* Cambridge: Cambridge University Press.

Topalov, Christian. 1991. "Patriotismes et citoyennetés." *Genèses* 3: 162–176.

Traugott, Mark, ed. 1995. *Repertoires and Cycles of Collective Action.* Durham, N.C.: Duke University Press.

Trexler, Richard C. 1981. *Public Life in Renaissance Florence.* New York: Academic Press.

Tuominen, Mary. 1994. "The Hidden Organization of Labor: Gender, Race/Ethnicity, and Child-Care Work in the Formal and Informal Economy." *Sociological Perspectives* 37: 229–246.

Turner, Mark. 1996. *The Literary Mind.* New York: Oxford University Press.

U.S. Department of Labor. 1975. *Jobseeking Methods Used by American Workers.* Washington, D.C.: U.S. Government Printing Office.

Vail, Leroy, ed. 1989. *The Creation of Tribalism in Africa.* London: James Curry; Berkeley: University of California Press.

Vogel, Morris J. 1980. *The Invention of the Modern Hospital: Boston, 1870–1930.* Chicago: University of Chicago Press.

Walder, Andrew G. 1996. "Markets and Inequality in Transitional Economies: Toward Testable Theories." *American Journal of Sociology* 101: 1060–1073.

Waldinger, Roger D. 1986. *Through the Eye of the Needle: Immigrants and Enterprise in New York's Garment Trades.* New York: New York University Press.

————. 1986–1987. "Changing Ladders and Musical Chairs: Ethnicity and Opportunity in Post-Industrial New York." *Politics and Society* 15: 369–401.

————. 1989. "Immigration and Urban Change." *Annual Review of Sociology* 15: 211–232.

————. 1994. "The Making of an Immigrant Niche." *International Migration Review* 28: 3–30.

————. 1996. *Still the Promised City? African-Americans and New Immigrants in New York, 1940–1990.* Cambridge: Harvard University Press.

Waldinger, Roger, and Mehdi Bozorgmehr, eds. 1996. *Ethnic Los Angeles.* New York: Russell Sage Foundation.

Waldinger, Roger D., Robin Ward, and Howard Aldrich. 1985. "Ethnic Business and Occupational Mobility in Advanced Societies." *Sociology* 19: 586–597.

Waldmann, Peter. 1989. *Ethnischer Radikalismus: Ursachen und Folgen gewaltsamer Minderheitenkonflikte.* Opladen: Westdeutscher Verlag.

Ward, Bernard. 1912. *The Eve of Catholic Emancipation, 1803–1829.* London: Longmans.

Wasserman, Stanley, and Katherine Faust. 1994. *Social Network Analysis: Methods and Applications.* Cambridge: Cambridge University Press.

Watkins, Susan Cotts, ed. 1994. *After Ellis Island: Newcomers and Natives in the 1910 Census.* New York: Russell Sage Foundation.

Watkins-Owens, Irma. 1996. *Blood Relations: Caribbean Immigrants and the Harlem Community, 1900–1930.* Bloomington: Indiana University Press.

Way, Peter. 1993. *Common Labour: Workers and the Digging of North American Canals, 1780–1860.* Cambridge: Cambridge University Press.

Weber, Max. 1968. *Economy and Society: An Outline of Interpretive Sociology.* Edited by Guenther Roth and Claus Wittich. 3 vols. New York: Bedminster.

Weede, Erich. 1993. "The Impact of Military Participation on Economic Growth and Income Inequality: Some New Evidence." *Journal of Political and Military Sociology* 21: 241–258.

Weil, Patrick. 1994. "Immigration, nation et nationalité: regards comparatifs et croisés." *Revue Française de Science Politique* 44: 308–326.

Weinberg, Daniel H. 1996. "A Brief Look at Postwar U.S. Income Inequality." *Current Population Reports,* Series P-60, no. 191. Washington, D.C.: U.S. Government Printing Office.

Weiss, Andrew. 1995. "Human Capital vs. Signalling Explanations of Wages." *Journal of Economic Perspectives* 9: 133–154.

Wellman, Barry, and Steven Berkowitz, eds. 1988. *Social Structures: A Network Approach.* Cambridge: Cambridge University Press.

White, Harrison. 1992. *Identity and Control: A Structural Theory of Social Action.* Princeton: Princeton University Press.

Whitney, Joseph B. R. 1970. *China: Area, Administration, and Nation Building.* Research Paper 123, Department of Geography, University of Chicago.

Wial, Howard. 1991. "Getting a Good Job: Mobility in a Segmented Labor Market." *Industrial Relations* 30: 396–416.

Will, Pierre-Etienne. 1994. "Chine moderne et sinologie." *Annales: Histoire, Sciences Sociales* 49: 7–26.

Williams, Christine L. 1989. *Gender Differences at Work: Women and Men in Nontraditional Occupations.* Berkeley: University of California Press.

———. 1995. *Still a Man's World: Men Who Do Women's Work.* Berkeley: University of California Press.

———, ed. 1993. *Doing "Women's Work": Men in Nontraditional Occupations.* Newbury Park, Calif.: Sage.

Williams, Fiona. 1995. "Race/Ethnicity, Gender, and Class in Welfare States: A Framework for Comparative Analysis." *Social Politics: International Studies in Gender, State, and Society* 2: 127–159.

Williams, Lena. 1997. "The Battle of the Braid Brigade." *New York Times*, January 26, City, 4.

Williams, Robin. 1994. "The Sociology of Ethnic Conflicts: Comparative International Perspectives." *Annual Review of Sociology* 20: 49–79.

Williamson, Jeffrey. 1985. *Did British Capitalism Breed Inequality?* Boston: Allen and Unwin.

Williamson, Jeffrey, and Peter Linder. 1980. *American Inequality: A Macroeconomic History.* New York: Academic Press.

Williamson, Oliver. 1975. *Markets and Hierarchies, Analysis and Antitrust Implications: A Study in the Economics of Internal Organization.* New York: Free Press.

———. 1985. *The Economic Institutions of Capitalism.* New York: Free Press.

———. 1991. "Comparative Economic Organization: The Analysis of Discrete Structural Alternatives." *Administrative Science Quarterly* 36: 269–296.

Wilson, William Julius. 1980. *The Declining Significance of Race: Blacks and Changing American Institutions.* 2d ed. Chicago: University of Chicago Press.

———. 1996a. *When Work Disappears: The World of the New Urban Poor.* New York: Knopf.

———. 1996b. "Work." *New York Times Magazine*, August 18, 26–31, 40, 48, 52–54.

Wolff, Edward N. 1995. "How the Pie Is Sliced: America's Growing Concentration of Wealth." *American Prospect* 22: 58–64.

Wright, Erik Olin. 1985. *Classes.* London: Verso.

———. 1989. "Inequality." In *Social Economics*, edited by John Eatwell, Murray Milgate, and Peter Newman. New York: Norton.

Wright, Erik Olin, Janeen Baxter, and Gunn Elisabeth Birkelund. 1995. "The Gender Gap in Workplace Authority: A Cross-National Study." *American Sociological Review* 60: 407–435.

Wrightson, Keith and David Levine. 1979. *Poverty and Piety in an English Village: Terling, 1525–1700.* New York: Academic Press.

———. 1991. *The Making of an Industrial Society: Whickham, 1560–1765.* Oxford: Clarendon Press.

Wu, Jialu. 1994. "How Severe Was the Great Depression? Evidence from the Pittsburgh Region." In *Stature, Living Standards, and Economic Development: Essays in Anthropometric History*, edited by John Komlos. Chicago: University of Chicago Press.

Yans-McLaughlin, Virginia, ed. 1990. *Immigration Reconsidered: History, Sociology, and Politics.* New York: Oxford University Press.

Yi, Zung, et al. 1993. "Causes and Implications of the Recent Increase in the Reported Sex Ratio at Birth in China." *Population and Development Review* 19: 283–302.

Young, Iris Marion. 1990. *Justice and the Politics of Difference*. Princeton: Princeton University Press.

Zaslavsky, Victor. 1992. "Nationalism and Democratic Transition in Postcommunist Societies." *Daedalus* 121, no. 2: 97–122.

Zavella, Patricia. 1987. *Women's Work and Chicano Families: Cannery Workers of the Santa Clara Valley*. Ithaca: Cornell University Press.

Zdravom'islova, E. A. 1993. *Paradigm'i Zapadnoi Sotsiologii obschestvenn'ix dvizhenii*. St. Petersburg: Nauka.

Zelizer, Viviana. 1985. *Pricing the Priceless Child: The Changing Social Value of Children*. New York: Basic Books.

———. 1988. "Beyond the Polemics on the Market: Establishing a Theoretical and Empirical Agenda." *Sociological Forum* 3: 614–634.

———. 1994a. "The Creation of Domestic Currencies." *American Economic Review: Papers and Proceedings* 84: 138–142.

———. 1994b. *The Social Meaning of Money*. New York: Basic Books.

———. 1996. "Payments and Social Ties." *Sociological Forum* 11: 481–496.

———. 1998. "How Do We Know Whether a Monetary Transaction Is a Gift, an Entitlement, or a Payment?" In *Economics, Values, and Organization*, edited by Avner Ben-Ner and Louis Putterman. Cambridge: Cambridge University Press, forthcoming.

Zerubavel, Eviatar. 1996. "Lumping and Splitting: Notes on Social Classification." *Sociological Forum* 11: 421–433.

Zubrinsky, Camille L., and Lawrence Bobo. 1996. "Prismatic Metropolis: Race and Residential Segregation in the City of the Angels." *Social Science Research* 25: 335–374.

Zunz, Olivier. 1982. *The Changing Face of Inequality: Urbanization, Industrial Development, and Immigrants in Detroit, 1880–1920*. Chicago: University of Chicago Press.

———. 1990. *Making America Corporate, 1870–1920*. Chicago: University of Chicago Press.

Index

291

individualistic models of, 30–33
labor theory of value by, 87
education
 limited effect upon reducing categorical inequality of, 244
 typing in United States, 77
Eiselen, W. M., 121
Elias, Norbert, 18–19
elites
 create divisions to reduce threat, 93
 exploitation by, 94, 193–94
 goods and, 26
 nationalism and, 173
 opportunity hoarding by, 94
emulation, 9, 11
 categorical inequality and, 181
 contrasted with borrowing, 63, 95
 defined, 10
 goods and, 26
 by governments, 195
 as heart of nationalism, 174–75
 multiplies categorical inequality, 190–91
 in organizations, 59, 96–97
 scripting and, 53
 self-reproduces, 191
 in South African mining, 127–28
entitlements, 42, 43
entrepreneurship, 160
ethnicity
 durable inequality and, 161
 economic niches and, 160–61
 government-backed, 194
 opportunity hoarding and, 154–55, 160
 used in South Africa, 120, 122, 220
Ethnos Theory, 121
exploitation, 9, 11
 categories organize, 88–89, 138–39
 costs, 90
 defined, 10, 86–87
 by elite, 94, 193–94
 facilitated by categorical inequality, 81
 facilitated by well-marked boundaries, 76
 gender and, 132, 136, 139–41
 goods and, 26
 by government, 193
 Marxist theory of, 87
 nationalism and, 173
 by nonelite, 94
 opportunity hoarding and, 93, 155
 in organizations, 68, 138–39
 organized around categorical distinctions, 88–89
 organized medicine as, 184
 scripting, local knowledge, and, 54

segregation and, 137–38
self-reproduces, 191
seven elements of, 128–29, 130–32
in South Africa, 127, 128–29

feeding, as social process, 45–46
feminists
 on connection of categorical relationships and exploitation, 83
 as critics of capitalist work, 145–46
 on male/female wage inequality, 133–34
Fernández-Kelly, María Patricia, 153
firms. See also jobs; organizations
 boundary maintenance and exploitation in, 138–39
 defined, 103
 incentive systems in, 110–14
 job categorization in, 79–80, 104–5
 mobility in, 108–9
 opportunity hoarding in, 166–67, 168–69
 payment forms in, 44–45
 sex-typing of jobs in, 76
Fischer, Claude S. et al., 22–24
Flexner, Abraham, 184
Fogel, Robert W., 2
France
 Italian migration to, 149, 150
 nutrition level of work force in, 2
 professionalization in, 157
 promotion of opportunity hoarding in, 194–95
Fraser, Steven, 234–35
Fredrickson, George M., 124–25
Freeman, Richard B., 233
French Revolution, 223
frontiers. See also boundaries
 imported, 77, 78
 local, 77, 78
 male/female relations relative to, 140–43
 reduce cost of exploitation, 129

Gans, Herbert J., 66
gender, 14. See also women
 altering inequality in, 144–45, 241
 boundaries, 64
 categories in United States, 143–45
 contrasted with race as categorical distinction, 240–41
 cuts across other categories, 240
 discrimination, 31, 134
 exploitation and, 132–35, 136, 139–41
 as exterior category, 75
 incentive systems and, 136
 inequality, economists' explanation of, 133

Indexer: Andrew Christenson
Compositor: Maple-Vail Composition Services
Text: Palatino
Display: Snell Roundhand, Bauer Bodoni
Printer and Binder: Maple-Vail Book Manufacturing Group